MICROSOFT CERTIFIED SYSTEMS ENGINEER

MCSE Windows® 2000
Server Lab Manual

MCSE Windows® 2000 Server Lab Manual

C. Joe Blow
Lee Cottrell

McGraw-Hill/Osborne
New York Chicago San Francisco
Lisbon London Madrid Mexico City Milan
New Delhi San Juan Seoul Singapore Sydney Toronto

McGraw-Hill/Osborne
2600 Tenth Street
Berkeley, California 94710
U.S.A.

To arrange bulk purchase discounts for sales promotions, premiums, or fund-raisers, please contact **McGraw-Hill**/Osborne at the above address. For information on translations or book distributors outside the U.S.A., please see the International Contact Information page immediately following the index of this book.

MCSE Windows® 2000 Server Lab Manual

1234567890 FGR FGR 0198765432

ISBN 0-07-222301-4

Publisher	**Acquisitions Coordinator**	**Series Designer**
Brandon A. Nordin	Athena Honore	Roberta Steele
Vice President & Associate Publisher	**Technical Editor**	**Cover Series Designer**
Scott Rogers	Walter Merchant	Greg Scott
Acquisitions Editor	**Production and Editorial Services**	
Chris Johnson	Anzai!, Inc.	
Senior Project Editor	**Illustration Supervisor**	
Betsy Manini	Lyssa Wald	

This book was composed with Corel VENTURA™ Publisher.

I would like to dedicate this book to my wonderful family: Michael, Fernando, Markeil, Alexis, CJ, Melvin, Felicia, Mildred, Wendell, Lynnette, Tyrese, Shirley, Lois, and Fernando Sr. A special dedication to my wife Avis—without her loving support, timely encouragement, and loving home environment, this book would not have been possible.

—*C. Joe Blow*

This book has been a group effort between me and my family. My wife Laurie is the center of my world; she makes my success possible. My daughter Elizabeth can always place a smile on my face, regardless of deadline or work hassle. I dedicate this book to them. May they always enjoy happiness, health, and prosperity.

—*Lee Cottrell*

ABOUT THE AUTHORS

Joe Blow has 22 years of networking and wireless experience. His bachelor's degree is in electronics engineering technology from Sienna Heights College in Adrian, Michigan. He currently serves as assistant department head for information technology at the Electronic Computer Programming Institute (ECPI) and is faculty advisor for the Virginia Beach campus. He is responsible for program coordination at all campuses. In addition to his MCSE NT 4.0 Plus Internet, Visual Basic, C, and Oracle programming experience, Joe is a certified fiber optics instructor and a Windows 2000 instructor at ECPI's Virginia Beach campus.

Lee Cottrell has a master of science degree in information science from the University of Pittsburgh. He is also a certified teacher in the state of Pennsylvania. Currently, Lee is the program manager for the computer programming and networking program at the Bradford School in Pittsburgh. His teaching duties include networking, hardware, programming, database design, and web development. Lee also develops and writes curriculum for the ten Bradford Schools nationwide. During his free time, Lee consults for local small businesses, solving many computer problems.

CONTENTS

ACKNOWLEDGMENTS

I would like to thank

- the students of ECPI who gave me the drive and desire to create this lab book;
- Walter Merchant who added editorial and moral support;
- all the wonderful folks at McGraw-Hill/Osborne: Chris Johnson for his patience and professionalism, Athena Honoré for keeping me under her guidance, Tom Anzai and his entire team; and a special thanks to Bonnie McLaughlin and Robert Godseck, who recommended me to McGraw-Hill/Osborne;
- Julian Aiken, who continues to encourage me to always give my best effort;
- Ethel Hinton, Claudette Fuller, Chuck Goodman, and Wendy Krizek, whose inspiration has no boundaries;
- my colleagues at ECPI, who provided me with questions and real world experiences.

—C. Joe Blow

I would like to acknowledge the following people for their invaluable aid in this project:

- Tom Anzai and Ann Fothergill-Brown, for responding when I needed their help;
- Walt, for good comments on my labs;
- C. Joe Blow, Chris Brown, and Athena Honoré for giving me the honor of working on this project;
- and the students at Bradford School, Pittsburgh, for putting up with my mood swings due to lack of sleep.

—Lee Cottrell

INTRODUCTION

The term "IT professional" has many meanings. Throughout the networking world, the IT professional is often associated with designing, implementing, administering, or securing networks for a wide variety of businesses. Many of these terms eventually help to define the roles that an IT professional will play within a business or organization. But an IT professional's true worth to an organization can be defined by the one term that distinguishes their profession from all others—"solution provider." Whether you are designing a complicated network or implementing services throughout a Windows 2000 domain, you are providing a solution to the networking problems of some business or organization. The Chinese say, "A problem is merely a question not yet answered." IT professionals take that saying a step further: "A networking task is merely a question that needs an answer." And it is the sole requirement of all IT professionals to find a *solution* to the questions posed by those who employ them.

C. Joe Blow and Lee Cottrell would like to invite you into the real world of information technology. They have created a lab manual that will allow you to evaluate your progression from new administrator for a small package delivery company to reliable Windows 2000 Server solution provider.

The Get-It-Right small package delivery company would like to use Windows 2000 Server as a networking option. You have been selected as an administrator to move the company through a series of day-to-day issues that will arise as the company migrates to Windows 2000. The Get-It-Right management and information services staff members will be depending on your expertise to provide their network users with the best features and services provided by Windows 2000 Server.

This lab manual is designed to assist you in providing the Get-It-Right Company with solutions that are both cost-effective and efficient. The manual uses a four-step approach to providing solutions to issues presented by potential network users. The first step involves the requirements or tasks to be accomplished. That step is usually provided by the Get-It-Right management or IS staff members. The second step involves sitting down and planning a course of action. In the second step, you locate your resources, identify the requirements, and make notes that will help guide you to a solution. The third step is where most of the real work is done. In that step, you implement the solutions to the requirements set forth by the company. The last step, which is by far the most important, is the testing phase. In that step, you make sure that all requirements have been met and that all facets of the solution implemented work according to your plans. The four steps are always present in one form or another in any task that requires the services of a network professional.

This manual is designed to place the reader in the spotlight, working in a real information technology environment for a for-profit organization that demands that the job be done right the first time. Networking professionals at any level can attempt to provide the real-life solutions required by the Get-It-Right small package delivery company. IT employers will find that potential employees are better prepared to meet professional challenges after using this lab manual. Here, you learn the proven techniques that are required to stay marketable in the field of information technology as a Windows 2000 solution provider.

Chapter Components

Each chapter is designed to provide you, the reader, with hands-on practice in a realistic setting. Each lab exercise was designed from the authors' experiences as network administrators. The exercises are designed to teach necessary job skills. Those job skills will allow you to become a valued member of any organization.

Each chapter starts with a brief description of a problem facing the company. The problem is explained, and you are presented with courses of action. You are then asked to solve the problem using various Windows 2000 Server technologies.

Each chapter contains a series of lab exercises. The exercises are divided into four parts: an **Introduction** to the problem, **Learning Objectives**, **Lab Materials and Setup**, and **Getting Down to Business**. Each part has an important role in teaching the necessary skill.

The **Introduction** reiterates a portion of the problem discussed at the beginning of the chapter. It focuses on one particular portion of the problem, and explains the best course of action. This section is usually presented as a business problem.

The next section, the **Learning Objectives**, tells you what to expect to learn from the exercise. Many skills are presented in this book. Each skill is crucial to becoming a successful Windows 2000 admin. Often, skills are repeated over the course of several labs. One example is the use of Active Directory Users and Computers. In several chapters, that snap-in is used to create users or to apply user rights.

After the **Learning Objectives**, a list of **Lab Materials and Setup** is given. The list is essential to knowing what tools and settings will be needed to complete the lab. From personal experience, I know how frustrating it is to arrive at a server to complete a task, only to find that the 2000 Server CD is needed and is locked in the boss's desk. By listing the needed materials up front, the admin is prepared before starting the lab. If you take this skill and apply it in the workforce, then you will prove to be a competent and organized worker.

Finally, you reach the **Getting-Down-to-Business** section. That section is designed to provide a general course of action to solve the problem. It is not a "click by click" description For example, you may be asked to start the MMC. You will need to know how to start MMC in Windows 2000 Server.

It seems that no classroom lacks a test or quiz. This manual is no exception. Two quizzes are presented in each chapter.. Both are designed to apply new knowledge in a business setting. The first quiz, the **Lab Analysis Test,** consists of five open-ended short-answer questions. Open-ended questions often have more than one answer. The questions look back on the lab and probe the skills learned. They explore potential weaknesses in solutions, or alternate solutions. Additional questions involve describing the technologies used. Remember that the purpose of the question is not to trick you, but to help focus your knowledge for a business setting.

The second quiz, the **Key Terms Quiz**, contains 10 keywords and 5 fill-in-the-blank sentences. The sentences define or describe the use of one or more of the keywords. Your task is to insert the correct keyword. The questions are designed to focus your thoughts on the most important terms from the chapter of study. Esoteric terms are left out. Only terms with a high practical value are included.

The last section of each chapter is the **Lab Solutions.** Each lab is completely solved, step-by-step, complete with pictures. The lab solutions provide one manner of solving the problem at hand. The solution presented is by no means the only solution to the problem. You are encouraged to avoid reading the solutions before you have solved the problem independently. Of course, if you are stuck, then glance at the solutions for guidance. Answers to the quizzes are also presented.

In summary, each chapter is designed around solving a problem for an organization. Each lab exercise solves either one problem or a part of the problem. You will gain practice working on a "live" Windows 2000 Server. This experience will mean the difference between being hired as a network administrator or as a hamburger administrator ("would you like to upsize that order, sir?").

CONTENTS

Answers to Lab Analysis Test 276
Answers to Key Term Quiz 276

**12 Implementing User Security with Policies,
Profiles, and Encryption. 277**
Limiting Remote Access 278
Securing the Server and Workstations with a Group Policy 279
Linking Policies to the Domain. 281
Verifying Roaming Profile. 282
Switching Off Control Panel 282
Encrypting a Folder. 284
Lab Analysis Test 285
Key Term Quiz 286
Lab Solutions for Chapter 12 287
Answers to Lab Analysis Test 302
Answers to Key Term Quiz 302

**13 Auditing Folders, Simplifying User Creation,
and Modifying Security Settings 303**
Auditing a Folder. 304
Creating a User Template 305
Changing Password Policies. 307
Analyzing the Security Settings 308
Lab Analysis Test 310
Key Term Quiz 311
Lab Solutions for Chapter 13 312
Answers to Lab Analysis Test 323
Answers to Key Term Quiz 323

14 Using Terminal and Internet Information Services 325
Installing Terminal Services in Remote Administration Mode. 326
Monitoring Terminal Services 327
Installing Internet Information Services. 328
Configuring an FTP Site 329
Lab Analysis Test 331
Key Term Quiz 332

MCSE
MICROSOFT CERTIFIED SYSTEMS ENGINEER

1

Preparing for the Challenges of Windows 2000 Server Certification

E mployment opportunities in information technology can be found in businesses worldwide. As a potential job candidate, you should be aware of the skills and knowledge required for such positions, and be able to evaluate whether or not your experience provides the knowledge and skills that a particular job requires. (In the business world, this preparation is often called "doing your homework.")

Identifying your strengths and weaknesses before attempting a new project is essential for success in any work environment. The labs in this chapter help you to evaluate your current knowledge and skills as they compare to the knowledge and skills necessary to work with Windows 2000 Server and to pass the Windows 2000 Server certification exam. You'll use the Microsoft Windows 2000 Server exam objectives as a measurement tool.

LAB EXERCISE 1.01

Identifying and Assessing the Skills Needed for Windows 2000 Server Certification

30 Minutes

Imagine that you are pursuing a job opportunity with the Get-It-Right package delivery company. The firm is looking for a project leader with network administration experience to migrate their network to a Windows 2000 Server network environment. All potential candidates will be evaluated on their knowledge of Windows 2000 Server, and although certification in Windows 2000 Server is not an absolute requirement for the position, it is strongly recommended.

You are currently employed by Get-It-Right, and are responsible for helping to maintain the company's current network. Management is in the process of choosing the employee that should be responsible for the overall project. You are highly interested in the position of project leader, but you're not sure if you have the knowledge and skills to install a Windows 2000 network. Obviously, if you're going to apply for the job, you need to know that your skills are up to the task. Confidence in your skills is also a significant asset during the interview process and negotiations for the position of project leader.

Learning Objectives

In this lab, you learn how to determine the skills that are required for the job, and evaluate your skill set before you interview for the position. At the end of the lab, you'll be able to

- Locate Microsoft's current certification exam objectives
- Identify key features of Windows 2000 Server
- Identify the skills required to obtain Windows 2000 Server certification
- Understand how your skill set measures up to the certification requirements
- Develop a rough estimate of how much time you need to prepare for the exam.

Lab Materials and Setup

The lab requires these materials:

- Pen and paper or word processor
- Access to the Internet
- Access to *MCSE Windows 2000 Server Study Guide* (optional)

Getting Down to Business

You create a matrix to compare your skill set to the Window 2000 Server certification objectives. Using the matrix, you analyze the Microsoft certification objective requirements, and your skill set to anticipate your learning requirements.

Step 1. Connect to the Microsoft web site (http://www.microsoft.com/) and locate the current list of Microsoft 2000 Server exam objectives.

Step 2. Use the list that you find to complete the "exam objective" column of the skills evaluation matrix (Table 1-1).

Step 3. For each objective in the matrix, evaluate your current skills using these terms:

- Knowledge of the objective: none (N), somewhat (SW), or good (G)
- Objective already achieved: yes (Y), no (N), uncertain (U)
- Time needed to complete the objective: short (SH), long (L), unknown (U)

Step 4.   Once you are satisfied with the matrix, ask your instructor or another information technology professional to review it and to help you make an accurate assessment of your current skills.

TABLE 1-1			
Skill Set Evaluation Matrix			

Exam objective	Knowledge of objective	Have I achieved this objective?	Time needed to complete the objective

LAB EXERCISE 1.02

Identifying and Evaluating New Windows 2000 Features

25 Minutes

The Get-It Right management team is impressed with the answers that you gave during your interview. They feel that you may be able to lead their migration project. The chief financial officer (CFO) decides to tell you the reason that the firm is migrating to another platform. She says, "We've been experiencing tremendous growth over the last year, and we feel that we've outgrown our current network. We realize that our competitors will not stand still and allow us to enjoy our success for too long. We need a network that will allow us to sustain our growth and help us to remain a step ahead of our competitors." She also says that she has been reading about the new Windows—in particular the literature about some of the features that will supposedly make Windows 2000 Server more attractive to the users of the system.

The CFO would like you to tell the management team how you think the new Windows 2000 features will benefit Get-It Right. Are you prepared to answer the question?

Learning Objectives

In this lab, you identify the new features offered with Windows 2000 Server, and you explain how those features might be successfully used in a Windows 2000 network at the Get-It-Right package delivery company. At the end of the lab, you'll be able to

- Identify new Windows 2000 Server features and services
- Determine the possible benefits of Windows 2000 Server services
- Discuss the importance of the services that Windows 2000 Server offers.

Lab Materials and Setup

You need these materials:

- Pen and paper or word processor
- Access to *MCSE Windows 2000 Server Study Guide* (optional)
- Access to the Internet

Getting Down to Business

To identify the new Windows 2000 Server features and to determine the benefits that these features can offer to Get-It-Right, follow these steps:

Step I. First, determine the resources that you will use in your research. Decide how to best document and present your findings to the management team. Remember that your audience will include many non-technical people: make sure that your documentation speaks for itself.

Step 2. Use Table 1-2 to organize the information that you will present about Windows 2000 Server.

- Choose the most important features and services offered with Windows 2000 Server.
- Briefly describe each feature.
- Explain how each feature addresses a need of the Get-It-Right package delivery company.

Step 3. Present your findings to your instructor or evaluator for review. Be prepared to offer any insights that may help to substantiate your views.

TABLE 1-2	Windows 2000 feature	Description	Benefits
Features List for Windows 2000 Server			

LAB ANALYSIS TEST

1. An information technology employee at your company is trying to decide if he has the prerequisites to pursue the Windows 2000 Server certification exam. Where would you suggest that he obtain the information?

   _____

   _____

2. Your boss would like to provide hands-on training for employees who lack networking experience but who would like to learn Windows 2000 Server. What suggestions would you offer?

   _____

   _____

3. A department head within your organization is not as thrilled as the rest of the staff about a possible upgrade to Windows 2000 Server. He still has nightmares about the general protection fault errors that were associated with Windows 95. What satisfaction can you offer him regarding some of the new features of Windows 2000 that address the causes for his concerns?

   _____

   _____

4. The Information Services (IS) staff at a small technology company is considering a move from Novell Netware 5.0 to Windows 2000 Server. They are wondering if Microsoft has addressed some of the inadequacies of its previous operating systems. One such inadequacy involves the ability of the IS staff to manage the storage requirements of network users. How would you answer their questions?

   _____

   _____

5. Everyone at a local Internet service provider is excited about the possibilities and opportunities that a new operating system can bring to their workplace. However, many of the staff members who will be involved in the actual change process are dreading the time that will be required to configure all the PCs in the various departments in a consistent way. What features of Windows 2000 Server might help them join in the excitement surrounding the new network operating system?

   _____

   _____

KEY TERM QUIZ

Use the following vocabulary terms to complete the sentences below. Not all of the terms will be used.

       segment

       RIS (Remote Installation Service)

       implement

       EFS (encrypting file system)

       DFS (distributed file system)

       NTFS (NT file system)

       administer

       driver signing

       protocols

1. A Windows 2000 Server Microsoft Certified Professional should have the ability to _____ and troubleshoot information systems that incorporate Microsoft Windows 2000 Server.

2. Using _____ , an administrator can configure a PC with all of the desktop properties and applications required by a user, can capture an image of that PC, and can then deploy the captured image to other PCs within the department or workgroup.

3. Using _____ , an administrator can simplify the organization of the network resources located on various servers by permitting them to be accessed from a single server.

4. To prevent faulty applications from overwriting system-level files, Windows 2000 Server uses a procedure called _____ . As a result, the operating system permits only Microsoft-approved software to be loaded onto the server.

5. Windows 2000 Server requires a thorough understanding of NTFS 5.0. One of the new features associated with the enhanced file system allows users to secure personal data by encoding and decoding their files with the _____ .

LAB SOLUTIONS FOR CHAPTER 1

The sections that follow walk you through the steps to solve the lab exercises. You should avoid looking at these sections unless you are stuck on a particular exercise.

Lab Solution 1.01

Your analysis of the skill set required of a Windows 2000 Server Professional should help you prepare for the questions that you may be asked during your interview with the Get-It-Right management team. Using the exam objectives as a guideline helps you to identify where you need to concentrate your attention before attending the interview. Your assessment should look similar to the one in Table 1-3.

Exam objective	Knowledge of the objective	Have you achieved this objective?	Time needed to complete the objective?
Installing Windows 2000 Server	N	Y	SH
Troubleshooting access to resources	N	U	U
Installing access to resources	N	U	U
Configuring access to resources	N	U	U
Configuring hardware devices	G	Y	SH
Configuring hardware drivers	G	Y	SH
Troubleshooting hardware devices	G	Y	SH
Troubleshooting hardware drivers	G	Y	SH
Managing system performance	SW	Y	L
Monitoring system performance	SW	Y	L
Optimizing system performance	SW	Y	L

TABLE 1-3

Sample Skill Set
Evaluation Matrix
(continued)

Exam objective	Knowledge of the objective	Have you achieved this objective?	Time needed to complete the objective?
Managing system reliability	SW	Y	L
Monitoring system reliability	SW	Y	L
Optimizing system reliability	N	U	U
Optimizing system availability	N	U	U
Managing system availability	SW	Y	SH
Monitoring system availability	SW	Y	SH
Troubleshooting storage use	G	Y	SH
Managing storage use	G	Y	SH
Configuring storage use	G	Y	SH
Configuring network connections	G	Y	SH
Troubleshooting network connections	G	Y	SH
Implementing security	N	U	U
Troubleshooting security	N	U	U
Monitoring security	N	U	U

Lab Solution 1.02

Most job candidates are usually quite knowledgeable about their areas of expertise.
However, many a job is lost because the candidate cannot identify the benefits that
their employment will bring to the business. Managers often like to ask why you feel
that you are the right candidate for the position being offered.

You have investigated the many new features that are associated with migrating a network to Windows 2000 Server. You are now better prepared to convince your audience of the benefits that you and Windows 2000 Server can offer the company. You have thought carefully about the audience that will be evaluating your findings, and so you have created a chart similar to the one in Table 1-4 that identifies new features, provides a brief description, and identifies associated benefits offered by Windows 2000 Server.

TABLE 1-4   New Windows 2000 Server Features

Windows 2000 feature	Description	Benefits
Remote Installation Service (RIS)	Using RIS, you can create an image of a Windows 2000 Professional computer and then use that image to install Windows 2000 Professional to various departmental computers.	RIS was created to ease deployment throughout an enterprise network. It eliminates the need to physically attend to each client computer.
Distributed File System	Features of the file system help system administrators by simplifying user access to files and by managing files that are physically distributed across a network.	Users no longer need to know or specify the physical location of a file to be able to access it.
Driver signing	Driver signing is a Windows 2000 procedure that allows the operating system to recognize Microsoft-approved third-party files, such as device drivers.	Driver signing reduces the chance that a faulty or corrupted printer driver, video driver, or other application will disable a computer.
System Monitor (SM)	System Monitor is an improved administrative tool that helps you to monitor the performance of a network	Enhancements in the performance logs and the Alerts add-on make it easier to configure and record network activity and warnings. Using System Monitor, an administrator can easily identify devices that may affect network performance.
Disk quotas	The disk quota feature allows an administrator to control disk consumption by users on a per-user or volume basis.	Administrators can set disk-space limits on individual users and can track users who exceed defined disk-space levels. As a result, unnecessary storage purchases are avoided.
Local Group Policy (LGP)	With Local Group Policy, an administrator can manage and control a user's desktop, including the applications available to the user.	Local Group Policy makes enforcement of desktop policies easier. The software and content of company PCs can be managed.

ANSWERS TO LAB ANALYSIS TEST

1. According to the documentation at Microsoft's web site, exam candidates are presumed to possess at least 1 year of experience in implementing and administering a medium-to-large network. You should have the employee reference to the Microsoft web site (http://www.microsoft.com/trainingandservices/exams/examasearch.asp?PageID=70-215) or a Windows 2000 study guide such as the *MCSE Windows 2000 Server Study Guide.*

2. Recommend purchasing several computers to create computer labs that consist of two to three computers each. Purchase several study guides to be used by students in the new program, and secure copies of the Windows 2000 Server operating system for evaluation and testing. If this approach is not feasible, then suggest that your boss purchase special software—such as Vmware—that will enable you to install multiple instances of the Windows 2000 Server operating system on a single computer.

3. Provide the department head with information regarding driver signing. Explain to him that, with this new Windows 2000 Server feature, the operating system will recognize files that have been approved by Microsoft as being functional and of high quality. Furthermore, explain to the department head that he can choose the level of protection for various PCs.

4. Windows 2000 Server comes with a disk quota feature that allows disk usage to be tracked and controlled on a per-user, per-volume basis. Using disk quotas, you can monitor the hard disk space consumed by users, and the amount that they have left in their quota. Monitoring helps the IS staff to identify users who may potentially be consuming an inappropriate amount of disk space, and to add space when users really need it.

5. Using the Remote Installation Service, you can set up new client computers remotely without having to visit each client. Selected administrators can configure a PC in their department, capture one or more images, and then deploy them to various PCs within the department or on the network.

ANSWERS TO KEY TERM QUIZ

1. implement (or administer)
2. RIS
3. DFS
4. driver signing
5. EFS

2

Performing an Attended Installation of Windows 2000 Server

I n this chapter, you perform the steps required to properly install Windows 2000 Server. Microsoft has made the installation of its operating systems in Windows 2000 much easier by enhancing certain features that were available in Windows NT 4.0 and by providing some additional features.

Before you actually start the installation process, you should plan ahead. Many network solutions have started out with tasks that seemed simple in nature, but that soon mushroomed into problems with many symptoms. Those headaches can easily be avoided by properly planning the network implementation. The skills of planning and implementation form the foundation of successful network administration.

LAB EXERCISE 2.01

Determining Resource Names and Network Layout

40 Minutes

Get-It-Right is a small package shipping company that has grown from a garage-based operation to its own office building, housing four divisions. Get-It-Right has decided to invest financially to improve access to company resources.

The Get-It-Right office building has been configured to support a 100MB Ethernet backbone. All offices have been wired to support access to the new company LAN. The company would like to move its network to a Windows 2000 platform. To accomplish that task, Get-It-Right has purchased additional computers and printers. You need to begin by providing the Get-It-Right management with these organizational aids:

- Naming convention for resources
- Network diagram/drawing showing naming convention

Learning Objectives

In this lab, you plan for the creation of a small network that will include personal computers, printers, file servers, and print servers. You name and identify computers and network resources, and you provide a sketch or diagram that supports the proposed naming conventions. At the end of the lab, you'll be able to

- Create naming conventions for computers and printers
- Create a resource allocation chart/table
- Design/draw a small network.

Lab Materials and Setup

The lab requires these materials:

- A pen and paper
- A drawing program (optional)

Getting Down to Business

You are going to provide Get-It-Right management with a naming convention for company resources and a diagram that represents those resources. Use this procedure:

Step 1. **Plan** your approach by first familiarizing yourself with the current Get-It-Right network and network resources.

- Review the Get-It-Right resources shown in Table 2-1.

Step 2. **Implement** your organizational approach.

- Use the information in Table 2-1 to create naming conventions for the Get-It-Right company resources.
- Enter your chosen conventions into Table 2-2.

lab
Hint *Whenever you provide technical documentation to management, remember the KIS ("keep it simple") principle. If you have to explain your documentation, then the design is probably unnecessarily complex.*

- Draw a diagram that represents the Get-It-Right network and that lists the names created in Table 2-2.

TABLE 2-1	The Get-It-Right Network Resource List			
Division	**Employee name**	**Number of computers**	**Number of printers**	**Operating system**
Administration	Avis Reed Godfrey Avents Michael Cross Felecia Ellis	Four	Two 17 ppm laser printers	Windows NT 4.0 workstation
Sales	Ron Jones Robert Smith Cynthia Wright Helen Oliver Shirley Smith	Five	Three Inkjet printers	Windows 95
Shipping	Sam Sneed Darryl Greene Bobby Orr Mike Jordan Willis Reid	Five	Two 6 ppm laser printers	Windows 95
Information Services	Fernando Murray Ron Carr Barbara Jones	Three	Two 24 ppm laser printers	Windows 2000 Server to be installed

Step 3. **Test** your approach by presenting your completed work to your instructor or evaluator.

   ■ Give the evaluator of your work the opportunity to make suggestions and changes. Your work is not complete until you provide the evaluator with a correction-free network diagram that meets with full approval.

LAB EXERCISE 2.02

Determining Hardware Requirements   **60 Minutes**

The Get-It Right management team is anxious to see the network come to life. They are quite impressed with the network diagrams that you created.

   The Get-It-Right resource list included old and new equipment. The managers have been reading that the hardware requirements of Windows 2000 are quite

| TABLE 2-2 | Naming Conventions for the Get-It-Right Network Resources |

Division	User name	Workgroup name	Computer name	Printer name	Operating system recommended
Administration					
Sales					
Shipping					
Information Services					

different from previous Windows operating systems. They are concerned that some of the equipment they own may not meet the needs of the new operating system. Can you provide the Get-It-Right management team with the information they need to make the proper decisions about the equipment needed for this project?

Learning Objectives

In this lab, you determine whether the computer hardware meets the requirements for installation of Windows 2000. You must record the current hardware configurations of the various computers and compare them against Microsoft's Hardware Compatibility List (HCL). At the end of the lab, you'll be able to

- Use administrative tools to determine hardware configurations
- Document hardware information for a personal computer
- Locate and use the Windows 2000 HCL.

Lab Materials and Setup

You need these materials:

- Access to a Windows 95, 98, NT 4.0, or Windows 2000 computer
- Access to the Internet
- Pen and paper

Getting Down to Business

You are going to provide the Get-It-Right managers with a written report of the equipment that fails to meet Microsoft's HCL standards. You'll add your recommendations on how to resolve the problem of non-compliant hardware. Here's how:

Step 1. Begin **planning** the content of your report by recording the hardware configurations of the equipment used by the Get-It-Right Company.

- Log on to the Windows 95/98 computer. Open Device Manager, and record the manufacturer or model number of these devices:

Device	Manufacturer\Model number
Disk drive controller(s)	
Disk drive(s)	
Display adapter(s)	
Display monitor	
CD-ROM drive(s)	
Processor(s)	
Network adapter(s)	

■ Log on to the Windows NT 4.0 computer, and record the manufacturer or model number of these devices:

Device	Manufacturer\Model number
Disk drive(s)	
Display adapter(s)	
Display monitor	
CD-ROM drive(s)	
Processor(s)	
Network adapter(s)	

■ Log on to the Windows 2000 computer, and record the manufacturer or model number of these devices:

Device	Manufacturer\Model number
Disk drive(s)	
Display adapter(s)	
Display monitor	
CD-ROM drive(s)	
Processor(s)	
Network adapter(s)	

■ Check the current HCL. Browse to http://www.microsoft.com/hcl/, and compare your hardware to the that shown in the hardware compatibility list located at the Microsoft web site.

■ Use the hardware legend at the web site to support your findings. (The legend should resemble Figure 2-1.)

lab
ⓘint

For the management team, remember to make notes that clearly reveal the meaning of the icons in the legend.

Step 2. Implement your research by recording your findings in Table 2-3.

Step 3. Test your research by presenting your completed work to your instructor or evaluator.

■ Give the evaluator the opportunity to make suggestions. Explain the risks involved if management should choose not to comply with your HCL findings. If your documentation is good, then you should easily be able to defend your findings.

FIGURE 2-1 Microsoft's HCL Legend

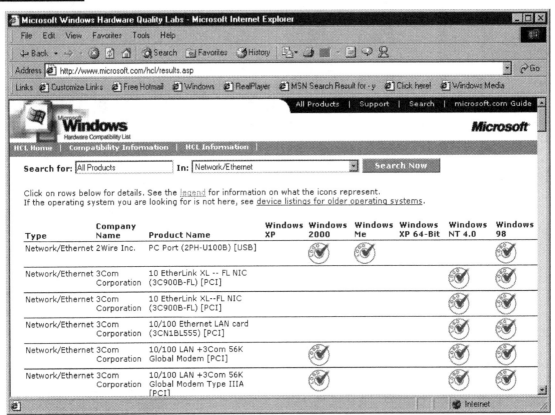

Computer name	Processor	Memory	Network adapter	Hard drive	HCL_LOGO	Meaning

TABLE 2-3 Results of Checking Microsoft's Hardware Compatibility List

LAB EXERCISE 2.03

Choosing a File System

15 Minutes

The Get-It-Right management team would like you to help them choose the proper file system for their new network. The company plans to use three Windows 2000 servers to support three database applications. One database is for payroll information; one database is for customer support information; and one database is for the shipping records that track package delivery. The managers would like to know the pros and cons of the various file systems available for use with Windows 2000 Server.

Choosing a file system and partitioning the hard drive go hand-in-hand. The file system that you choose determines the disk partitioning schemes that you can use. Certain file systems limit flexibility and restrict options for protecting data. Companies such as Get-It-Right are depending upon your expertise in these areas to choose the proper file system for their environment.

Can you help Get-It-Right make the proper decisions with regard to choosing a file system?

Learning Objectives

In this lab, you provide the Get-It-Right managers with the documentation that they need to make the proper file system choice for their network. At the end of the lab, you'll be able to

- Identify the three file systems available for Windows 2000
- Identify the strengths and weaknesses of each file system
- Determine the best file system to use in a network.

Lab Materials and Setup

The lab requires these items:

- Access to a Windows 2000 Server CD
- Access to a computer with the hardware listed on the HCL
- Access to the Internet (optional)

Getting Down to Business

To choose an appropriate file system for Get-It-Right, use this procedure:

Step 1. **Plan** by reviewing the factors that will affect your decision about which file system is best for the Get-It-Right network environment. Use this list as a guide:

■ Will the server be used to support additional operating systems such as NT 4.0 or Windows 98?

■ Do you need to support file names longer than 8 characters?

■ What role will file security play in the new network?

■ How much control over user data will be needed?

■ How much storage space can you give over to supporting the operating system?

Step 2. **Implement** by documenting your recommended file system choices in Table 2-4. You'll need this information for the next lab exercise, "Partitioning the Drive."

TABLE 2-4 Considerations for Selecting a File System

Server name	Dual boot?	Long filename support?	File security required?	Control user storage?	FAT32 or NTFS?

Step 3. **Test** your understanding of file system choices by having your instructor or evaluator check your selections.

■ Your evaluator should verify that you have addressed all of the items of concern listed in your planning step.

■ Your evaluator should consult the Microsoft web site or a Windows 2000 Study Guide to verify that you have addressed all areas of concern regarding your partition choices.

■ Remain open to suggestions and be able to show support for your findings.

LAB EXERCISE 2.04

Partitioning the Drive

30 Minutes

The closer you get to the actual implementation of the network, the more cautious the Get-It Right management team becomes.

The company has three PCs that they plan to dedicate as network servers. They plan to purchase three 10GB drives to support database applications (one for each server). The space requirements for the applications to be installed on each server will not exceed 4GB. The managers think that these purchased drives will allow for adequate application growth, but they are not sure of the storage requirements for the Windows 2000 Server operating system. Because the managers plan to install Windows 2000 Server on each machine, they would like to know if the operating system's requirements will affect their current storage requirements. They want answers to these questions:

- How much space does the Windows 2000 operating system need?
- What partitions will be required to support the operating system?
- Are special disk configurations needed?
- What utilities are needed to partition the disk?
- Can you provide management with the information that they need?

Learning Objectives

In this lab, you learn how to allocate hard disk space to support the requirements of Windows 2000 Server. You are able to identify the location of the operating system files and to use utilities that allow for the creation of disk partitions. At the end of the lab, you'll be able to

- Identify various ways to partition a hard disk drive
- Identify the two types of partitions required by Windows 2000 Server
- Determine the partition size for the Windows 2000 Server partition.

Lab Materials and Setup

This lab requires these materials:

- Access to a Windows 2000 Server CD
- Access to a computer with the hardware listed on the HCL
- Access to the Internet (optional)
- DOS boot disk with the FDISK utility (optional)

Getting Down to Business

To provide the Get-It-Right managers with information that will help them to determine their hard disk storage and partition requirements, use these steps:

Step 1. **Plan** by deciding your process for partitioning the hard drives that will support Windows 2000 Server.

Your plan should address these issues:

- Which utility will you use to create and delete partitions?
- Where will the system partition and boot partition reside on the hard drive?
- What will be the size of the partitions that you create?

You may want to search the Microsoft web site (located at http://www.microsoft.com) using the keywords "Windows 2000 Server." Such a search will locate documentation about Windows 2000 Server partitioning and disk storage. Record your findings, and use that information to complete Table 2-5.

cross
Reference *See Chapter 2 of the* **Windows 2000 Server Study Guide** *by Tom Shinder and Deb Litttlejohn Shinder (McGraw–Hill/Osborne, 2000).*

TABLE 2-5   Disk Partitions and Their Sizes

Server name	Disk partition utility	Number of partitions	Size of OS partition	Size of application partition	Location of system and boot partitions
IS-Server1					
IS-Server2					
IS-Server3					

Step 2. **Implement** your plan by creating a partition for storing the Windows 2000 Server operating system.

- Use a disk partitioning utility such as FDISK (DOS) or Disk Administrator (NT 4.0), or partition the drive during the installation of Windows 2000 Server.

- Use the information that you entered in Tables 2-4 and 2-5 when creating your partitions.

Step 3. **Test** your work by having your instructor or evaluator check your findings.

- Your evaluator should verify that you have addressed all of the items of concern listed in your planning steps.

- Your evaluator should also access the Microsoft web site or a Windows 2000 Study Guide to verify that you have addressed all areas of concern regarding your partition choices.

LAB EXERCISE 2.05

Choosing a Licensing Mode

15 Minutes

Using unlicensed or pirated software exposes your company to risks—legal and otherwise. The Get-It-Right management team has read several business articles related to companies suffering huge financial losses that were related to pirated or unlicensed software. A company can be financially crippled. They realize that any employee can turn in a company that has violated software license agreements. They also know that some companies offer incentives to whistle blowers who are willing to identify violators of license agreements. Fearing the worst, the Get-It-Right managers would like you to identify the current license situation at the company. You should identify currently licensed software, and calculate the licenses that you need to support the network.

Licensing is such an important issue with Microsoft that they have included a Licensing snap-in with the Administrative Tools to assist you in monitoring your purchased licenses. Can you help protect the company from violating Microsoft's licensing agreements?

Learning Objectives

In this lab, you learn the about the various license modes available with Windows 2000 Server. You also learn about Microsoft's Software Inventory Analyzer. At the end of the lab, you'll be able to

■ Distinguish between a per-server license and a per-seat license

■ Determine which license mode you should use

■ Familiarize yourself with Microsoft's Software Inventory Analyzer.

Lab Materials and Setup

To complete the lab, you need these items:

■ Access to a Windows 2000 Server CD

■ Access to a computer running Windows 2000 Professional or Server

■ Access to the Internet

Getting Down to Business

Here's how to check the current status of licenses on the system, and to plan for additional licenses, if necessary.

Step 1. **Plan** your approach by identifying the various types of licenses available and the utilities available to list the licenses that you currently own.

You can find the necessary information by using the Windows 2000 help utility, the Microsoft web site, or a Windows 2000 Server Study Guide. Make sure that your research identifies:

■ the various types of licenses,

■ when the licenses should be used,

■ the purpose of a Client Access License (CAL), and

■ how to determine your current licenses.

Step 2. To **implement** your organization of licenses, create a chart that identifies and describes the various licensing modes.

- Ensure that the chart includes an item pertaining to CALs.

- Include a section that you can use as a quick reference when deciding which environments require a particular licensing mode.

- Record your findings in Table 2-6.

- Now, connect to http://www.microsoft.com/piracy/samguide/tools/sat.asp and download and install the Microsoft Software Inventory Analyzer. Use that software to generate a current license report.

TABLE 2-6   Licensing Guide for Get-It-Right

Server name	Number of users	Multiple server access (per seat)	Single server (per server)	Number of CALs required (equal users)	Not sure of license? (per server)
IS-Server1					
IS-Server2					
IS-Server3					

Step 3. **Test** your findings by presenting them to your instructor or evaluator for inspection.

- If your documentation is sufficient, it should supply answers to the questions about licensing that the Get-It-Right managers have raised.

LAB EXERCISE 2.06

Joining a Workgroup or Domain

25 Minutes

Decisions, decisions, decisions. Will this task never end! What type of network security group should the new server be involved in—a workgroup or a domain? When and under what circumstances should that choice be made? What other requirements are needed to complete the task? The answers to those questions are required for successful implementation of the new network.

The Get-It-Right management team is not familiar with the concepts of workgroups and domains. They would like you to answer these questions:

- What is the classification of a workgroup?
- What is the classification of a domain?
- What are the requirements for joining a workgroup or domain?

Learning Objectives

In this lab, you learn how to differentiate between the requirements for joining a workgroup and those for joining a domain. At the end of the lab, you'll be able to

- Identify the differences between a server in a workgroup and a server in a domain
- Know the requirements for joining a server to a domain
- Identify a member server and a standalone server.

Lab Materials and Setup

The lab requires these materials:

- Access to a Windows 2000 Server CD
- Access to a Windows 2000 computer running Windows Professional or Server
- Access to the Internet (optional)
- A Windows 2000 domain controller with DNS installed (optional)

Getting Down to Business

To choose a workgroup or domain configuration for the network, use this procedure:

Step 1. **Plan** your approach by deciding whether this computer will be part of a decentralized group or part of an existing Windows 2000 domain.

- You need to research the requirements for joining a Windows 2000 workgroup or domain. You can perform a keyword search on "workgroup" and "domain" at the Microsoft web site located at http://www.microsoft.com.
- You can also use the Help selection on the Windows 2000 Start menu to access information regarding workgroup and domain joining requirements.

Step 2.   **Implement** your research by documenting the information that will be needed before a computer can successfully join an existing domain or workgroup.

■ Draw two diagrams that represent a small workgroup and a small domain that could exist at Get-It-Right.

■ List the requirements for joining a workgroup or domain within each drawing.

Step 3.   **Test** your work by presenting your findings to your instructor or evaluator.

■ Your evaluator can help you determine if all of the requirements for joining a workgroup or a Windows 2000 domain have been addressed. If you have documented your drawings well, your evaluator should be able to quickly approve your research.

LAB EXERCISE 2.07

Performing an Attended Installation of Windows 2000 Server

60 Minutes

The Get-It-Right management team would like to proceed with the installation of the server that will eventually host the Get-It-Right domain. The managers have used the pre-installation information that you gathered to accumulate a list of options that they would like you to use during installation of the first domain controller. Here it is:

Server name	Columbus (location of the company)
Workgroup name	Test1
Domain name	Get-It-Right.com
Administrator password	security
Licensing mode	Per server (count = 50)
File system	NTFS
Partition size	4000MB

You've researched and gathered all of the pre-installation information that you need to proceed with the installation of Windows 2000 Server. You'll need to install Windows 2000 Server as a standalone device using the Windows 2000 Server CD ROM. After successful completion of the server install, you'll need to promote the server to a Windows 2000 domain controller that will host the Active Directory for the new domain.

Are you ready to install the first server in the Get-It-Right domain?

Learning Objectives

In this lab, you learn how to perform an attended installation of Windows 2000 Server. You work with predefined options to create the Windows 2000 Server that will eventually be used to host the Get-It-Right domain. At the end of the lab, you'll be able to

- Install Windows 2000 using a bootable CD-ROM
- Configure a Windows 2000 Server as a standalone server
- Create a Windows 2000 NTFS file system
- Configure a Windows 2000 server to use a predetermined licensing mode
- Promote a Windows 2000 server to domain controller.

Lab Materials and Setup

You need these materials:

- A Windows 2000 Server CD
- Access to a computer running Windows 2000 Server or Professional
- A personal computer that has no operating system and that meets the requirements of your HCL documentation
- Access to the Internet

Getting Down to Business

An attended installation of Windows 2000 Server requires you to complete these steps:

Step 1.   **Plan** by securing the materials necessary to complete the installation of Windows 2000 Server and the promotion of the server to domain controller.

You must have this information at your disposal:

- How to obtain Internet access for the new server
- Product key for Windows 2000 Server
- Name of the server
- Initial workgroup name
- Administrator's password
- Licensing mode
- Networking components required
- Domain name
- Domain controller promotion requirements

Step 2.   **Implement** by installing Windows 2000 Server to meet the requirements that were defined by the Get-It-Right managers.

- Locate the information that details the requirements for promoting a Windows 2000 server to domain controller.
- Create a checklist to use as a guideline when you start the domain controller promotion process. You may decide to check the http://support.microsoft.com/support/kb/articles/q238/3/69.asp URL for information regarding the DCPROMO utility.
- Log on to the new server and perform the DCPROMO utility.
- Create the domain controller based on the information that you obtained.

Step 3.   **Test** by logging on to the new domain controller as the administrator. After you have logged on to the new domain controller, verify these items:

- DNS is installed on the server.
- The new domain controller has access to the Internet.
- You can ping the server name and receive the FQDN.
- The Active Directory snap-ins are available under Administrative Tools.
- The partition that you created is a 4000MB NTFS partition.
- The Get-It-Right management team (your instructor/evaluator) is satisfied with your results.

LAB ANALYSIS TEST

1. A small research and development company is trying to decide whether to build a domain-based network or a peer-to-peer (workgroup) network. What information could you provide to that company to help them make a decision?

   _____

   _____

2. The IS staff of Why.Now.org is considering a move to Windows 2000 Server. They have been debating for days about how to name the resources on their network. They are leaning toward names such as PRN-1 and WS-1. What recommendations can you offer the IS staff before they implement that plan?

   _____

   _____

3. A manager within the Accounting department at the Keep-It-Clean window washing company is having problems understanding Microsoft's licensing policy. He does not understand why his department might have to include additional money in its budget for server licenses. He feels that, because he has purchased the server software, then the licenses should be included. What information can you offer the manager to help him prepare for the additional expense?

   _____

   _____

4. Tom, an IS manager at a small Novell shop, would like to know why Microsoft has placed so much emphasis on hardware. He wants to know if Microsoft is trying to hide something. How would you address his suspicions?

   _____

   _____

5. Martha is the IS manager for a large enterprise network that is running Windows NT 4.0 Enterprise Server. She feels that she know all she needs to know about NTFS because she is using it within her Windows domain. What information can you give her so that she will know that NTFS has changed in Windows 2000?

   _____

   _____

KEY TERM QUIZ

Use the following vocabulary terms to complete the sentences below. Not all of the terms will be used.

> CAL
>
> DNS
>
> FAT
>
> FAT32
>
> NTFS
>
> seat
>
> server

1. You plan to install Windows 2000 Server and Windows 98 on the same computer. If you use a 3GB partition, then you will have to use the _____ file system.

2. If your network includes a Windows 2000 application, printer, and database server, you should use the per-_____ licensing mode. This mode of licensing allows users to connect to all servers simultaneously.

3. You are in the process of creating the first domain controller in your new network. You are not sure how your company plans to deal with the licensing requirements that Microsoft offers. You should use the per-_____ licensing mode, because that license mode can be changed at a later time.

4. Several users on the network are experiencing problems when trying to log on to the Exchange server. Some users are receiving messages that say the server is not available. These users all require a(n) _____ if they want access to the Exchange server services.

5. For a PC to be able to join a Windows 2000 domain, you need a Windows 2000 domain controller, a computer name, and the _____ service.

LAB SOLUTIONS FOR CHAPTER 2

The sections that follow walk you through the steps to solve the lab exercises. You should avoid looking at these sections unless you are stuck on a particular exercise.

Lab Solution 2.01

Here's how to decide on a naming convention and diagram your decision.

Step 1.   Review the information in Table 2-1.

Step 2.   In creating a resource naming scheme, always use descriptive names similar to those in Table 2-7.
Your network diagram should be similar to that in Figure 2-2.

TABLE 2-7   Naming Scheme for Get-It-Right Network Resources

Department or division	User name	Workgroup name	Computer name	Printer name	Operating system
Administration	AReed GAvents MCross FEllis	Admin	Admin1 Admin2 Admin3 Admin4	Admin- laser1-17ppm Admin-laser2-17ppm	Windows Professional
Sales	RJones RSmith CWright HOliver SSmith	Sales	Sales1- Sales2 Sales3 Sales4 Sales5	Sales-Inkjet1 Sales-Inkjet2 Sales-Inkjet3	Windows 98
Shipping	SSneed DGreene BOrr MJordan WReid	Shipping	Ship1 Ship2 Ship3 Ship4 Ship5	Ship-laser1-6ppm Ship-Laser2-6ppm	Windows Professional
Information Services	FMurray RCarr BJones	IS	IS-Serv1 IS-Serv2 IS-Serv3	IS-Laser1-24ppm IS-Laser2-24ppm	Windows 2000 Server

FIGURE 2-2   Diagram of the Get-It-Right Network

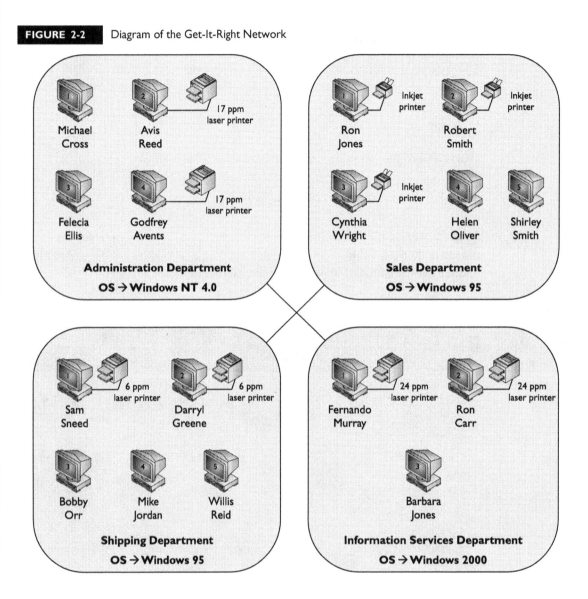

Lab Solution 2.02

Your answers in this exercise will depend on the equipment available to you.

Step 1.   To find hardware information about a computer running Windows 95/98, click Start | Settings | Control Panel. Double-click the System icon, and in the resulting System Properties dialog, click the Device Manager tab.

To find hardware information about a computer running Windows NT 4.0, click Start | Settings | Control Panel. Double-click the System icon, and in the resulting System Properties dialog, click the Device Manager tab.

To find hardware information about a computer running Windows 2000, click Start | Settings | Control Panel. Double-click the System icon, and in the resulting System Properties dialog, click the Device Manager tab.

Step 2.   Your hardware research at the Microsoft web site should lead you to create a chart similar to that in Table 2-8.

Lab Solution 2.03

Many variations are possible in completing this task. If you plan to use any partitions that have existing data, then you should back up the data on those partitions before you proceed with the creation of new partitions. Once you have a backup, you should complete these steps:

Step 1.   Decide on the disk utility for creating your partition. Do you create the partition as part of the installation, or will you use a utility such as FDISK or disk management? If this is a new installation, creating the partition during the installation process is the easier choice.

The partition for the OS should not be less than 2GB, which is Microsoft's recommended size. If you use only one partition, then the boot and system partitions will both reside on it. You should also create a second partition for the applications that the servers will support. Because the application software will not exceed 4GB, you could create one 8GB partition or two 4GB partitions. The additional partitions will allow adequate storage for the application software and any data that may be produced by the applications. Whichever combination of partitions you use, remember that the system partition must reside on the active partition. The best choice is to create three partitions. One 2GB partition to hold the OS, one 4GB partition to hold the application software, and one 4GB partition to hold the application data. Place the system and boot partitions on the first partition, and mark that partition as the active one.

Step 2.   Choose whether you might want to use special disk configurations such as RAID or Dynamic Disk. Remember that you cannot convert a disk from "dynamic" back to "basic." Do not make the choice if you are not familiar with the configurations.

Computer name	Processor	Memory	Network adapter	Hard drive	HCL_LOGO	Meaning
Admin-01						Indicates that the product has met all of the Windows Logo requirements for the logo program.
Sales-01						Indicates that the product has met all of the Windows Logo requirements for the logo program and that a driver is available for download.
Sales-02						Indicates that the product has met all of the Windows Logo requirements for the logo program and that a driver is available on the Windows operating system CD.
Ship-01						Indicates that the product may not meet all of the Windows Logo requirements for the logo program, but that it has been deemed compatible with Windows by the team that developed the operating system, and that a driver is available on the Windows operating system CD
Serv1						Indicates that the product has met all of the Windows Logo requirements for the logo program on a beta version of the specified operating system.

TABLE 2-8   Hardware Compatibility List Results for the Get-It-Right Hardware

Lab Solution 2.04

How to partition a hard drive strongly depends on the server's working environment.

Step 1.   Unless you plan to dual-boot the PC, you should select the NTFS file system, taking advantage of the features that it offers. You need a chart similar to this one to assist in the final decision:

Dual boot?	Yes/No
File security required?	Yes/No
Long filename support needed?	Yes/No
Partition greater than 2GB?	Yes/No
Encryption required?	Yes/No
Disk quotas?	Yes/No

Step 2.   Partition the drive as planned, according to the instructions supplied with your third-party partitioning tool. (Or choose the partitions in lab exercise 2.07 during the attended install procedure.)

Lab Solution 2.05

You should select a licensing mode that reflects the licenses required to access the resources in your network.

Step 1.   If you are not sure about the licenses that will be needed, then choose the per-server mode, because that mode can be changed at a later time. Remember these rules when dealing with server licenses:

1. Use the per-seat licensing mode if clients will be required to use multiple servers.

2. Use the per-server mode of licenses if you do not have a license for each client or if you are not sure which licensing mode should be used on your network.

Step 2.   Use the Software Inventory Analyzer to create a report on your server similar to the one in Figure 2-3.

FIGURE 2-3 Reviewing a report from the Software Inventory Analyzer

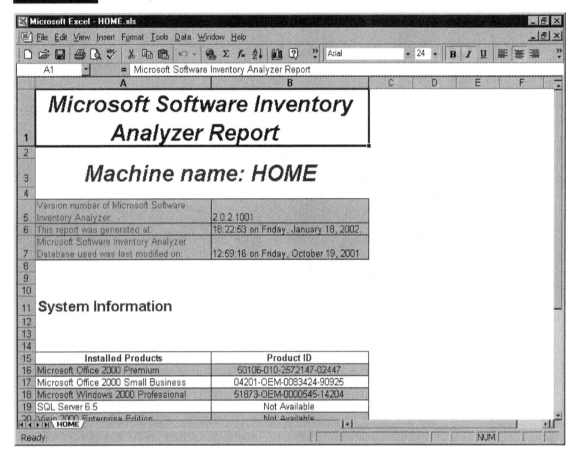

Lab Solution 2.06

You should know whether the server will become a member server in an existing domain or whether it will provide resource access to a small workgroup.

Step 1. Regardless of the choice you make, you should be armed with the domain name, computer name, or workgroup name that will be used to complete the task.

Step 2. Your drawing of the small workgroup should look like the one in Figure 2-4. For joining the workgroup, the requirements are these:

- Name of the existing or new workgroup
- Administrative privileges on the server

FIGURE 2-4

Creating the
workgroup
drawing

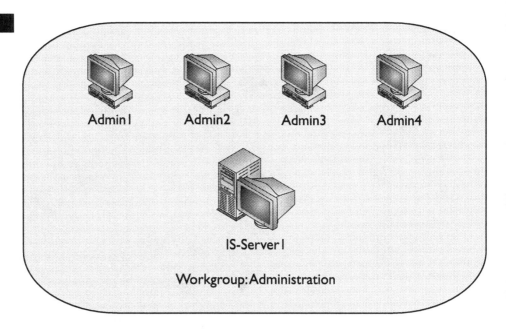

Windows 2000 Workgroup

Your drawing of the domain should look like the one in Figure 2-5. For joining
the domain, the requirements are these:

- Domain controller on the network
- Computer account for new server
- DNS server to resolve domain names
- Administrator privileges on the server

Lab Solution 2.07

During this exercise, you should have assembled your required materials and
information, and performed an installation in a way that resembles that described here.

Step 1.   Because the computer that you are using is on the hardware
compatibility list (HCL), you should install Windows 2000 Server using the

FIGURE 2-5

Creating the
Get-It-Right
domain drawing

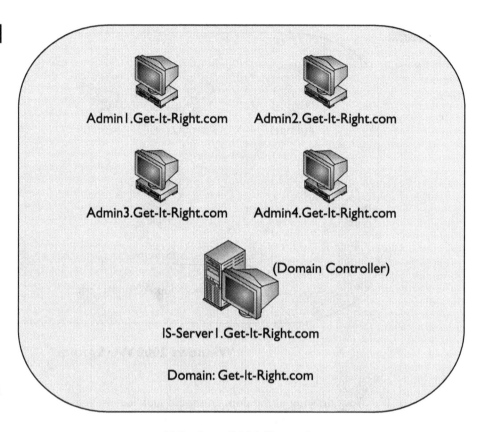

Admin1.Get-It-Right.com Admin2.Get-It-Right.com

Admin3.Get-It-Right.com Admin4.Get-It-Right.com

(Domain Controller)

IS-Server1.Get-It-Right.com

Domain: Get-It-Right.com

Windows 2000 Domain

bootable CD-ROM. You should use the information provided by the Get-It-Right management to complete the installation requirements for Windows 2000 Server:

1. Server name: Columbus (location of the company)

2. Workgroup name: Test1

3. Domain name: Get-It-Right.com

4. Administrator password: security

5. Licensing mode: per server, count = 50

6. File system: NTFS

7. Partition size: 4000MB

Step 2.   To start the installation from the CD, put the Windows 2000 Server CD into the CD-ROM drive, and then switch on the PC. Press SPACEBAR to boot from the CD-ROM.

At the Setup Notification Screen, acknowledge by pressing ENTER.

At the Windows 2000 Server Setup screen, press ENTER to install Windows 2000 Server.

Because this is a new partition, when the Windows 2000 Server Setup screen opens, press C to continue with setup.

At the Windows 2000 License Agreement, read the license agreement and press F8 to accept it.

At the Windows 2000 Server Setup screen, choose to create a new partition or to use an existing partition.

If you chose to create, you must enter the partition size (4000MB). Press ENTER to create. Select the new partition, and then press ENTER to install Windows 2000 Server.

At the Windows 2000 Server Setup screen, choose to format the partition as NTFS. Press ENTER to format. Windows 2000 formats the drive and copies files to the installation folders. The Setup process counts down 15 seconds, and then restarts the PC.

The GUI phase of installation starts, and the Welcome to the Windows 2000 Setup wizard opens. Click Next to continue.

The Installing Devices screen opens, and the Regional Settings screen appears. Verify that the settings reflect the location of the company, and then click Next.

At the Personalize Software screen, type Get-It-Right into the Name and Organization fields, and then click Next.

At the Your Product Key screen, enter the 25 alphanumeric product key found on the Windows 2000 CD case, and then click Next.

At the Windows 2000 Licensing Mode screen, choose the per-server licensing mode. Enter 50 concurrent connections.

At the Computer Name and Administrator Password screen, enter **Columbus** for the server name. Enter **security** for the administrator account password, and then click Next.

At the Windows 2000 Component screen, review the list, and then click Next.

At the Date and Time Settings screen, enter the correct date and time for Columbus, Ohio. Choose to automatically adjust clock for daylight savings time, and then click Next.

At the Network Settings screen, review the components that are installed with the Typical settings, and then click Next.

At the Workgroup and Computer Domain Name screen, click No, to not join a domain. Enter **Test1** for workgroup name.

Complete the Windows 2000 Setup wizard by clicking Finish.

Now, complete promoting the server to a domain controller. Log on to the server as administrator with the password **security**.

To run DCPROMO, click Start, and then click Run. Type **DCPROMO** into the Run box, and then click OK.

The Active Directory wizard opens. Click Next.

Review the selections on the Domain Controller Type screen (Figure 2-6). Click Domain Controller for a new domain, and then click Next.

At the Create Tree or Child Domain screen, click "Create a new domain tree," and then click Next.

At the Create or Join Forest screen (Figure 2-7), choose to create a new forest of domain trees. Click Next.

At the New Domain Name screen, type **Get-It-Right.com**, and then click Next.

At the NetBIOS Domain Name screen, accept the default entry, and then click Next.

Specifying
the domain
controller type

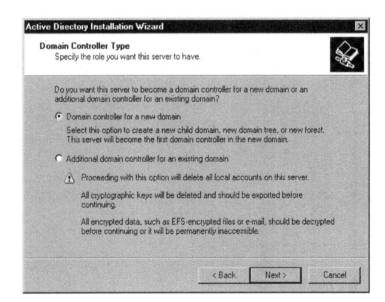

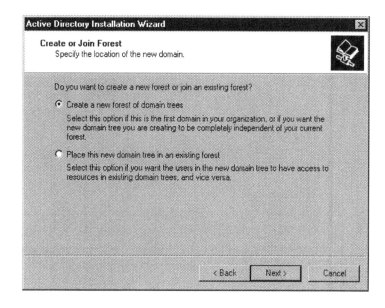

FIGURE 2-7

Choosing
to create
or join a forest

Review the location of the database and log files (Figure 2-8). Accept the default, and then click Next.

FIGURE 2-8

Reviewing
the locations
of the database
and log files

Review the Shared System Volume screen carefully. Accept the default by clicking Next.

Review the information message that now appears concerning DNS:

When you are done reading, click OK.

The Configure DNS screen now asks if you want to configure the Domain Name System service for the new domain. Choose the Yes option, and click Next.

Review the information on the Permissions screen (Figure 2-9). Choose permissions compatible with pre-Windows 2000 servers, and click Next.

At the Directory Services Restore Mode Administration Password screen, leave the password blank, and then click Next.

At the installation Summary screen (Figure 2-10), review all of the selections, and, if you are satisfied, click Next. Afterward, click Finish.

When prompted to reboot, click Restart Now.

FIGURE 2-9

Setting
the default
permissions
for objects
in the domain

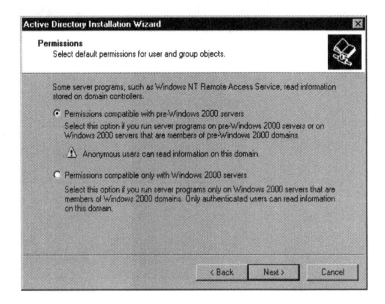

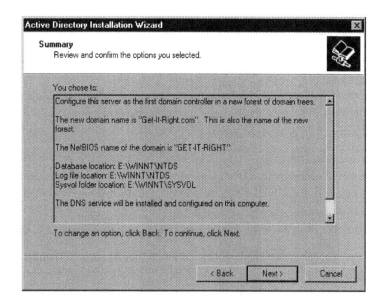

FIGURE 2-10

Reviewing
the installation
summary screen
for the new
domain controller

Step 3. Verify the installation by logging on as administrator using the
password **security**.

Is DNS installed on the server? Does the new domain controller have access to
the Internet? Can you ping the server name and receive the FQDN? Are the Active
Directory snap-ins available under Administrative Tools? Is the partition that you
created a 4000MB NTFS partition? Are the Get-It-Right management team (your
instructor/evaluator) satisfied with your results?

ANSWERS TO LAB ANALYSIS TEST

1. Inform the company that, if they are considering a Windows 2000 domain, they need to be familiar with Windows 2000 Active Directory. Any Windows 2000 Server that is acting as a domain controller will have Active Directory installed. Active Directory requires extensive knowledge of directory services and a thorough knowledge of DNS. If they lack that expertise and do not wish to contract out the service, then they should consider building a workgroup.

2. You should explain to the IS staff that resource names in Windows 2000 should be designed with the end user in mind. It is important to use names that are descriptive in nature. Failure to create names that easily identify the purpose and location of resources could lead to unnecessary delays in responding to end user problems. Resource names should be similar to these: Account_01 (PC), Account_Laser_1 (printer), and MailServer_1 (e-mail).

3. Before trying to explain the licensing issues to the manager, refer him to the Microsoft web site. Give him the opportunity to read Microsoft's licensing policy before trying to explain the requirements. Once the manager has read the information, you can explain to him that Microsoft requires a server access license before clients can use resources on a Windows 2000 server. You can then proceed to explain the pros and cons of the two licensing modes. Be sure to mention that Windows 2000 Professional includes a CAL as part of the operating system software.

4. You might start off your explanation by saying "Microsoft is a quick learner." Microsoft has learned that untested device drivers can cause an operating system to hang or crash. They have realized that although they do not make hardware drivers, users of their software often feel that the operating system is the cause of their problems. In an effort to make the operating system more reliable in the eyes of their users, Microsoft recommends loading only device drivers that have been thoroughly tested by the manufacturer. Microsoft has included a procedure called Driver Signing that allows the operating system to recognize files that have been approved by Microsoft.

5. Instead of reinforcing her views about NTFS, you may save yourself a lot of time by identifying the new features of NTFS 5.0 that will offer her the most benefits as a network administrator. You may want to point out that NTFS 5.0 offers disk quotas that an administrator can use to control user storage requirements. That feature is not available in NT 4.0. In addition, Microsoft's Active Directory helps users and administrators to manage and search the network much more easily than in Windows NT 4.0. However, the Active Directory will work only with NTFS 5.0.

ANSWERS TO KEY TERM QUIZ

1. FAT32

2. seat

3. server

4. CAL

5. DNS

MICROSOFT CERTIFIED SYSTEMS ENGINEER

3

Automating the Deployment of Windows 2000

Thisᵗ chapter discusses various ways to automate the deployment of Windows 2000. Windows 2000 Server offers several features that make the installation of Windows Professional or Server much easier for an administrator. Microsoft has designed these new features and capabilities to reduce the total cost of ownership, which includes the amount of money and time spent installing and configuring software. The proper deployment of Windows 2000 requires good planning and adequate preparation.

Windows 2000 Server deployment options allow for the total or incremental deployment of operating system and application software. They significantly reduce user downtime and increase the chances of successful deployment. You'll investigate some of the methods of Windows 2000 deployment such as System Preparation Tool, Remote Installation Preparation, and the Remote Installation Service. You will also explore using the Windows 2000 Setup Manager to create unattended installation files to help automate Windows 2000 deployment.

Understanding the features and capabilities of Windows 2000 deployment will make you a valuable asset to any organization. Proper planning and preparation will help you develop deployment options that are cost effective and successful. The goal of any good administrator should be to save the company money and to reduce the time associated with change management. The skills that you learn in this chapter will help you properly plan and deploy Windows 2000.

LAB EXERCISE 3.01

Using the System Preparation Tool (SysPrep) to Deploy Windows 2000

30 Minutes

You are the new administrator for the Get-It-Right package shipping company. The company has recently invested financially to improve employee access to company resources. The company has purchased several hundred computers that they would like to allocate to different divisions within the company. They would like to use the most time and cost-effective methods to prepare those computers for use.

The managers have been investigating the benefits associated with automated deployment and would like you to evaluate the different Windows 2000 deployment features. They want you to create a computer image that will be used as the foundation for each department. It has been suggested that you start with the Windows System Preparation tool.

Do you have the know-how to plan and prepare for the proper deployment of Windows 2000 using the SysPrep utility?

Learning Objectives

In this lab, you plan for the successful deployment of Windows 2000 Professional by using the Windows System Preparation tool. On a master computer, you install Windows 2000 Professional and any applications that are to be installed on the destination computers. You then run SysPrep to prepare for the transfer of the image to the other computers. The major advantage of SysPrep installation is speed: only the files required for the specific configuration are created as part of the image. At the end of the lab, you'll be able to

- Locate and extract the Windows 2000 deployment tools
- Know the requirements that must be met before using the SysPrep utility
- Know the files that are associated with the SysPrep utility
- Create an image to be used for deployment.

Lab Materials and Setup

The lab requires these materials:

- Access to a computer that has a clean installation of Windows 2000 Server
- Windows 2000 Server CD
- Pen or pencil
- Access to Windows 2000 help utility
- Access to the www.microsoft.com web site (optional)
- Access to a third-party imaging tool (optional)

Getting Down to Business

In this lab, you are going to create an image that will be used to deploy Windows 2000 Professional or Server to various departments at Get-It-Right. You will use the SysPrep utility to create an image of Windows 2000 Professional or Server. Using an image means time and money savings for the company as they deploy Windows 2000 to various company departments. Use this procedure:

Step 1. **Plan** for image creation by determining the requirements for running the SysPrep utility.

■ Make sure that SysPrep is a viable deployment option for Get-It-Right. Use Table 3-1 to complete the list of requirements that must be met before you can use the SysPrep Utility.

TABLE 3-1	Requirements	Notations
SysPrep Utility Requirements	Hardware Abstraction Layer (HAL)	
	Advanced Configuration and Power Interface (ACPI)	
	Mass storage devices	
	Plug and Play devices	
	Third-party utility	

■ Next, complete Table 3-2 so that you can provide the Get-It-Right management with a description of the components that are used by the SysPrep utility.

TABLE 3-2	Component	Description
SysPrep Utility Components	SYSPREP.EXE /QUIET	
	SYSPREP.EXE /NOSIDGEN	
	SYSPREP.EXE /REBOOT	

lab
Hint

You may want to use the Windows 2000 help utility or the Microsoft web site (located at www.microsoft.com) to complete Tables 3-1 and 3-2.

Step 2.   **Implement** image creation by using the information that you collected in Tables 3-1 and 3-2 to create an image of a Windows 2000 server.

- Make any necessary changes to the Windows 2000 server—for example, the desktop configuration, application installations, or service pack updates.

- Do not join the computer to a domain. Verify that the applications and components on the PC work as expected.

- Locate the DEPLOY.CAB file located on the Windows 2000 Server CD. Extract all the files, including the SYSPREP.EXE and SETUPCL.EXE files, to a folder called **deploy**.

- Run the SYSPREP.EXE utility with the reboot option.

Step 3.   (Optional) **Test** the image.

- If you have a third-party disk imaging utility such as Power Quest's Drive Image or Storage Soft's ImageCast, you can capture the image of the source computer. Once you have captured the image, you can then deploy it to a computer that meets the requirements you listed in Table 3-1.

LAB EXERCISE 3.02

Using Setup Manager to Create Answer Files for Unattended Installation of Windows 2000

30 Minutes

The Get-It Right package delivery company currently comprises three divisions: Sales, Administration, and Shipping. The management team would like you to create answer files to help deploy Windows 2000 Server to computers that may not all be configured in the same way. Management would like you to involve the departmental users as little as possible and to complete the installs in a timely manner.

Are you capable of handling those requirements?

Learning Objectives

In this lab, you use the Windows 2000 Setup Manager utility to create answer files to automatically deploy Windows 2000 Server. The utility simplifies the addition of user or computer-specific configuration information. You reduce the possibility of syntax errors in your answer files by using the graphical interface of the Windows 2000 Setup Manager. At the end of the lab, you'll be able to

- Locate the Windows 2000 Setup Manager utility
- Use the Windows 2000 Setup Manager to create unattended installation answer files
- Use the Windows 2000 unattend.doc to create custom answer files.

Lab Materials and Setup

You need these items for the lab:

- Access to a personal computer running Windows 2000 Server or Professional
- Windows 2000 Server CD
- Microsoft Office CD (optional)
- Pen or pencil
- 1.44MB disk
- Access to Windows 2000 help utility
- Access to Microsoft's web site (optional)

Getting Down to Business

You are going to create a custom answer file for the Get-It-Right Sales division. The file that you create will be used at a later time to automatically deploy Windows 2000 Server to a PC within the Sales division of the company. You locate the Deploy.cab file on the Windows 2000 Server CD, and you extract the Setup Manager utility. You then use the Setup Manager utility to create an answer file to deploy Windows 2000 Server unattended. That process will save Get-It-Right significant time and money. In addition, the utility eliminates the need for user intervention. Here's how:

Step 1. **Plan** the creation of the answer file.

- Locate the Windows 2000 Server CD, and extract the Setup Manager and the unattend.doc file from the Deploy.cab file. You will use the Setup

Manager and the unattend.doc file to create a custom answer file for the Sales division.

■ Examine the information in the various lists that follow. They will aid you in creating the custom answer file.

Initial settings	
Default name	Avis Reed
Organization	Get-It-Right
Licensing mode	Per server
Concurrent connections	50
Computer name	Sales-Server
Administrator password	sales
Auto logon	2
Display colors	True color (24-bit)
Screen Area	800x600

Network settings, custom	
IP address	10.10.1.1
Subnet mask	255.248.0.0
Default gateway	10.10.1.20
DNS address	208.27.168.7
WINS address	10.10.1.16
Enable NetBIOS over TCP/IP	
Client for Microsoft Networks	
File and print sharing for Microsoft Networks	
Internet protocol (TCP/IP)	
Time zone	Eastern Time

Proxy settings	
Proxy server	10.10.1.76
Port	80

Browser settings	
Home page	http://get-it-right.com/
Search page	http://yahoo.com/

Installation folder	
TargetPath	Sales
Workgroup	Sales
File system	NTFS
Install Office 2000	D:\Office\Setup.exe (optional)
Install Windows 2000 Server	From CD
Answer file name and location	a:\winnt.sif

Step 2. **Implement** by creating a custom answer file based on the information provided in step 1.

- Use the Windows 2000 help utility and the unattend.doc file that you extracted from the Deploy.cab file to meet the requirements listed in step 1.

- Having created the answer file, you will use the Windows 2000 CD and the winnt.sif file in lab exercise 3.05 to automatically deploy Windows 2000 Server to a partition on a PC.

Step 3. **Test** by having your instructor or Windows 2000 Professional check your winnt.sif file for completeness.

- Use the list provided in step 1 to insure that all requirements have been addressed in your unattended answer file.

- Show your instructor how to use the find command to locate key words in the unattend.doc file. That process will help you quickly create more sophisticated custom answer files in the future.

LAB EXERCISE 3.03

Configuring the Remote Installation Service

60 Minutes

Deploying the operating system and application software to the various users and departments within a company can be very challenging. Many IS staff members have lost many a night's sleep trying to anticipate and to prepare for the variations of user desktop configurations that they may have to install and support. Microsoft has promoted the use of remote OS installation to deploy software to various desktops throughout a company's infrastructure to drastically reduce the need for IS staff involvement.

You are one of the IS staff administrators for the Get-It-right network. You are being asked to configure the Remote Installation Service (RIS) for the company's network. Windows 2000 Professional will be deployed to various departments within the company. You must configure a RIS server that will be used at a later time to deploy Windows 2000 Professional to a test environment.

Are you capable of handling this challenge?

Learning Objectives

In this lab, you set up and configure a RIS server. RIS Server is a bundled component of the Windows 2000 Server operating system. Your configuration of RIS will include the supported services of DHCP, DNS, and the Windows 2000 Active Directory. You will need to authorize the RIS Server and create a remote installation boot disk for client PCs that are not PXE (Preboot Execution Environment)–compliant. The RIS server that you create will be used in the next lab exercise to automatically deploy Windows Professional to a client PC within a predefined department. At the end of the lab, you'll be able to

- Install and configure RIS
- Authorize a RIS server to respond to a client request
- Create a remote installation boot disk.

Lab Materials and Setup

The lab requires these materials:

- A 1.44MB disk
- A Windows 2000 server that has access to the Active Directory, DHCP, and DNS services. The server must also have a blank NTFS partition, 800MB to 1GB in size
- A PC running Windows 2000 Professional
- Windows 2000 Server CD
- Windows 2000 Professional CD
- Crossover cable to connect two NICs (network interface cards)
- Small hub to connect two PCs (optional)

Getting Down to Business

You are going to install Windows 2000 Remote Installation Service on an NTFS partition. That partition cannot contain the Windows 2000 Server operating system. Successful completion of this lab requires that the additional services DNS, DHCP, and Active Directory be already installed and configured. To install RIS, use this procedure:

Step 1.   **Plan** for the installation and testing of Windows 2000 services.

- Locate the Windows 2000 Server CD.
- Join the Windows 2000 client to your Active Directory domain. By doing so, you verify that clients are able to use the name resolution service of DNS, contact the Active Directory domain controller, and successfully obtain an IP address from the DHCP server.
- All of the requirements set forth in the plan section must be completed successfully before you attempt to install and configure RIS.

Step 2.   **Implement** the RIS installation.

- RIS must be installed on a Windows 2000 server using the DHCP, DNS, and Active Directory services.
- Install RIS on a NTFS partition that does not contain the Windows 2000 Server OS. Choose a folder in which to store the remote installation.

- Configure the server to respond to client requests for service
- Use default responses during the installation.
- Authorize the RIS server via the DHCP snap-in.
- Use the Active Directory Users and Computers snap-in to delegate control to all users to create computer accounts in the domain.
- Generate client computer names using first initial and full last name.
- Place any new computers in the same Active Directory container as the user setting up the computer.
- Choose the Automated Setup option for all client installations.
- Create a remote installation boot disk using the Remote Boot Disk Generator.
- Install Windows Professional using the RIS server.

Step 3. **Test** the RIS server by using your Windows 2000 client PC to verify the services of RIS, DHCP, and the DHCP Boot Information Negotiation Layer (BINL) extensions.

- Boot the client computer using the remote installation boot disk.
- Verify that the client received an IP address from the DHCP server.
- Verify that the RIS server prompts the user to "Press F12" to download the client installation wizard.
- Follow the screen prompts, and install Windows 2000 by selecting the appropriate image.

LAB EXERCISE 3.04

Using Remote Installation Preparation (RIPrep) to Prepare a Computer for Deployment

40 Minutes

Many deployment scenarios may arise when a company attempts to install and configure Windows 2000. The Remote Installation Preparation wizard (RIPrep.exe) provides the ability to prepare an existing Windows 2000 Professional installation, including user-specific applications and desktop settings, and to duplicate that image to various RIS servers on a network. All applications, including the Windows 2000 Professional OS, must reside on drive C. Once the client PC has been properly configured and tested, RIPrep must be run from the RIS server that will store the image.

Get-It-Right is a prime candidate for the benefits of Remote Installation Preparation. As the IS administrator responsible for RIS deployment at Get-It-Right, you are required to replicate an image of a pre-configured computer to your RIS server.

Are you prepared to accomplish this task?

Learning Objectives

In this lab, you run the Remote Installation Preparation wizard (RIPrep.exe) from the RIS server that will store the image of the source computer. You will store the image of the source computer to your RIS Server as a RIPrep image. After this image has been properly gathered on the RIS server, any PXE-compliant PC or PC with a remote installation boot disk can access the server to copy the new image. At the end of the lab, you'll be able to

■ Connect to a RIS server from a client PC

■ Create an image of a working PC using RIPrep utility.

Lab Materials and Setup

You need these items for the lab:

■ Windows 2000 Server running the Remote Installation, DHCP, DNS, and Active Directory services

■ Windows 2000 Professional client configured with various applications and desktop settings

■ A PC that has a hard drive with a 2GB partition and no operating system installed (optional)

■ Crossover cable to connect two NIC cards

■ Small hub to connect two PCs (optional)

Getting Down to Business

You are going to capture an image of a Windows 2000 client using the Remote Installation Preparation wizard. Once you have successfully captured the image, it can be deployed to other PCs within the company or to a specific department. Use this procedure:

Step 1. **Plan** your approach to the image capture.

- Verify that the source computer selected for the RIPrep image capture has been properly configured.
- Check to make sure that all applications have been properly installed and tested on the source computer.
- On the source computer, configure any desktop settings that are required by the company or department that will host the new PCs.
- Make sure that the source computer has a good network connection to the RIS server and that the DHCP, DNS, and Active Directory services are performing properly on the RIS server.

Step 2. **Implement** by capturing the image.

- Start the Remote Installation Preparation wizard.
- Log on to the source computer, and then click Start, click Run, and type this command into the Open text box:

```
\\RISservername\Reminst\Admin\I386\RIPrep.exe
```

- Accept the default answers for the wizard screens that appear, but change the friendly name of the image to **Get-It-Right RIPrep image**.

Step 3. **Test** by using the remote installation boot disk to connect to the RIS server.

- Install Windows 2000 Professional on a new client PC.
- Select the proper image file name and install the image to the PC.
- Once the installation is complete, verify that all applications and desktop settings are identical to those of the source computer.

LAB EXERCISE 3.05

Performing an Unattended Installation of Windows 2000 Server

40 Minutes

The financial success of Get-It Right can be directly attributed to their savvy business practices. It has been said that the management of the company evaluates all operational procedures in a continuing effort to improve the company's return on investment. The deployment of Windows 2000 will not be an exception to these practices. Time is money, and every effort should be taken to reduce the time required to implement change in the working environment.

You will deploy Windows 2000 Server unattended to show the Get-It-Right management that automated deployment of Windows 2000 significantly reduces the time and personal required to implement change in their working environment. Are you ready to demonstrate the savings that automated deployment will offer Get-It-Right?

Learning Objectives

In this lab, you use the custom answer file that you created in lab exercise 3.02 to automatically deploy Windows 2000 Server. You will use the custom answer file, and the Windows 2000 CD to quickly install a computer in Get-It-Right's Sales division. The installation will be performed fully unattended to show the company's management the cost savings associated with automated installation procedures. At the end of the lab, you'll be able to

- Perform a fully automated installation of Windows 2000 Server
- Install and configure proxy and browser settings during an automated installation
- Install applications during an automated installation (optional)
- Verify that the installation meets all requirements.

Lab Materials and Setup

For this lab, you need these materials:

- Floppy disk with the winnt.sif file located in the root directory
- Access to a personal computer running Windows 2000 Server or Professional that has a second 2GB blank partition

- Access to a computer that meets the requirements of Windows HCL, but that does not have Windows 2000 installed (optional)
- Windows 2000 Server CD

Getting Down to Business

You are going to install Windows 2000 Server using an unattended installation file and the Windows 2000 Server CD. Here's how:

Step 1. **Plan** by ensuring that you have the Windows 2000 Server CD and the floppy disk with the winnt.sif file located in its root directory. You will use that custom answer file to help automatically deploy Windows 2000.

Step 2. **Implement** by launching the automated install.

- Insert the Windows 2000 Server CD into the CD-ROM drive.
- Insert the disk that holds the winnt.sif file into disk drive A.
- Restart the computer and let the installation proceed without your intervention.

Step 3. **Test** by checking these locations to verify that all the requirements of the unattended installation have been achieved:

- Check the system properties of My Computer.
- Check the program menu for Microsoft Word, Excel (optional).
- Check Disk Manager for the file system and partition size.
- Check the NIC properties.
- Check the TCP/IP properties.
- Check the display settings.
- Check the Internet browser settings.

LAB ANALYSIS TEST

1. Mike, the IS manager for the Southeast Manufacturing division would like to use RIS for the deployment of client PCs in his department. Mike would prefer to use the PXE option rather than the remote installation boot disk. Mike would like to know if his PCs will support the PXE options. How would Mike know if the PCs in his division have the correct PXE ROM version, and what can he do if the version is wrong?

   _____

   _____

2. Joe is an administrator in charge of supplying client computers to sales representatives throughout his company. He likes the benefits associated with the System Preparation tool. He feels that the mini-wizard associated with SysPrep will save his staff valuable time. However he does not know if his PCs all have the same hardware. What information can you provide Joe so that he can determine whether SysPrep is the right deployment option for him to use?

   _____

   _____

3. Mark is the IS manager for the European division of his company. He would like to use the Remote Installation Preparation tool to deploy client operating systems to PCs in several locations throughout Europe. He would like to know if he can place the RIPrep images on CDs to be distributed to his IS staff. What information can you provide Mark before he invests resources in this project?

   _____

   _____

4. Sarah is the IS manager for Safe Foods, a large food processing company in the Midwest. Many of her IS staff members have multiple partitions on their PCs. Sarah would like to know if she can use the Remote Installation Preparation tool to image one of the PCs belonging to a staff member as a model for all IS staff members. Can she accomplish this task?

   _____

   _____

5. Randy is the IS administrator for a remote region of his company. He has been patiently listening to all of the deployment decisions that the company has been discussing over the past months. Management seems to be leaning toward using SysPrep as the deployment option for his region. He is not so enthused about the new strategy, because he knows that the equipment in his location have a minimum of five different configurations. What information could you provide to Randy to help him prepare for the deployment of Windows 2000 in his region?

   _____

   _____

KEY TERM QUIZ

Use the following vocabulary terms to complete the sentences below. Not all of the terms will be used.

> remote installation preparation
>
> Remote Installation Service (RIS) server
>
> Setup Manager
>
> setupcl.exe
>
> sysprep.exe
>
> sysprep.inf
>
> System Preparation tool
>
> Total Cost Ownership (TCO)

1. During preparation of a computer in the Sales department, you notice that the mini-setup wizard has failed to start. Which system preparation file is responsible for your problems? _____

2. If an administrator is able to lower the _____ involved in maintenance and administration of software installations and upgrades, he or she may receive a bonus at the end of the year because of the total savings to the company.

3. The _____ allows administrators to install software in various locations by allowing them to create files that provide the responses that appear during software installations or upgrades.

4. A type of image configured on a(n) _____ requires several Windows 2000 services such as DNS, DHCP, and Active Directory to function properly.

5. _____ is an answer file used during the duplication process that provides configuration information for target computers. It is possible to confuse this file with the unattend.txt file that is created with the Setup Manager.

LAB SOLUTIONS FOR CHAPTER 3

The sections that follow walk you through the steps to solve the lab exercises. You should avoid looking at these sections unless you are stuck on a particular exercise.

Lab Solution 3.01

The requirements that must be met and the answers about using the System Preparation tool (SysPrep) to prepare a computer for deployment are given on the next couple of pages.

Step 1. Although your answers may vary, your information summary should resemble that in Tables 3-3 and 3-4. Table 3-3 lists the complete requirements of a SysPrep installation. Table 3-4 lists the components that comprise the SysPrep utility.

TABLE 3-3	Requirements	Notations
Requirements for Using the System Preparation Tool	Hardware Abstraction Layer (HAL)	Hardware Abstraction Layer driver must be the same on the source and destination computers.
	Advanced Configuration and Power Interface (ACPI)	ACPI must be identical on the source and destination computers.
	Mass storage devices	Mass storage devices such as SCSI/IDE hard drives must be the same on source and destination computers.
	Plug and Play devices	The SysPrep master image automatically runs Plug and Play detection on the destination computer. These devices do not have to be the same on the source and destination computers.
	Third-party utility	You will need some type of third-party utility to copy and distribute the image. The SysPrep tool only prepares the source PC for imaging.

Step 2. To extract the deployment tools, log on with administrative privileges to your Windows 2000 Server or Professional PC. Insert the Windows 2000 Server or Professional CD into the CD-ROM drive.

Start Windows Explorer, and create a folder named **Deploy** in the root folder of the system drive (which should be C).

Select Start | Run, and click Browse. Browse to the Support\Tools folder on the Windows 2000 CD. Double-click the Tools folder, and then double-click the Deploy.cab file. Click OK.

TABLE 3-4

Components of
the System
Preparation Tool

Component	Description
SysPrep.exe /quiet	This option does not show messages on the screen.
SysPrep.exe /nosidgen	This option will not generate security IDs. This option allows each computer to generate its own IDs during the mini-wizard.
SysPrep.exe /reboot	This options forces a restart of the source computer after the image has been completed.
SysPrep.inf	Answer file
Setupcl.exe	Runs the mini-setup wizard and regenerates the security IDs on the source and destination computers.
Mini-setup wizard	Adds user-specific parameters on the destination computer.

Select all of the files listed in the Deploy.cab file. Right-click any one of the highlighted files, and then click Extract on the pop-up menu.

The Browse for Folder screen opens. Select the Deploy folder on the system drive, and then click OK. After the files are copied, use Windows Explorer to view the Deploy folder. There should be seven files in the folder.

lab
Warning *The steps given here assume that the SysPrep utility has been extracted from the Deploy.cab file to a folder named Deploy.*

To create a master image using the SysPrep utility, log on to the source computer with administrative privileges.

Select Start | Run, and then type **C:\deploy\Sysprep.exe –reboot**.

A warning message opens on the screen. Click OK.

The source computer prepares the image and automatically restarts the PC.

Lab Solution 3.02

The solution provided here creates an unattended answer file using the Windows 2000 Setup Manager utility. Also shown is a sample answer file that has been customized to meet the requirements of the Get-It-Right company and that has been renamed to winnt.sif. Although your answers may vary, your work should resemble the work outlined here.

Step I.   If you haven't yet extracted the deployment tools and placed them on the local machine (lab exercise 3.01), do so now.

Step 2. To create a customized winnt.sif answer file using the Windows 2000 Setup Manager, log on with administrative privileges to your Windows 2000 Server or Professional PC.

Select Start | Run. Into the open dialog box, type **C:\deplot\setupmgr.exe**. Click OK. The Windows 2000 Setup Manager wizard opens. Click Next.

At the New or Existing Answer File screen, accept the default answer "Create A New Answer File," and click Next.

At the Product to Install screen, accept the default answer "Windows 2000 Unattended Installation," and click Next.

At the Platform screen, select "Windows 2000 Server," and click Next.

At the User Interaction Level screen, select "Fully Automated," and click Next.

At the License Agreement screen, click "I Accept the Terms of the License Agreement," and click Next.

At the Customize the Software screen, enter **Avis Reed** in the Name box. Enter **Get-It-Right** for the organization name. Click Next.

At the Licensing Mode screen, select "Per Server." Type **50** into the "Number of concurrent connections" box. Click Next.

At the Computer Name screen, type **Sales-Server**, then click Add. Click Next.

At the Administrator Password screen, select "Use the following Administrator Password," and then type **sales** (in lowercase letters) into the Password and Confirm Password boxes. Select "When the computer starts, automatically log on as administrator," and then type **2** into the "Number of times to auto logon" box. Click Next.

At the Display Settings screen, set the display colors to True Color (24 Bit). Set the screen area to 800x600. Click Next.

At the Network Settings page, select Custom Settings, and then click Next.

At the Number of Network Adapters screen, accept the default setting "One network adapter," and click Next.

At the Network Components Screen, verify that the Client for Microsoft Networks, the File and Printer Sharing for Microsoft Networks, and the Internet Protocol (TCP/IP) components will all be installed by default.

Double-click Internet Protocol (TCP/IP). The TCP/IP Properties window opens. Select "Use the following IP address," and then enter these values:

- IP address: **10.10.1.1**
- Subnet Mask: **255.248.0.0**
- Preferred DNS server: **208.27.168.7**

Click the Advanced button, and then select the Wins tab. Select "Enable NetBIOS over TCP/IP," and then click the Add button. Into the WINS Server address box, type **10.10.1.16**, and click Add. Click OK, and then click OK again. Click Next when the Network Component screen reopens.

At the Workgroup Or Domain screen, accept the default option of "workgroup." Into the Workgroup box, type **Sales**, and then click Next.

At the Time Zone screen, set the time zone to "Eastern Time (U.S. and Canada)." Click Next.

At the Additional Settings screen, accept the default "Edit additional settings." Click Next.

At the Telephony screen, accept the defaults. Click Next.

At the Regional Settings screen, click Next to accept the defaults.

At the Languages screen, you do not want to add support for other languages. Click Next.

At the Browser and Shell Settings screen, select "Individually specify proxy and default home page settings." Click the Proxy Settings button. Select "Use a Proxy Server." Into the Address box, type **10.10.1.76**. Into the Port box, type **80**. Click OK.

Select the Browser Settings button. For the Home Page, type **http://get-it-right.com**. For the Search Page, type **http://yahoo.com**. Click OK, and then click Next.

At the Installation Folder screen, select "This Folder." Type **sales**, and then click Next.

At the Install Printers screen, you have no printers to add, and so click Next.

If you have an application to install at the Run Once screen, you must type the path to the install file. For example: **\\server1\office\setup.exe** or **D:\office\setup.exe**. Click Add, and then click Next.

At the Distribution Folder screen, select "No, this answer file will be used to install from CD." Click Next.

The Answer File Name screen opens. If you like, you can accept the default file name and location; otherwise, enter a path and name of your choice. If you don't enter a different path or filename, click Next to accept the defaults. Click Finish.

To rename and further customize the unattend.txt answer file once you have completed the Setup Manager utility, use Windows Explorer to locate the file that you created. Double-click the unattend.txt file. Notepad, which is a text editor, opens.

Customize the unattend.txt file to meet the requirements of the Get-It-Right company. When you are finished editing the file, save it in the root folder of disk drive A as "winnt.sif." (The quotation marks prevent Notepad from adding a TXT extension to the file.)

Step 3.   Here is an example of the custom winnt.sif file that you should have created:

```
;SetupMgrTag
[Data]
AutoPartition=1
MsDosInitiated="0"
UnattendedInstall="Yes"
[Unattended]
UnattendMode=FullUnattended
OemSkipEula=Yes
OemPreinstall=No
TargetPath=Sales
FileSystem = ConvertNTFS
[GuiUnattended]
AdminPassword=sales
AutoLogon=Yes
AutoLogonCount=2
OEMSkipRegional=1
TimeZone=35
OemSkipWelcome=1
[UserData]
FullName="Avis Reed"
OrgName=Do-It-Right
ComputerName=Sales-Server
[Display]
BitsPerPel=24
Xresolution=800
YResolution=600
[LicenseFilePrintData]
AutoMode=PerServer
AutoUsers=50
[TapiLocation]
AreaCode=757
[Branding]
BrandIEUsingUnattended=Yes
[URL]
Home_Page=http://Do-It-Right.com
Search_Page=http://yahoo.com
[Proxy]
Proxy_Enable=1
Use_Same_Proxy=1
HTTP_Proxy_Server=10.10.1.76:80
Proxy_Override=<local>;<local>
[GuiRunOnce]
Command0=D:\Office\Setup.exe
[Identification]
JoinWorkgroup=Sales
```

```
[Networking]
InstallDefaultComponents=No
[NetAdapters]
Adapter1=params.Adapter1
[params.Adapter1]
INFID=*
[NetClients]
MS_MSClient=params.MS_MSClient
[NetServices]
MS_SERVER=params.MS_SERVER
[NetProtocols]
MS_TCPIP=params.MS_TCPIP
[params.MS_TCPIP]
DNS=No
UseDomainNameDevolution=No
EnableLMHosts=Yes
AdapterSections=params.MS_TCPIP.Adapter1
[params.MS_TCPIP.Adapter1]
SpecificTo=Adapter1
DHCP=No
IPAddress=10.10.1.1
SubnetMask=255.248.0.0
DefaultGateway=10.10.1.20
DNSServerSearchOrder=208.27.168.7
WINS=Yes
WinsServerList=10.10.1.16
NetBIOSOptions=1
```

Lab Solution 3.03

The procedure to install and configure RIS and RIS Server is outlined here.

Step 1.   Verify that clients are able to use the name resolution service of DNS, contact the Active Directory domain controller, and successfully obtain an IP address from the DHCP server.

Step 2.   Insert the Windows 2000 Server CD into the CD-ROM drive. Click Start | Settings | Control Panel. Click Add/Remove Programs. Click the Windows Components tab. Select the Remote Installation Service check box.

When the installation completes, restart the PC.

To configure RIS, click Start |Run, and type **RISetup.exe** into the Run box. Press ENTER. When the Remote Installation wizard opens, click Next.

At the Remote Installation Folder Location window, type the designation for the drive that will hold the installation folder structure. Type the correct path to the folder as shown in Figure 3-1.

lab

Warning *The remote installation folder cannot be located on the same partition as the operating system files. The partition where you place the Remote Installation folder must be formatted with the NTFS 5.0 file system. The partition must have enough disk space to support multiple images.*

At the Initial Settings window, select "Respond to client computers requesting service,", and then click Next.

The Installation Source Files Location window opens. Indicate the location of the Windows 2000 Professional installation files as shown in Figure 3-2, and then click Next.

At the Windows Installation Image Folder Name window, accept the default name **Win2000.pro**. Click Next.

At the Friendly Description and Help Text window, type into the Friendly Description box the name of the division or department that will use the image. Then, type any necessary help information into the Help Text box. Click Next.

The Review Settings window opens (Figure 3-3). Review the Summary information shown in the window, and click Finish.

To authorize the RIS server, log on as a domain administrator to the server where the DHCP service is installed. Click Start | Programs | Administrative Tools | DHCP. The DHCP Manager Window opens.

FIGURE 3-1

Specifying
the path to
the remote
installation folder

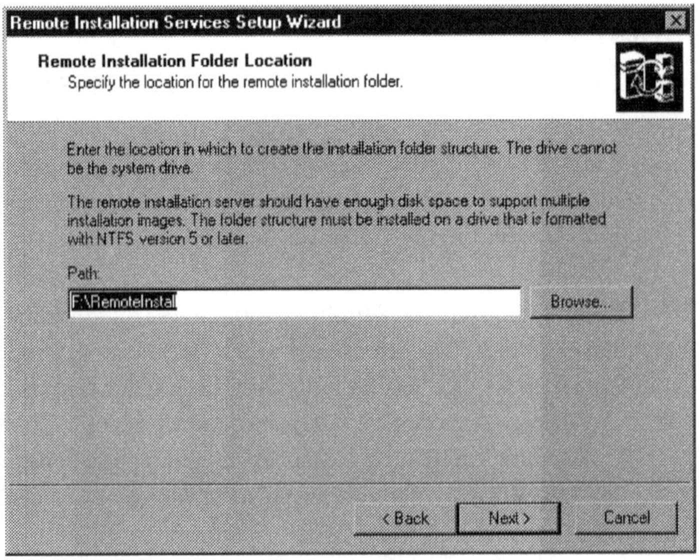

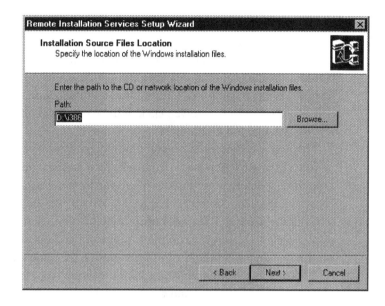

FIGURE 3-2

Specifying
the path to
the installation
source files

Now, right-click DHCP in the left-hand pane, and click Add Server. Type the IP address of the RIS server, and then click OK.

Right-click DHCP again, and click Manage Authorized Servers. Select your RIS server, and click Authorize. Click OK.

FIGURE 3-3

Reviewing
the RIS server
settings

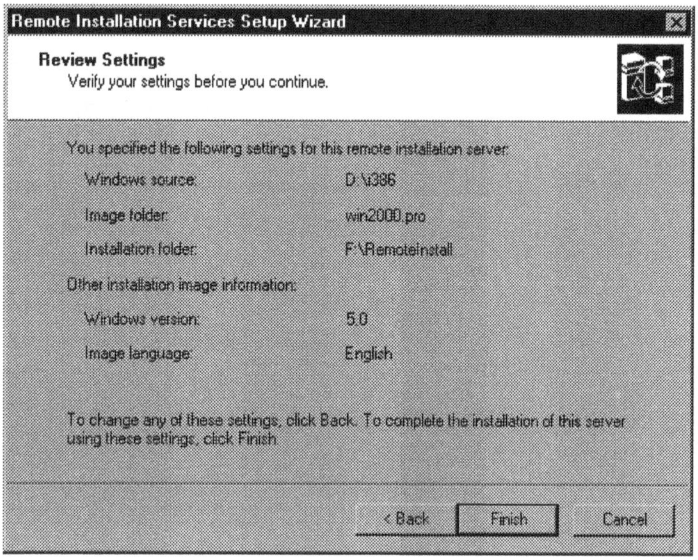

To create a remote installation boot disk, click Start | Run, and type **\\server_name\ RemoteInstall\Admin\I386\RBGF.EXE** into the Run box. Click OK.

When the Windows 2000 Remote Boot Disk Generator screen opens, insert a blank, formatted 1.44MB disk into drive A. Select your network interface adapter from the Adapter list. Click Create Disk, and then close the window.

To configure the RIS server, click Start | Programs | Administrative Tools | Active Directory Users and Computers.

The Active Directory Users and Computers window opens.

Click Domain Controllers. Right-click the name of your server, and select Properties. Click Remote Install. When the Remote Install tab appears, select "Respond to client computers requesting service," as shown in Figure 3-4.

Click the Advanced Settings button. On the New Clients tab of the RIS Properties screen, choose to name the computer based on the username of the user setting up computer. Now, select the Customize button in the same section of the window.

At the Computer Account Generation window, type **%1First%Last** as shown in Figure 3-5, and click OK, and then Apply, OK again, and then OK once more.

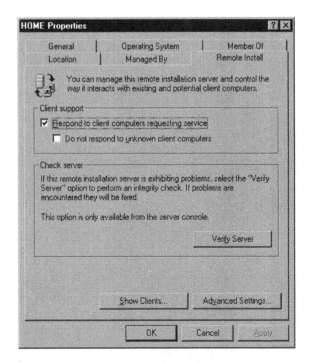

FIGURE 3-4

Permitting unknown client computers to request RIS service

FIGURE 3-5

Computer
Account
Generation

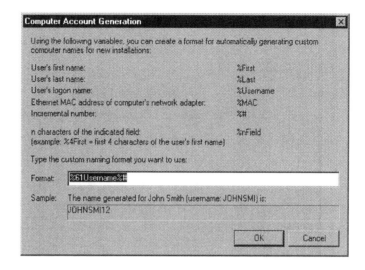

Lab Solution 3.04

Here's how to capture a Remote Installation Preparation (RIPrep) image for later use in deployments.

lab
Warning *The personal computer to be used as the master/source computer must be a RIS client and the Windows 2000 Professional Operating system must be installed on Drive C.*

Step 1. Carefully check the source computer's configuration. The image that you capture will exactly reproduce the current state of this computer.

Step 2. To create an image from the master (source) computer, log on to the computer (Windows Professional Client) with administrative privileges.

Connect to the RIS server where you want to copy the image. Select Start | Run, and then type the UNC path to the RIS server. The UNC path will resemble the one shown here:

```
\\RISservername\Reminst\Admin\I386\RIPrep.exe
```

The welcome screen for the Remote Installation Preparation wizard opens. Click Next.

At the Server Name Screen, enter the RIS server's name or IP address as shown in Figure 3-6, and then click Next.

At the Image Folder Name screen, enter the name of the folder that is to hold the image, and then click Next.

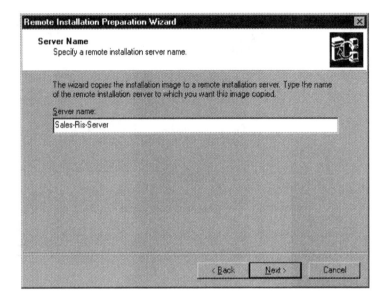

FIGURE 3-6

Specifying
the RIS server
name

At the Friendly Description and Help Text screen, type a user-friendly description such as **Sales user image**, and then type some helpful text such as **Please contact the IS department for additional help.**. Click Next.

The Review Settings Screen now opens (Figure 3-7). Review the summary information presented. If the information is correct, click Next.

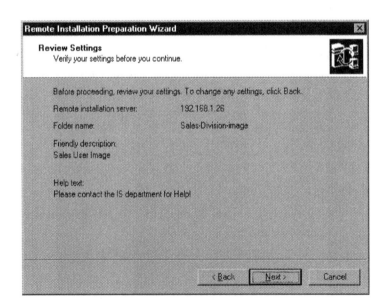

FIGURE 3-7

Reviewing the RIS
server settings

The Completing the Remote Installation Preparation Wizard screen now opens. If you are ready to proceed to capture the image, click Next. The wizard starts copying the image.

Lab Solution 3.05

Performing an unattended installation of Windows 2000 Server using a custom answer file involves two major steps.

Step 1. Make sure that the answer file has been renamed to winnt.sif and that the file is stored in the root directory of the floppy disk.

Step 2. Ensure that the destination computer supports bootable CDs and has at least a 2GB partition available. When you insert the CD into the CD-ROM drive, the automated installation of Windows 2000 server should now proceed as dictated in the custom answer file.

Step 3. To verify that the file system is NTFS, that the installation folder is Sales, and that the partition size is 2000MB, log on with administrative privileges to your Windows 2000 server.

Double-click the My Computer icon on the desktop. Right-click the system partition (which should be drive C), and then click Properties. Verify that the file system is NTFS and that the Capacity is 2GB (2000MB = 2GB). Click OK.

Double-click the system partition (drive C) and look for the Sales folder. Close the My Computer window.

(Optional) To verify that Microsoft Office installed successfully, look on the Windows 2000 server desktop for the Microsoft Outlook icon. Alternatively, select Start | Programs. Check the program menu for Microsoft Word and Excel.

To verify that the user name, organization name, workgroup, and computer name have been configured as required, right-click the My Computer icon on the desktop. Click Properties. On the General tab, verify that the software is registered to Avis Reed and Get-It-Right.

Click the Network Identification tab and verify that the workgroup is set to Sales and that the name of the computer is Sales-Server. Click OK.

To verify the Network settings, right-click the My Network Places icon on the desktop. Select Properties. Right-click the local area connection. Select Properties. Verify that Client for Microsoft Networks, file and print sharing for Microsoft networks, and the Internet protocol (TCP/IP) have been installed.

Double-click the Internet protocol (TCP/IP). The TCP/IP Properties window opens. Verify that the IP address is set to 10.10.1.1, that the subnet mask address is set to 255.248.0.0, that the Default gateway address is set to 10.10.1.20, and that the Preferred DNS server address is set to 208.27.168.7.

Click the Advanced button. Click the WINS tab. Verify that the WINS server address has been set to 10.10.1.16, and that the Enable TCP/IP over NetBIOS option has been selected. Click OK.

To verify the time zone, double-click the computer clock in the tray at the far right-hand end of the task bar. Click the Time Zone tab. Verify that the time zone is set to Eastern Time (U.S. and Canada). Click OK.

To verify the display settings, right-click an open area on the desktop. Click Properties, and then select the Settings tab. Verify that the colors are set to True Color (24 Bit) and that the screen area is set to 800×600 pixels. Click OK.

To verify the proxy and browser settings, right-click the big "e" (Internet Explorer icon) on the desktop. Select Properties. Verify that the home page address is set to http://get-it-right.com.

Click the Connections tab, and then click the LAN Settings button. Verify that the Proxy Server Address is set to 10.10.1.76 and that the Port Address is set to 80. Click OK.

Double-click the Internet Explorer icon on the desktop. Right-click the Search button on the toolbar. Select Properties. Verify that the search page is set to http://yahoo.com. Close the Internet browser window.

To verify the licensing mode, select Start | Settings | Control Panel. Double-click the Licensing icon. Verify that the Per Server option has been selected and that the number of concurrent connections is set to 50. Click OK.

ANSWERS TO LAB ANALYSIS TEST

1. When a PXE-compliant PC boots, a PXE ROM message appears on the screen. Mike can check the PXE ROM code version that is displayed during the boot sequence of each client machine. Mike may have to invoke the BIOS ROM menu and select PXE rather than TCP/IP or BOOTP to see the version number. Windows 2000 RIS supports .99c or greater PXE ROMs. You may be required to obtain a newer version of the PXE-based ROM code from the manufacturer of your PC. You may also refer Mike to the Microsoft web site located at http://www.microsoft.com (keyword PXE), for more information on the Remote Installation Service and PXE.

2. To be able to use SysPrep, the source and destination computers must have identical mass storage devices, Hardware Abstraction Layers (HALs), and Advanced Configuration and Power Interfaces (ACPIs). Plug and Play devices such as network interface cards (NICs), and video adapters do not have to be identical because the source image will run Plug and Play device detection on the destination computer. The HAL driver used on the source and destination computers must be the same.

3. Remote Installation Preparation–based operating system images cannot be copied to CDs or to other removable media. Microsoft is considering making these options available in the near future. Suggest to Mark that he watch for news related to new Windows 2000 features at Microsoft's web site.

4. The Remote Installation Preparation tool that ships with Windows 2000 supports only a single disk with a single partition (C drive). The disk size at the destination PC must be equal to or larger than the disk used to create the image at the source computer.

5. Inform Randy that the Remote Installation Preparation tool will allow him to store multiple images of client PCs. Randy can store the various images with friendly names that will help his staff members to easily decide which image would be appropriate for each of the five hardware configurations located in his region. Refer Randy to the Microsoft web site located at http://www.microsoft.com (keywords: deployment, RIPrep, and Remote Installation).

ANSWERS TO KEY TERM QUIZ

1. setupcl.exe
2. Total Cost Ownership (TCO)
3. Setup Manager
4. Remote Installation Service (RIS) server
5. sysprep.inf

4

Upgrading from Windows NT 4.0

This chapter discusses how to upgrade Windows NT 4.0 Server to Windows 2000 Server. Compared to performing a clean install, upgrading a network server ensures that all current network settings are retained. The process is often called *migration*. To improve the success of a migration from one OS to another, certain guidelines should be followed. Following those guidelines ensures minimal user down time, and the ability to roll the migration back to the original operating system.

The Windows NT 4.0 upgrade/migration process involves several key steps. In the first step, you determine the role that the current NT 4.0 servers will play in the new Windows 2000 environment. In the second, you determine which operating system fixes or service packs have to be installed to support the servers in the Windows 2000 environment. In the last and most important step, you troubleshoot or verify the success of the migration process.

In this chapter, you'll investigate some of the methods that ensure a successful migration to Windows 2000, including determining the proper time for the migration, deciding which service packs to install, and locating log files to help troubleshoot failed installations.

Understanding the migration process from Windows NT 4.0 to Windows 2000 server is a vital skill set for any Windows professional. The Microsoft Windows NT 4.0 operating system is so popular that Microsoft has decided to continue the Windows NT 4.0 certification process. Many organizations that may currently lack the resources or expertise to move to the Windows 2000 environment are therefore likely to retain their NT 4.0 operating systems for some time. A Windows professional should remain prepared to offer networking solutions to a variety of networking environments. The skills that you will learn in this chapter will help you to properly prepare to offer services to organizations that are considering the migration to Windows 2000.

LAB EXERCISE 4.01

Upgrading a Server from Windows NT Server 4.0

60 Minutes

You are a Windows 2000 professional who has been hired by the Get-It-Right package shipping company as a migration consultant. The company would like to upgrade one of their remote office locations, which is currently supported by Microsoft's Windows

NT 4.0 server, to Windows 2000. That office location is vital to the daily operations of the company.

The management at Get-It-Right want you to use the most time-efficient and cost-effective methods available during the migration process. The network resources must remain available to the users Monday through Friday from 9:00 A.M. to midnight. Failure to meet those requirements is unacceptable. Also, the company data must be protected at all times.

Are you prepared to proceed with the challenges that this job offers? Can you provide the services that Get-It-Right requires? Is migration one of your professional assets?

Learning Objectives

In this lab, you coordinate a time to upgrade the current NT 4.0 server to Windows 2000. To protect the integrity of the network, you must perform a full backup of the Windows NT Server 4.0 to another computer on the network before you start the upgrade. After completing the backup, and before you start the upgrade, you create an emergency repair disk. You repeat the creation of the repair disk after you finish the installation of the server. Finally, you review the various log files created during the migration process to verify that the process completed successfully. At the end of the lab, you'll be able to

- Create a Windows NT emergency repair disk
- Perform a full backup of NT 4.0 Server
- Upgrade/migrate a Windows NT 4.0 Server to Windows 2000 Server
- Deploy service packs
- Troubleshoot potential problems with a Windows NT 4.0 migration
- Know the log files that are created during the migration process.

Lab Materials and Setup

The lab requires these materials:

- Access to a computer running Windows NT 4.0 as a primary domain controller (PDC)
- Access to a computer running Windows 2000 Server
- Windows 2000 Server CD

- Small 4-port hub or crossover cable
- 1.44MB floppy disk
- Pen or pencil
- Writing pad (optional)
- Access to the www.microsoft.com web site (optional)

Getting Down to Business

You are going to upgrade a Windows NT 4.0 primary domain controller to a Windows 2000 domain controller without affecting business operations at Get-It-Right. You must protect the company's data and take steps to ensure a smooth transition between Windows NT 4.0 and Windows 2000. The upgraded domain controller will join the Get-It-Right domain. Use this procedure:

lab
Hint *Whenever you are implementing changes to a working network, always make the changes during times that will not affect the users of the network. Use the formula that follows to determine the time that will be required for implementing changes: Total time = Time required for change + Time required to remove change + Time required to test change.*

Step 1. **Plan** the upgrade/migration by consulting the chart that the management of Get-It-Right have created to guide the process.

- The chart (Table 4-1) will help you determine the information that should be backed up, the time when the migration process should begin, and the steps that you must perform to properly complete the process.

TABLE 4-1		
Details of the Remote NT 4.0 Server	**Working hours**	8 A.M. – Midnight, Monday–Friday
	Server information	Primary domain controller (PDC) Server name: Distribution Administration password: password
	Partition 1 (4GB)	NTFS 4.0, running Windows NT 4.0 Server Contains the distribution database software
	Partition 2 (2GB)	Compressed Contains the database data files
	Virus software	Norton AntiVirus

■ Table 4-2 specifies (in no particular order) the tasks that should be performed to ensure integrity of the company's data, access to the data during working hours, access to the data after migration, and recovery of the server if the migration process fails. You need to organize the checklist before proceeding.

cross
Reference

Chapter 4 of the **Windows 2000 Server Study Guide** *by Tom Shinder and Deb Litttlejohn Shinder (McGraw–Hill/Osborne, 2000).*

TABLE 4-2	
Windows NT 4.0 to Windows 2000 Migration Tasks (Unorganized)	Start the upgrade process @ 12:30 A.M.
	Test the new Windows 2000 domain controller @ 3:00 A.M.
	Install service pack
	Create emergency repair disk 1
	Create emergency repair disk 2
	Perform complete post-migration backup of server
	Uncompress partitions or folders
	Compress partitions or folders
	Take an inventory of the current configuration
	Perform complete pre-migration backup of server
	Install TCP/IP (if not installed)
	Switch to Native mode
	Install Office and database applications
	Perform a disk scan, a current virus scan, and a defragmentation on all partitions
	Verify the post-migration configuration
	Delete unnecessary files or applications
	Verify that the computer meets the requirements for an upgrade

Step 2.   **Implement** by performing the steps on your checklist.

Step 3.   **Test** your work by logging on to the new Windows 2000 domain controller.

■ Verify the configuration.

■ Next, use the Active Directory Domains and Trusts snap-in to switch the new domain controller from Mixed mode to Native mode to take full advantage of the Windows 2000 features.

■ Have your instructor or evaluator check your work.

LAB EXERCISE 4.02

Deploying Service Packs

60 Minutes

An operating system that has been released to the public may not always contain all the files necessary to successfully support the environment in which a network operates. From time to time, software manufactures release updates or fixes to their operating systems to address problems that may be experienced on a network.

Microsoft releases security fixes, new system administration tools, drivers, and various other support items for their operating system as *service packs*. Microsoft recommends installing the latest service packs as soon as they are released. Experienced administrators know that, although service packs fix many network problems, they also have a tendency to create new problems. Formerly, after initial deployment, Microsoft's service packs had to be redeployed each time a new component or service was added to the system. In Windows 2000, service packs do not have to be redeployed because the operating system tracks the service packs that have been installed and the files that have been deleted or added as a consequence. In this way, the operating system automatically retrieves the necessary files from the service pack when a new component is added.

Service packs can enhance or degrade the performance of a network. The network administrator has the vital responsibility of knowing when to apply service packs and when to avoid them. Successful network administrators create test environments where they test network applications before and after service pack deployment. They read the software release notices or the readme.txt files that accompany service pack releases. They make themselves aware of the potential hazards or benefits of service pack updates.

Are you able to successfully deploy the correct service packs to the Get-It-Right server? Do you know which areas of a service pack apply to your network? Can you deploy and test service packs on the Get-It-Right server?

Learning Objectives

In this lab, you use the Microsoft web site http://windowsupdate.microsoft.com/ to download Windows 2000 Service Packs 1 and 2 to your server. You save the files on the server for possible deployment at a later time. You use the ReadMe file that accompanies the service packs to find locations within the Microsoft web site that will give you a detailed description of what is fixed or enhanced by the various service packs. You then use that information to create a checklist of items that may affect the services or applications being used on the Get-It-Right server.

By using the checklist that you create, you will decide if you should deploy Service Pack 1, 2, or none. If you decide to deploy the service packs, then you will verify that the system still functions after the deployment. At the end of the lab, you'll be able to

- Locate the Windows 2000 update web site
- Download service packs
- Understand the fixes and enhancements of Service Packs 1 and 2
- Deploy service packs
- Understand the importance of using a testing environment.

Lab Materials and Setup

You need these materials for the lab:

- Access to a personal computer that has been recently upgraded from a Windows NT 4.0 PDC to Windows 2000 Server
- Access to a second personal computer that has been recently upgraded from a Windows NT 4.0 PDC to Windows 2000 Server (optional)
- Access to Windows 2000 help utility
- Access to the Internet (Microsoft's web site)
- Pen or pencil
- Writing pad (optional)

Getting Down to Business

You are going to download the Microsoft Windows 2000 Service Packs 1 and 2. You will then research the benefits or enhancements that deploying those service packs on your new Windows 2000 server will bring.

The management of Get-It-Right have asked you to protect the integrity of their data and to avoid making the network inaccessible to the users. To fulfill that obligation, you will complete your research of the service pack deployment, and you will then install one or both service packs on a server in a test environment. (If you do not have an additional upgraded PDC, proceed in this lab as if you created a testing server.) Once the service packs are loaded, log on to the server and test its functionality. Here's the procedure you need:

Step 1. **Plan** your work by reviewing the information in Table 4-3.

■ The information provided in the table represents applications, services, and hardware that could be found on typical Windows 2000 networks. The items listed could be affected by your failure to install necessary service packs.

■ After reviewing the information, use the Windows 2000 help utility to explore information concerning updates to Windows 2000.

■ Verify that you have access to the Internet, and a pen or pencil handy to record your findings.

lab

ⓘint *Service pack enhancements can relate to thousands of applications or operating system issues. To help you focus your research on items that may pertain to your network environment, I've created a list of applications, services, and hardware that are commonly deployed on networks.*

Step 2. **Implement** by logging on to the test environment server.

■ Record the current service pack information.

■ Locate the Windows 2000 update button to connect to the Microsoft web site. You must research the service pack information to find articles or bug fixes that may relate to your application, service, or hardware.

■ Use the information in Table 4-3 as a research project guideline to find enhancements or bug fixes relating to applications, services, and hardware found on your Windows 2000 server.

■ Record your findings in Table 4-3.

■ Based on your findings, deploy the appropriate service packs.

Step 3. **Test** by having your instructor or Windows 2000 Professional evaluator review your findings.

■ Log on to the Windows 2000 server, and check that it still performs to your expectations.

■ Check that the high encryption pack has been loaded in addition to the appropriate service pack.

TABLE 4-3	Applications, services, or hardware	Service Pack related to the application, service, or equipment	Knowledge Base article # (QXXXXXX) or Bulletin # (MSXX-XXX)
Windows 2000 Server Applications, Services, and Hardware	Internet Explorer 5.5		
	Windows Media Player 6.4		
	VeriSign Certificate Services		
	128-Bit encryption		
	File Replication Service (FRS)		
	Toshiba computers and utilities		
	Administrator controls the Registry size		
	Virus software		
	E-mail services (Exchange 5.5)		
	Distributed file system utilities (dfsutil.exe)		
	Windows 2000 hibernation		
	DNS service		
	HP Office Jet Fax machines		
	Offline file and folders		
	DNS dynamic updates		

■ Run the appropriate utility to show your instructor or evaluator which service pack is now running on your test environment server.

LAB EXERCISE 4.03

Troubleshooting Failed Installations

60 Minutes

If you properly plan for the upgrade/migration of Windows NT 4.0 to Windows 2000, the process should complete successfully. However, things can always occur that were not planned. When such situations arise, they can lead to many hours of lost time and production.

Because the possibility that a migration will not go according to plan is ever present, good network administrators know that their worth will become evident during these critical situations. The ability to troubleshoot network or installation problems is a vital asset to any network professional.

Successful troubleshooters know where to look for help in diagnosing network or installation problems. Many IS managers list the ability to troubleshoot network and installation problems as a plus for potential employees. The money and resources that are wasted by managing symptoms instead of locating the source of a problem can be staggering. Many IS managers believe that troubleshooting skills are developed over time. But the foundation for good troubleshooting skills is simply to know where to look for help in locating the source of the problem.

You are an IS staff administrator for the Get-It-Right network. You are being asked to troubleshoot a failed upgrade of a Windows NT 4.0 domain controller. The IS manager would like to know what steps you will take to locate the source of the problems.

Are you capable of handling this challenge?

Learning Objectives

In this lab, you familiarize yourself with the various files that are created to assist you in solving problems created by failed installations. You will also make yourself aware of some of the installation errors that you may encounter during an upgrade/migration process. Further, you'll familiarize yourself with the requirements of a Windows 2000 domain controller. At the end of the lab, you'll be able to

- Troubleshoot failed installations with setup logs
- Identify some of the common errors that may occur during an upgrade/ migration process
- Know the requirements of a Windows 2000 domain controller.

Lab Materials and Setup

This lab requires these materials:

- A Windows NT 4.0 PDC that has recently been upgraded to a Windows 2000 domain controller
- Windows 2000 help utility
- Access to the Internet.

Getting Down to Business

You are going to troubleshoot a Windows NT 4.0 PDC–to–Windows 2000 upgrade. You will create a checklist of potential upgrade/migration errors and use it to help detect and identify installation problems. You will then check the SETUPERR and SETUPACT logs for problems that may have occurred during the setup process. Here's the procedure:

Step 1. **Plan** for troubleshooting by locating a source you can use to identify the problems associated with a Windows 2000 installation.

- Familiarize yourself with the requirements of a Windows 2000 domain controller.

- Use the information that you have gathered to complete Table 4-4 during the next (implementation) step.

Step 2. **Implement** your troubleshooting approach by connecting to the Microsoft web site located at www.microsoft.com.

- Locate information concerning the Windows 2000 installation process and the Windows 2000 domain controller requirements.

- Use the information that you find to list, in Table 4-4, five possible Windows 2000 installation errors that you may experience.

TABLE 4-4	Installation error	Description of error
Research into Windows 2000 Installation Errors		

■ In Table 4-5, list some of the Windows 2000 domain controller requirements.

Chapter 4 of the **Windows 2000 Server Study Guide** *by Tom Shinder and Deb Litttlejohn Shinder (McGraw–Hill/Osborne, 2000).*

TABLE 4-5	Hardware or services
Research into Windows 2000 Domain Controller Requirements	

Step 3. Test by locating and identifying the log files that are associated with the Windows 2000 installation process.

■ In Table 4-6, identify the location, name, and description of the log files that are created during the installation/migration of Windows 2000 Server.

| TABLE 4-6 | Research into Windows Installation Setup Log Files |

Log file name	Log file location	Description

LAB ANALYSIS TEST

1. Rob, the IS manager for Give-It-A-Try.com is ready to start the migration process from Windows NT 4.0 to Windows 2000. He has created a checklist of the steps that he feels must be completed to ensure a smooth migration. He feels that he is properly prepared for the migration, but not prepared to handle any failures. What suggestions can you offer Rob so that he can safely return the network to its original configuration if the migration to Windows 2000 fails?

   _____

   _____

2. A small research and development company is considering upgrading their Windows NT 4.0 backup domain controller (BDC) to a Windows 2000 domain controller. They have been told that Windows 2000 does not have an uninstall feature, and now they would like to proceed with extreme caution. To help ease their fears, what steps should they take to prepare their computer for the upgrade?

   _____

   _____

3. Shirley is the administrator of a Windows NT 4.0 domain that consists of one PDC and one BDC. She has heard conflicting statements regarding the upgrade of her network to Windows 2000. She would like to know which domain controller to upgrade first: the PDC or the BDC? When will she have to run the DCPROMO utility, and which option does she choose? Can you provide Shirley with the information that she will need to upgrade her domain controllers successfully?

   _____

   _____

4. Martha is an administrator of a Windows NT 4.0 network. The network consists of four Windows NT 4.0 domain controllers. One of the domain controllers is a PDC; the three other domain controllers are BDCs. Martha would like to know if she should upgrade all of her domain controllers to Windows 2000 if she decides to upgrade. What can you tell her?

   _____

   _____

5. Wendell is considering upgrading his PDC to a Windows 2000 domain controller. He would like to know if he can retain his FAT file system. What can you tell him?

   _____

   _____

KEY TERM QUIZ

Use the following vocabulary terms to complete the sentences below. Not all of the terms will be used.

cross
Reference
Chapter 4 of the **Windows 2000 Server Study Guide** *by Tom Shinder and* **Deb Litttlejohn Shinder (McGraw–Hill/Osborne, 2000).**

DCPROMO.EXE	Mixed
Native	SETUPACT.LOG
SETUPAPI.LOG	SETUPERR.LOG
SETUPLOG.TXT	UPDATE.EXE
WINVER	

1. During the migration of a Windows NT 4.0 network to Windows 2000, you discover that all of the primary domain controllers cannot be upgraded to Windows 2000 domain controllers. Certain applications will not function properly in Windows 2000. Because you must now support Windows NT 4.0 and Windows 2000 domain controllers the Windows network should be run in _____ mode and then switched to _____ mode when the applications can be supported in Windows 2000.

2. Susan is an administrator that has recently upgraded a Windows NT member server to Windows 2000 Server. She would like to add all local user and group accounts to the Active Directory and to maintain their permissions for local resources. She must run _____ to accomplish this task.

3. Mark has been an administrator in the Windows NT 4.0 environment for a long time. He is not very familiar with Windows 2000, but he thinks that the upgrade process is simple. However, he has some reservations about the service packs that will be required to support Windows 2000. He should run the _____ utility program to determine the service pack version that he is running, and the _____ program to install service packs.

4. During the upgrade of a Windows NT 4.0 member server to Windows 2000 Server you are not sure if the proper device drivers have been copied to the new Windows 2000 server. Which setup log file will provide details about the device driver files that were copied during setup? _____ (This file will also contain errors and warnings with a time stamp for each issue.)

5. Which Windows 2000 setup log file would an administrator use to get details about the files that are copied to an NT 4.0 member server during the migration process to Windows 2000 Server? _____

LAB SOLUTIONS FOR CHAPTER 4

The sections that follow walk you through the steps to solve the lab exercises. You should avoid looking at these sections unless you are stuck on a particular exercise.

Lab Solution 4.01

A smooth migration will use a process resembling the one described here.

Step 1. Your organized Windows NT 4.0 migration checklist should resemble the one in Table 4-7.

TABLE 4-7	Verify that the computer meets the requirements for an upgrade
	Take an inventory of the current configuration
Organized	Delete unnecessary files or applications
Windows NT 4.0	Perform a disk scan, a current virus scan, and a defragmentation on all partitions
Migration	Create emergency repair disk 1
Checklist	Perform complete pre-migration backup of server
	Uncompress partitions or folders
	Install TCP/IP (if not installed)
	Start the upgrade process @ 12:30 A.M.
	Install service pack
	Install Office and database applications
	Compress partitions or folders
	Create emergency repair disk 2
	Test the new Windows 2000 domain controller @ 3:00 A.M.
	Verify the post-migration configuration
	Switch to Native mode
	Perform complete post-migration backup of server

Step 2. To upgrade a Windows NT 4.0 PDC to a Windows 2000 domain controller, begin by logging on to the Windows NT 4.0 domain controller with administrative privileges. Insert the Windows 2000 Server CD into the CD-ROM drive.

Select Start | Run, and type **D:\I386\winnt32.exe** in the Run box (where D: is the drive letter of your CD-ROM drive). Click the Browse button. Click OK.

The Welcome to Windows 2000 Setup wizard opens. Select "Upgrade to Windows 2000 (Recommended)," Click Next.

The License agreement dialog opens. Click the option that accepts the License agreement.

At the Product Key dialog, type the 25-character product key found on the Windows 2000 server CD case. Click Next.

At the Upgrading to the Windows 2000 NTFS File System screen, select "Yes; upgrade my drive," so that the partition will be formatted as a NTFS 5.0 partition.

During the upgrade, the Active Directory wizard starts and provides you with the opportunity to join an existing domain tree or forest, or to start a new one. Specify that you want to join an existing domain (Get-It-Right.com).

Step 3.   When the automated upgrade is complete, you should verify that everything was upgraded according to your checklist.

To switch Windows 2000 Server from Mixed mode to Native mode, log on to the Windows 2000 server with administrative privileges. Select Start | Programs | Administrative Tools | Active Directory Domains and Trusts. Right-click the domain name, and select Properties.

Click the General tab. Click the Change Mode button. Read the warning, and then click the Yes button on the warning message box. Click OK.

Lab Solution 4.02

Although you findings may vary, your answers should be similar to those shown here.

Step 1.   Table 4-8 shows service pack–related information pertaining to bug fixes or enhancements for some common applications, services, and hardware. Your answers may vary because various service pack fixes or enhancements usually pertain to different aspects or features of applications, services, and hardware found on your particular server.

To create your list, you should have connected to the Microsoft web site located at www.microsoft.com, and searched for service packs relating to Windows 2000. You also should have searched pertinent articles (like those shown) for additional information.

TABLE 4-8	Applications, services, or hardware	Service Pack related to the application, service, or equipment	Knowledge Base article # (QXXXXXX) or Bulletin # (MSXX-XXX)
Completed Research into Windows 2000 Server Applications, Services, and Hardware	Internet Explorer 5.5	Service Pack 2	Q255669 or MS01-051
	Windows Media Player 6.4	Service Pack 2	MS01-029
	VeriSign Certificate Services	Service Pack 2	MS01-017
	128-Bit encryption	Service Pack 2	Q285782
	File Replication Service (FRS)	Service Pack 2	Q272567
	Toshiba computers and utilities	Service Pack 2	Q259169
	Administrator controls the Registry size	Service Pack 2	Q260241
	Virus software	Service Pack 2	Q272734
	E-mail services (Exchange 5.5)	Service Pack 2	Q272590
	Distributed file system utilities (dfsutil.exe)	Service Pack 2	Q293114
	Windows 2000 hibernation	Service Pack 2	Q261601
	DNS service	Service Pack 2	Q292300
	HP Office Jet Fax machines	Service Pack 1	Q256859
	Offline file and folders	Service Pack 1	Q253618
	DNS dynamic updates	Service Pack 1	Q262188

Step 2. The procedure to download and install Windows 2000 Service Packs 1 and 2 follows. (Note that you are not required to install Service Pack 1 before Service Pack 2. Service Pack 2 includes all of the bug fixes and enhancements found in Service Pack 1.)

Log on to the Windows 2000 testing server with administrative privileges. Double-click the Windows Internet Explorer icon located on the Windows 2000 desktop.

Type **www.microsoft.com** into the address bar.

Select Downloads, and choose Download Center. Locate Service Pack 1. Select "SP1 Express Installation for Windows 2000 Server." Run that program from its current location.

lab
ⓗint

Windows 2000 Service Pack 1 is no longer found on the Windows Update page. It has been archived to the download center on the Microsoft web site page.

Return to the Microsoft web site and search for Windows 2000 Service Pack 2. Select "Windows 2000 SP2 Express Installation," and "Run this file from its current location."

Step 3. Discuss your findings and installations with your instructor or evaluator. Log on to the Windows 2000 server with Administrative privileges.

Click Start, and then Run. Type **cmd** into the Run box. Press ENTER to open a command prompt window.

To display information about the Windows 2000 service pack deployed on your server, type **WINVER**, and press ENTER. When you are done, close the command prompt window.

Lab Solution 4.03

The information that you locate as you complete this exercise may vary depending on your source.

Step 1. Table 4-9 shows common installation errors that may be encountered during installation of Windows 2000 Server. Your answers may vary and may not be listed in the same order.

Step 2. Table 4-10 shows some of the requirements that must be met to successfully deploy a Windows 2000 domain controller. Your list may vary somewhat, but the information should closely resemble the Windows 2000 Domain Controller requirements listed in the table.

Step 3. Table 4-11 lists the setup installation files that were created during the installation or migration to Windows 2000 Server. Your completed exercise should resemble that table.

TABLE 4-9	Installation error	Description of error
Possible Windows 2000 Installation Errors	Media errors	Defective or damaged CDs
	Insufficient disk space	Windows 2000 needs 1GB free space for the installation to proceed properly; 2GB is recommended.
	Hardware configuration problems	Non Plug and Play devices not configured as manufacturer intended.
	Hardware driver not supported by Windows 2000	Device not listed on the Windows 2000 HCL.
	Insufficient memory	128MB RAM is required for Windows 2000 Server; 256MB is recommended for domain controllers.
	Insufficient processing power	Pentium 133 MHz processor is the minimum required.
	Incorrect product key	Product key must match installation CD.
	Cannot contact domain controller	DNS server may not be available, or wrong domain name used.
	Network connection	TCP/IP not properly configured, or DHCP server not available.

TABLE 4-10	Hardware or services
Windows 2000 Domain Controller Requirements	133 MHz or higher Pentium-compatible processor
	Access to the Internet (DNS)
	256MB RAM recommended
	2GB hard disk space, 1GB free

TABLE 4-11	Windows Installation Setup Log Files

Log file name	Log file location	Description
SETUPACT.LOG	Windows 2000 installation folder (Winnt)	The Action file contains details about all the files copied during the installation. These actions are listed in chronological order.
SETUPLOG.TXT	Windows 2000 installation folder (Winnt)	The Log file contains information about the device drivers copied during installation.
SETUPERR.LOG	Windows 2000 installation folder (Winnt)	The Error log lists errors encountered during installation, if any. The severity of the error and a description are also included.
SETUPAPI.LOG	Windows 2000 installation folder (Winnt)	The API log contains errors and warnings pertaining to device driver files that were copied during setup.

ANSWERS TO LAB ANALYSIS TEST

1. For Rob to create a contingency plan to protect his network from problems that may arise if he cannot complete the migration to Windows 2000, he should

    - Back up all Windows NT 4.0 servers

    - Thoroughly test his backup of Windows NT 4.0 servers. Rob should see if he can re-create his network from the backup medium

    - Create an emergency repair disk on each Windows NT 4.0 server before and after the migration.

    You could also refer Rob to the Microsoft web site located at http://www.microsoft.com. Have him perform a keyword search for "Upgrade," to find more information on upgrading a Windows NT 4.0 server to a Windows 2000 server.

2. Helping this organization succeed in upgrading to a Windows 2000 domain controller requires two steps. First, refer the research company to the Microsoft web site located at http://www.microsoft.com. Have them do a keyword search on "rollback of a Windows NT 4.0 server," so that they can read information about preparing computers for upgrade. Second, you should provide a checklist of tasks to perform prior to the upgrade. The list should include these items:

    - Check the hardware compatibility list at the Microsoft web site. Identify the latest Windows 2000 drivers for the hardware listed in your BDC. If necessary, contact the manufacturer of the PC for the latest BIOS.

    - Perform a full backup of the Windows NT 4.0 BDC.

    - Scan for viruses before starting the upgrade.

    - Uncompress any compressed drives on the Windows NT 4.0 BDC.

    - Remove all virus protection and third-party software from the BDC.

    - Unplug any uninterruptible power supplies (UPSs) from the BDC.

3. Inform Shirley that she must upgrade the PDC to the first Windows 2000 domain controller if she plans to upgrade more than one Windows NT 4.0 server in a domain. When you upgrade a Windows NT 4.0 server PDC to Windows 2000 Server, the computer automatically starts the Active Directory Installation wizard. Once the Active Directory wizard starts, it gives you the opportunity to join an existing domain tree or forest, or to start a new one. Because this is the PDC, Shirley should choose to start a new domain. Next, upgrade each Windows NT 4.0 server BDC to be a Windows 2000 domain controller.

4. In the existing network, Martha should create an extra BDC that matches the last BDC before it is converted. Then, she should remove the backup BDC from the network and keep it offline and secured until she is satisfied with the upgrade to Windows 2000 domain controllers.

5. Wendell will be able to keep the user account database and the log files on the FAT file system. He must place only the system volume (SYSVOL), which is a requirement for a Windows 2000 domain controller, on an NTFS 5.0 volume.

ANSWERS TO KEY TERM QUIZ

1. Mixed, Native

2. DCPROMO.EXE

3. WINVER, UPDATE.EXE

4. SETUPAPI.LOG

5. SETUPACT.LOG

5

Using
Network Services

his chapter discusses some of the administrative tools available in Windows 2000 for managing the TCP/IP-based Windows 2000 Directory Services infrastructure. Microsoft has improved the functionality and reliability of TCP/IP services and now ships those services as part of the standard package. The World Wide Web, with all of its information services and business links, is based on the TCP/IP protocol stack. Service-oriented organizations (including Microsoft) who wish to take advantage of the World Wide Web's unlimited business opportunities have shifted their business focus to include the development of applications and services that depend on the TCP/IP protocol suite. Microsoft's Windows 2000 networks are primarily TCP/IP-based.

This chapter focuses on three of the TCP/IP-based administrative tools available in Windows 2000:

- The Dynamic Host Configuration Protocol (DHCP) is responsible for automatically assigning IP addresses within the infrastructure.

- The Windows Internet Naming Service (WINS) provides name-to-address translations for NetBIOS networks.

- The Domain Name System (DNS) Service provides Internet-based network name resolution services.

Networks based on TCP/IP can be very complex and can require a lot of accumulated knowledge and experience to maintain effectively. Many companies use TCP/IP concepts to gauge the understanding and experience levels of potential employees. Administrators who can provide effective and efficient access to a company's resources are uncommon. Many companies are therefore willing to compensate such individuals quite well. Understanding and effectively using TCP/IP tools such as DHCP, WINS, and DNS eases the management of TCP/IP-based networks. The exercises that follow use the primary domain controller that was upgraded in Chapter 4 to a Windows 2000 domain controller.

LAB EXERCISE 5.01

Working with the Dynamic Host Configuration Protocol Service

60 Minutes

You are an administrator working for the Get-It-Right package shipping company. The company has recently made many changes to its network infrastructure in an effort to improve services to network users. Information Service (IS) staff have continually been advising management about all of the benefits that the company will gain by implementing Windows 2000 in the infrastructure.

To continue with the process, management would like you to find a way to effectively manage the distribution of IP addresses within the network. They would also like you to integrate the DHCP service with other services that are currently on the network. Most importantly, they would like you to develop implementation strategies that are easy to understand and cost-effective.

Are you prepared to add the DHCP service to Get-It-Right's infrastructure? Will management be able to understand your procedures? Can you effectively manage the distribution of the company's IP addresses?

Learning Objectives

In this lab, you install the DHCP service on a Windows 2000 server, and you configure the DHCP server to support various divisions within Get-It-Right.

The DHCP service must integrate with the DNS service and provide support for non–Windows 2000 clients. You will need to reserve and exclude IP addresses for specific clients on the network. You will also need to create a Microsoft Management Console (MMC) that is easy to find, for use by the IS staff to maintain the DHCP service. Once you have successfully completed those tasks, you will authorize the DHCP server and test the functionality of the DHCP service.

At the end of the lab, you'll be able to

- Install the DHCP service
- Create a Microsoft Management Console
- Configure a DHCP server to meet specific requirements
- Create DHCP scopes
- Create a client reservation
- Integrate the DHCP and DNS services
- Authorize a DHCP server
- Test the functionality of the DHCP server.

Lab Materials and Setup

The lab requires these materials:

- Access to a computer functioning as a Windows 2000 domain controller
- A computer running Windows 2000 Server or Professional attached to the domain controller
- Small hub or crossover cable
- Pen or pencil
- Writing pad (optional)
- Windows 2000 help utility
- Access to the www.microsoft.com web site (optional)

Getting Down to Business

You are going to install and configure the DHCP service to an existing Windows 2000 domain controller. You will create scopes and client reservations to support various divisions within Get-It-Right. (You will receive a list of the IP addresses and subnets that are to be used to support the network.) You will also create a DHCP MMC that Information Services staff at Get-It-Right can use to maintain and administer the service. Finally, you will authorize and test the DHCP service.

lab
Hint

Whenever you are given a list of tasks to perform on a network, organize the list into a reasonable order. Check off the tasks one by one as they are completed. Never assume that you have completed all requirements; always determine a method to verify your assignments.

Use these steps:

Step 1. **Plan** for the implementation of the DHCP service on a Windows 2000 domain controller.

- The Information Systems staff of the Get-It-Right company have created a chart (Table 5-1) that you will use to help implement IP address assignments on the network. Refer to the chart to properly design and assign the IP address format that the Get-It-Right company will use.

TABLE 5-1		
	Company's DNS name	Get-It-Right.com
Information for Implementing Dynamic Host Configuration Protocol Service on the Network	**Company's assigned IP address**	192.168.1.0/24
	Subnet mask	255.255.255.240
	Management console	IS DHCP
	Routers	4
	DNS servers	1
	WINS servers	1
	Sales database server (Saledb1) MAC address	00-40-30-AC-D3-56
	Shipping database server (Shipdb1) MAC address	00-40-30-C9-39-03

Here is some additional information that you will use to implement DHCP requirements on the Get-It-Right network:

1. Database server IP addresses should be automatically assigned, but always the same.

2. The network should be divided into four consecutive scopes. These scopes are to be assigned:

   ■ Administration: 192.168.1.17 – 192.168.1.30/28

   ■ Personnel: 192.168.1.33 – 192.168.1.46/28

   ■ Shipping: 192.168.1.49 – 192.168.1.62/28

   ■ Sales: 192.168.1.65 – 192.168.1.78/28

3. All scopes should support 14 devices.

4. The DHCP server IP address is part of the administration scope. It should be assigned as the first IP address in the scope, and it should be manually assigned.

5. The DNS server IP address is part of the sales scope. It should be assigned as the second address in the scope. It should also be manually assigned.

6. The WINS server IP address is the same as the DHCP server address.

7. Configure DHCP to support WINS. Set the WINS resolution node to "hybrid."

8. A router address should be the last excluded IP address in each scope. Each router address should be assigned manually.

9. The IS DHCP management console should be stored under "administrative tools."

10. Four addresses should be excluded from the beginning of all scopes. These addresses are reserved for routers, DHCP servers, WINS servers, DNS servers, domain controllers, and other network devices that require statically assigned IP addresses.

11. Set the lease duration time for 10 days on all scopes.

12. Activate the administration scope, but not the other three scopes.

Step 2. **Implement** the changes, installing and configuring the DHCP service as required by the IS staff of the Get-It-Right company.

■ Use the information provided in step 1 to complete the assignment. You can use the Windows 2000 help utility or the Microsoft web site to help you navigate the configuration of the DHCP service and the creation of the IS DHCP management console.

cross
Reference

See Chapter 5 of the **Windows 2000 Server Study Guide** *by Tom Shinder and Deb Litttlejohn Shinder (McGraw–Hill/Osborne, 2000).*

Step 3. **Test** the configuration by logging on to the Windows 2000 domain controller.

■ Make sure that the IS MMC can be found under the Administrative Tools snap-in. Check the IS DHCP MMC to see if the DHCP server has been authorized.

■ Once you are satisfied with your findings, log on as an administrator to the Windows 2000 Professional or Server computer that is connected to the DHCP server. See if you have received an IP address from the server. If not, make sure that the computer's TCP/IP configuration is set to automatically receive an IP address from a DHCP server.

■ Review the information that the IS staff provided and ensure that you have met all requirements. Once you have completed those tasks, have your instructor or evaluator check your work.

LAB EXERCISE 5.02

Resolving NetBIOS Names Using the Windows Internet Naming Service

60 Minutes

By default, browsing on TCP/IP-based networks involves NetBIOS broadcasts. Browsing provides network users with a list of available shared network resources, from which the user can select a resource to access. In a pure Windows 2000 TCP/IP network, DNS handles name resolution. However, most networks, including that of Get-It-Right.com, interact with clients that still rely on NetBIOS for resolving computer names into network addresses.

In your efforts to integrate the appropriate network services within the Get-It-Right company, you must include the Windows Internet Naming Service (WINS). That service allows all users to quickly locate network resources on Windows 2000 machines. Because the Get-It-Right company is slowly migrating to a Windows 2000 network, you must still provide support for all the users that have not participated in the migration process. Your implementation of WINS must ensure that all users are able to register and renew their names automatically in the WINS database. In addition, all users must be able to query the WINS database to be able to resolve the NetBIOS names of other computers on the network.

Can you successfully implement WINS within the Get-It-Right company? Will all users be able to locate and access resources on the network?

Learning Objectives

In this lab, you install and configure the WINS service on an existing Windows 2000 domain controller. You configure the WINS server to support WINS clients, and non-WINS clients alike, on the Get-It-Right network. All WINS clients must be able to register, renew, release, and query the WINS Server. The WINS server must support replication to other WINS servers and manual additions to the WINS database.

At the end of the lab, you'll be able to

- Install the WINS Service
- Configure WINS proxy agent
- Create WINS replication partners
- Create static mappings
- Test the WINS service.

Lab Materials and Setup

You require these materials:

- Access to a computer functioning as a Windows 2000 domain controller
- A computer running Windows 2000 Server or Professional attached to the domain controller
- Small hub or crossover cable
- Windows 2000 help utility
- Access to the www.microsoft.com web site (optional)

Getting Down to Business

In this lab, you install and configure WINS to a Windows 2000 domain controller. The management of the Get-It-Right company have asked you to support Unix and Novell NetBIOS applications that require NetBIOS client support on the network. Although you could use DNS to resolve NetBIOS names on the network, you are being requested to provide the fastest and most efficient process for NetBIOS name resolution. You will also have to support the non-WINS clients by installing a WINS proxy agent and creating manual entries for the Novell and Unix servers on the network. Once you have accomplished those tasks, you will test the functionality of the WINS server by using the ping utility. Use these steps:

Step 1. **Plan** for the implementation of the WINS service on a Windows 2000 domain controller.

- The IS staff of the Get-It-Right company have provided a chart (Table 5-2) that will help you implement NetBIOS name resolution on the network. Refer to the information in the chart to help properly design and implement WINS for the Get-It-Right company.

TABLE 5-2	Object	Name	IP Address
Implementing the Windows Internet Naming Service on the Network	Unix server	UNIX01	192.168.1.35
	Novell server	NOV02	192.168.1.51
	WINS replication partner	WINS02	192.168.1.67
	WINS proxy agent	—	Configure on available Professional/Server

Step 2. **Implement** your plan by installing and configuring the WINS service as required by the IS staff of the Get-It-Right company.

▪ Use the information provided in step 1 to complete the assignment. You can also use the Windows 2000 help utility or the Microsoft web site to help you navigate the configuration of the WINS service.

lab
Warning

You do not need an additional WINS server to configure WINS replication. You will not be able to test replication, but you will know how to configure a replication partner on a network that has more than one WINS server.

Step 3. **Test** by logging on to the Windows 2000 Server or Professional computer that is connected to your domain controller.

▪ Try to verify that the WINS server is functioning properly. Ping the computer name of the domain controller, the Unix server, the Novell server, and your computer.

▪ Review the list of information that the IS staff has provided to ensure that you have met all requirements. Once you have completed those tasks, have your instructor or evaluator check your work.

LAB EXERCISE 5.03

Resolving Host Names Using the Domain Name System Service

60 Minutes

The Domain Name System (DNS) Service provides name-to-address translations for an Internet-based network. The Internet name given to a computer identifies it within the vast network of networks that comprise the Internet. In a Windows 2000 network, DNS clients, also known as *resolvers,* query DNS servers to look up and resolve names into the type of resource record specified in the query. In the process of resolving a name, DNS servers sometimes function as DNS clients, querying other servers to fully resolve the queried name. To help identify those other servers quickly, various companies are assigned authority by the Internet root servers for their domain name tree on the Internet.

To continue your efforts to integrate appropriate network services within the Get-It-Right company, you must now include DNS. That service will allow all users to quickly locate network resources on Windows 2000 machines. Once the Get-It-Right company fully migrates to Windows 2000, it will rely completely on DNS to locate all Internet-based network resources.

Your implementation of DNS must ensure that the DNS database can be modified automatically to integrate with the DHCP service. You must create both forward and reverse lookup zones to support queries by network users. In addition, you must create pointer records for clients that cannot use the DNS service.

Can you help the network users at the Get-It-Right company access Internet-based resources? Will network users be able to resolve names to IP addresses (and IP addresses to names)? Can you continue to successfully implement networking services for the Get-It-Right company?

Learning Objectives

In this lab, you install the DNS service on a Windows 2000 computer. You will need to create forward and reverse lookup zones to support host name and IP address resolution. The DNS server must be configured to support automated registration of host names within the DNS database, as well as manual registration of host names. Once the DNS server has been properly configured, it must be tested before allowing it to be used on the Get-It-Right network.

At the end of the lab, you'll be able to

- Install DNS
- Configure forward and reverse lookup zones
- Create resource records
- Configure DNS to support dynamic registration
- Test the DNS.

Lab Materials and Set-Up

You need these materials:

- Access to a computer functioning as a Windows 2000 domain controller (optional)
- A computer running Windows 2000 Server

■ Windows 2000 help utility

■ Access to the Internet

Getting Down to Business

The management of Get-It-Right have asked you to provide Internet and local access to resources. They would like DNS and other services to be integrated so that users can quickly and efficiently use all available company resources. You therefore install and configure DNS on a Windows 2000 server. (If you do not have an additional Windows 2000 server, then delete and reinstall the service on your Windows 2000 domain controller.) Once you have accomplished those tasks, you test the functionality of DNS on the DNS server. Use these steps:

Step 1. **Plan** for the implementation of DNS on a Windows 2000 server or domain controller.

■ The IS staff of the Get-It-Right company have provided information that will help you provide IP host name–to–IP address name resolution:

DNS IP address	192.168.1.66
Dynamic DNS support	Yes
Resource record for Unix database server	Host name: UNIX01 IP address: 192.168.1.35
WINS integration	Allow WINS integration on forward lookup zone WINS server IP address: 192.168.1.17
Forward lookup zone	Zone type: Primary Zone name: Get-It-Right.com
Reverse lookup zone	192.168.1.0

■ Refer to the foregoing information to properly design and implement DNS for the Get-It-Right company.

Step 2. **Implement** your plan by installing and configuring the DNS service as required by the IS staff of Get-It-Right.

■ Use the information provided in step 1 to complete the assignment. Use the Windows 2000 help utility or the Microsoft web site to help navigate the configuration of the DNS service.

Step 3. Test the functionality of the DNS service.

■ Use the DNS snap-in to perform simple and recursive queries on the DNS server to make sure that it can resolve local and Internet host names.

■ Review the information provided by the IS staff to ensure that you have met all requirements.

■ Once you have completed the preceding tasks, have your instructor or evaluator check your work.

LAB ANALYSIS TEST

1. Wendell has just joined a Windows 2000 Professional computer to his new domain. The computer's name is "rob1." When he tried to ping that computer name, he received four replies with the computer name showing as "rob1.get-it-right.com." Why did the name change?

_____

_____

2. Lynnette is an administrator for a large auto manufacturing company. The company is planning to use DHCP to manage the distribution of IP addresses on their Windows 2000 network. Lynnette understands how the DHCP server automatically distributes the IP addresses, but she does not know how to configure the DHCP server to handle the addresses that will be used by the routers, DNS servers, and WINS servers on her network. What information can you provide that will help her to properly implement DHCP service on her network?

_____

_____

3. Melvin is the administrator of a Windows 2000 domain that consists of several databases customized to support network users. The software applications have been written to look for specific server IP addresses. Melvin sees that approach as a potential administrative nightmare, and so he has decided to configure the DHCP server to lease all IP addresses unlimited. He knows that his solution is not a recommended procedure, but he does not know of any alternatives. What option can you offer to Melvin?

_____

_____

4. Fernando is an administrator on a Windows 2000 domain controller that has just been upgraded from being an NT 4.0 primary domain controller. Fernando feels that an NT 4.0 domain and a Windows 2000 domain are fairly similar. However, he is not familiar with dynamic DNS (DDNS). He does not understand why DDNS is so important in Windows 2000 when it was not important in Windows NT 4.0. What insight can you provide for Fernando regarding DDNS and Windows 2000?

_____

_____

5. Michael is an administrator who would like to use the features associated with Windows 2000 dynamic DNS. However, the company that he works for does no business that requires having a registered domain name. Michael thinks that he will be unable to use Microsoft's Windows 2000 DNS service unless he properly registers the company's domain name. What can Michael do, so that he can implement dynamic DNS on his network?

_____

_____

KEY TERM QUIZ

Use the following vocabulary terms to complete the sentences below. Not all of the terms will be used.

cross
Reference
See Chapter 5 of the **Windows 2000 Server Study Guide** *by Tom Shinder and Deb Litttlejohn Shinder (McGraw–Hill/Osborne, 2000).*

authorized

DHCPACK

DHCPREQUEST

DORA

FQDN

host

NetBIOS

1. During the _____ step of the request for an IP address, the DHCP server broadcasts a message that contains a valid lease for the IP address and can contain other configuration information. During this step, a client finishes initializing its TCP/IP network environment.

2. An administrator who has recently implemented DHCP services within her network cannot obtain an IP address from the DHCP server. The DHCP server has been properly configured, but the DHCP snap-in shows a red arrow next to the server name. The DHCP server has not been _____ to function as a DHCP server on the network.

3. If you would like to resolve _____ names to IP addresses on a Windows 2000 network that uses non-WINS clients, then you have to enable a WINS proxy agent on the subnet.

4. The acronym _____ is commonly associated with the four-step process used to request an IP address from a DHCP server in a Windows 2000 network.

5. Of the four address lease steps, it is during the _____ step that the client broadcasts a message to all DHCP servers indicating that it has accepted an offer from a specific DHCP server.

LAB SOLUTIONS FOR CHAPTER 5

The sections that follow walk you through the steps to solve the lab exercises. You should avoid looking at these sections unless you are stuck on a particular exercise.

Lab Solution 5.01

This section outlines the steps required to install the DHCP service, to create a custom management console, to configure DHCP scopes, to assign client reservations, to provide WINS support, and to test the WINS service (once the address and subnet mask for the domain controller are appropriately set).

Step 1. Before you can complete the exercise, you have to configure the Windows 2000 domain controller with a static address of 192.168.1.17 and a subnet mask of 255.255.255.240. That address will be the first in the administration scope.

Step 2. To install the DHCP service, log on to the Windows 2000 server as an administrator. Click Start, point to Settings, and click Control Panel.

Open the Add/Remove Programs utility, and click the Add/Remove Windows Components button. Select Networking Services from the list of components. Click Details.

Select the Dynamic Host Configuration Protocol (DHCP) check box. Click OK. Click Next.

You may be prompted for the Windows 2000 Server CD. Once the installation completes, click Finish.

To create the IS DHCP Microsoft Management Console, click Start, and then click Run. Into the Run box, type **mmc**, and then click OK.

On the console menu, click Add/Remove Snap-in, and then click Add. Under Snap-in, double-click the DHCP icon. Click Close, and then click OK

On the Console menu, click Save As. Into the File name window type **IS**, and then click Save.

To authorize a DHCP server, select your DHCP server in the console window. Right-click the server, and select Authorize.

lab
①int *The DHCP server is automatically authorized because it is installed on a Windows 2000 domain controller.*

To configure a DHCP scope, right-click your server, and click New Scope. Click Next when the "Welcome to New Scope" wizard opens.

The Scope name dialog opens, as shown in Figure 5-1. For the scope name, type **Administration Scope**. Type a comment such as **14 addresses to support Admin Division**.

The IP Address Range dialog opens. Type **192.168.1.17** into the Start IP Address box. Type **192.168.1.30** into the End IP Address box. Type **28** into the Length box. Click Next.

The Add Exclusions dialog opens. Type **192.168.1.17** into the Start IP Address box. Type **192.168.1.20** into the End IP Address box. Click Add, and then click Next.

The Lease Duration dialog opens (Figure 5-2). Into the Days box, type **10**. Click Next.

The Configure DHCP Options dialog opens. Accept the default choice: "Yes, I want to configure these options now." Click Next.

The Router (Default Gateway) dialog opens (Figure 5-3). Into the IP Address box, type the last IP address in the excluded range (**192.168.1.20**). Click Add, and then click Next.

The Domain Name and DNS Servers dialog opens. Type **get-it-right.com** into the Parent Domain box, and **192.168.1.66** into the IP Address box. Click Add, and then click Next.

FIGURE 5-1

Naming a scope

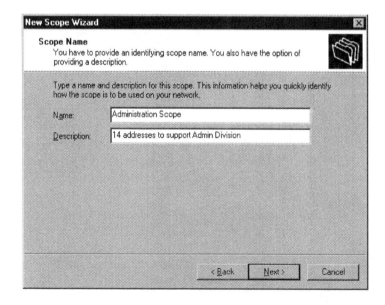

FIGURE 5-2

Setting the
lease duration
for a scope

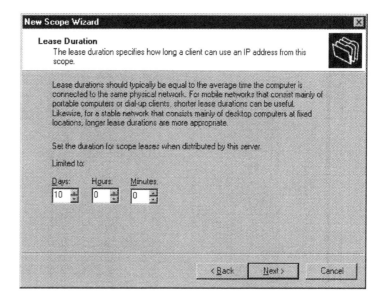

The WINS Servers dialog opens, as shown in Figure 5-4. Into the IP Address
box, type **192.168.1.17**. (The WINS IP address is the same as the DHCP server's
IP address.) Click Add, and then click Next.

The Activate Scope dialog opens. Accept the default "Yes, I want to activate the
scope now." Click Next, and then click Finish.

FIGURE 5-3

Setting the
address of the
server gateway

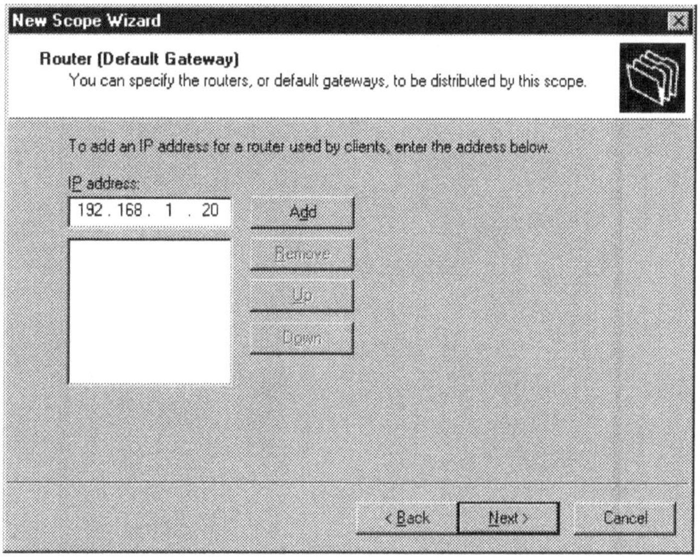

FIGURE 5-4

Setting the
IP address of the
WINS server

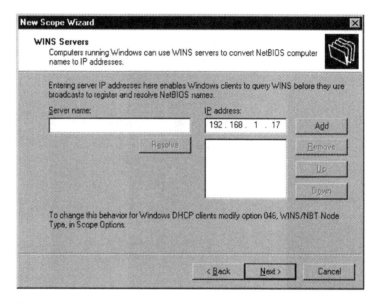

Repeat the procedure for the remaining three scopes. Make sure that you assign the appropriate scopes to the Sales, Shipping, and Personnel divisions. *Do not activate those scopes.*

To assign client reservations to the database servers, right-click the Reservations icon under the Sales scope. Click New Reservation.

At the New Reservation screen, type **Sales Database Server** into the Reservation Name box. Type **192.168.1.68** into the IP Address box, and **00-40-30-AC-D3-56** into the MAC Address box. Into the Description box, type a description such as **Reserved Sales address:**

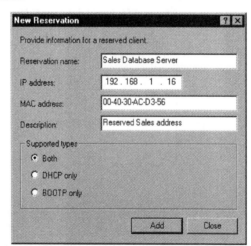

Click Add, and then click Close.

Under the Shipping scope, right-click the Reservations icon. Click New Reservation. When the New Reservation dialog opens, type **Shipping Database Server** into the Reservation Name box. Into the IP Address box, type **192.168.1.52**. Into the MAC Address box, type **00-40-30-C9-39-03**. Into the Description box, type a description such as **Reserved Shipping Address**. Click Add, and then click Close.

To configure DHCP to support WINS, right-click Server Options in the pane that shows the console tree. Now click Configure Options.

From the Available Options list, select the "046 WINS/NBT Node Type" check box. In the Byte box, change the entry to **0X8**. Click OK. Close the DHCP snap-in.

Step 3. To test the DHCP service, log on to the Windows 2000 Professional or Server computer with administrative privileges. Click Start, and then click Run. Into the Run box, type **cmd**, and then press ENTER. The DOS command prompt window opens.

Type **ipconfig/all**. You should see a listing of your TCP/IP configuration.

Verify that the computer has an IP address from the Administration scope. If you do not have an IP address, check the TCP/IP configuration to see if DHCP has been enabled. If DHCP is enabled, type **ipconfig/release**, then **ipconfig/renew** in the DOS window. If DHCP is not enabled, use the Windows 2000 help utility to configure the computer to receive an IP address from a DHCP server.

Lab Solution 5.02

Here are the steps required to install the WINS service, to perform static mappings, to configure replication partners, and to configure a proxy agent on a WINS client.

Step 1. WINS automatically starts and performs most of the basic configuration options once it is installed. Keep the chart supplied by the IS staff close at hand so that you can enter the necessary information when prompted.

Step 2. To install WINS, log on to the Windows 2000 server as an administrator. Click Start, point to Settings, and click Control Panel.

Open the Add/Remove Programs utility. Click the Add/Remove Windows Components button. Select Networking Services from the list of components. Click Details. Select the Windows Internet Name Service (WINS) check box. Click OK. Click Next.

You may be prompted for the Windows 2000 Server CD. Once the installation completes, click Finish.

To create static mappings, select your WINS server in the console window. In the pane that shows the console tree, click Active Registrations.

On the Action menu, click New Static Mapping. The New Static Mapping dialog opens. Complete the static mappings for the Unix and Novell Servers by entering the following information:

- Into the Computer Name box, type **UNIX01**, which is the NetBIOS name of the Unix server.

- In the Type list, click Unique. Into the IP Address box, type **192.168.1.35**. Click Apply.

- Into the Computer Name box, type **NOV02**, which is the NetBIOS name of the Novell server.

- In the Type list, click Unique. Into the IP Address box, type **192.168.1.51**.

Click Apply. Click Cancel.

To create a WINS replication partner, select your WINS server in the console window. In the pane that shows the console tree, click Replication Partners.

On the Action menu, click New Replication Partner. In the New Replication Partner dialog, type **192.168.1.67** for the IP address of WINS02. By default, replication partners are configured as push/pull type partners.

To configure the WINS proxy agent, log on to the Windows 2000 Professional or Server computer with administrative privileges. Click Start, and select Run. Into the Run box, type **regedit.exe** or **regedt32.exe**, and then press ENTER.

The Registry Editor window opens. Double-click the HKEY_LOCAL_MACHINE registry key, and navigate your way to the registry subkey HKEY_LOCAL_MACHINE\ SYSTEM\CurrentControlSet\Services\NetBT\Parameters.

Double-click EnableProxy in the results window on the right-hand side. Type a **1** in the value data window, and then click OK. Close the Registry Editor window.

Step 3.   To test WINS, log on to the Windows 2000 Professional or Server computer with administrative privileges. Click Start, and select Run. Into the Run box, type **cmd**, and then press ENTER. The DOS command prompt window opens.

Ping the computer names of your domain controller, Unix server, Novell server, and computer. Type the command

```
ping server_name
```

where *server_name* is the name of your domain controller, Unix or Novell Server. For example:

```
ping NOV2
```

You should receive four replies from your domain controller but none from the Unix or Novell servers. Those entries exist only in the WINS database, and not on the network.

Lab Solution 5.03

Here are the steps required to install the DNS service, to create forward and reverse lookup zones, to support dynamic updates, to create resource records, to allow WINS integration, and to test the DNS service.

Step 1.   Before you begin the exercise, you have to configure the Windows 2000 domain controller with a static address of 192.168.1.17 and a subnet mask of 255.255.255.240. Keep the information provided by the IS close at hand so that you can appropriately respond to prompts from the installation routine.

Step 2.   To install DNS, log on to the Windows 2000 server as an administrator. Click Start, point to Settings, and click Control Panel. Open the Add/Remove Programs utility.

Click the Add/Remove Windows Components button. Select Networking Services from the list of components. Click Details.

Select the Domain Name System (DNS) Service check box. Click OK, and then click Next.

You may be prompted for the Windows 2000 Server CD. Once the installation completes, click Finish.

To create a forward lookup zone, open the DNS Manager snap-in by selecting Start | Programs | Administrative Tools | DNS. Select the server icon in the left-hand pane, right-click the server icon, and then select New Zone, as shown in Figure 5-5.

FIGURE 5-5

Choosing
the New Zone
wizard

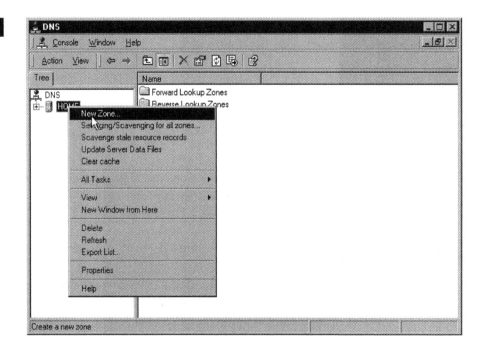

Your selection starts the New Zone wizard. Click Next.

When the Zone Type dialog opens, select Standard Primary, and click Next.

The Forward or Reverse Lookup Zone dialog now opens. Select Forward Lookup Zone. Click Next.

When the Zone Name dialog opens, type **Get-It-Right.com**, and then click Next.

The Zone File dialog now opens. Accept the default, and click Next. Then, click Finish.

To create a reverse lookup zone, begin the same way as for a forward lookup zone. Open the DNS Manager snap-in by selecting Start | Programs | Administrative Tools | DNS. Select the server icon in the left-hand pane, right-click the server icon, and then select New Zone. Click Next.

When the Zone Type dialog opens, select Standard Primary, and click Next.

The Forward or Reverse Lookup Zone dialog now opens. This time, select Reverse Lookup Zone. Click Next.

When the Reverse Lookup Zone dialog opens, type **192.168.1**. Click Next.

When the Zone File dialog opens, accept the default. Click Next, and then click Finish.

To allow dynamic updates for forward lookup zones, select the Get-It-Right.com forward lookup zone from the left-hand pane of the DNS snap-in window. Right-click the zone, and select Properties. At the General tab, set the "Allow dynamic update" list box to "Yes."

Click Apply, and then click OK.

To allow dynamic updates for reverse lookup zones, select the 192.168.1.x subnet reverse lookup zone from the left-hand pane of the DNS snap-in window. Right-click the zone, and select Properties. At the General tab, set the "Allow dynamic update" list box to "Yes." Click Apply, and then click OK.

To create a resource record, select the Get-It-Right.com forward lookup zone from the left-hand pane of the DNS snap-in window. Right-click the zone, and select New Host... When the New Host dialog opens, type **UNIX01** into the Name box. Into the IP Address box, type **192.168.1.35**. Select "Create associated pointer (PTR) record," as shown here:

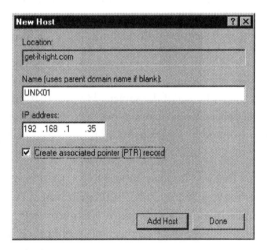

Click Add Host, and then click Done.

To allow WINS integration on forward lookup zones, select the Get-It-Right.com forward lookup zone from the left-hand pane of the DNS snap-in window. Right-click the zone, and select Properties. Select the WINS tab. Select Use WINS Forward Lookup. Into the IP Address box, type **192.168.1.17**.

Click Add, and then click Apply. Click OK.

Step 3. To test the DNS service, select the server icon in the left-hand pane, right-click the server icon, and then select Properties.

Select the Monitoring tab. Select a test type. Select a simple query against this DNS server and a recursive query to other DNS servers. Click the Test Now button. Once you are satisfied that DNS can resolve queries, click Apply. Click OK.

ANSWERS TO LAB ANALYSIS TEST

1. Whenever a computer joins a Windows 2000 domain, its computer name is automatically appended to that of the Windows 2000 domain. The domain name is added as a suffix to the computer (host) name. In our example, where the computer name is "rob1" and the domain name is "Get-It-Right.com," the FQDN of the computer is "rob1.Get-It-Right.com."

2. Microsoft recommends assigning static addresses to the Windows 2000 servers that will host routing, DNS, WINS, and DHCP services. To properly configure devices using the DHCP service, Lynnette should specify addresses to be excluded from a range of IP addresses that she plans to create. The DHCP manager will then not lease those addresses to any clients. Lynnette should create one continuous range of IP addresses that will support all clients on her network. She should then exclude IP addresses from the range to support the devices that must be statically configured. In addition to excluding IP addresses for DHCP, WINS, routers, and DNS, she should also exclude additional addresses for future expansion of the network.

3. Inform Melvin that he can assign the IP addresses to the database servers using client reservations. He will need to use the ipconfig utility on the database servers to list, and then to record the physical (hardware) addresses of the servers. He uses that information to assign the IP addresses that are being referenced by a custom application to the appropriate database server. In the process, he can also modify the lease duration times to reflect a reasonable lease period. Each database server will then be assigned the same IP address whenever its lease expires.

4. Inform Fernando that in Windows 2000, DNS is used to perform the functions that WINS once primarily performed in a Windows NT 4.0 environment. WINS was used in NT 4.0 to locate servers and computers within a network. In Windows 2000, Microsoft uses DNS to resolve computer host names and to locate computers within their local network and on the Internet. In addition, clients automatically register their names and IP addresses into the WINS database. In Windows 2000, dynamic DNS allows Windows 2000 clients or DHCP to automatically register clients into the DNS database. Fernando can therefore integrate the DHCP and DNS services to more easily manage address assignments and name resolution on his network.

5. The recommended approach in DNS design is to register the company's domain name if the company plans to have Internet access. If the company does not plan to have Internet access, then DNS can be configured with a namespace that is for internal use only. Michael should make sure that his root servers have not been created on his DNS servers. He should look for the "." zone on his DNS server. If the root servers exist, he may have to delete them before proper name resolution will occur on his network.

ANSWERS TO KEY TERM QUIZ

1. DHCPACK
2. authorized
3. NetBIOS
4. DORA
5. DHCPREQUEST

6

Installing, Configuring, and Troubleshooting Access to Resources

O n a Windows 2000 network, you control access to local resources by applying NTFS permissions. However, many of the resources needed by network users are located on network servers, and so the users will require network access to those resources. The resources need to be shared to network users, and the access by network users must be controlled. To effectively apply appropriate permissions to network and local resources, you must fully understand the resource-access process.

This chapter focuses on managing local and network access to resources, and configuring NTFS and network share permissions. For an organization to function effectively and efficiently, employees must be able to access the information they need to perform their jobs. But information also needs to be protected, and access to it should be given only on an as-needed basis. Furthermore, information within an organization does not always follow divisional or organizational boundaries. You therefore need tools to manage the many layers of access that may be required.

The job functions of many employees require access to information that "belongs to" other groups or divisions. These users create unique and challenging situations for giving proper access to required network resources. Failure to appropriately configure access to network resources can waste money and valuable employee time. Failure to properly secure resources can lead to theft or misappropriation of information.

In Windows 2000, you can use groups, NTFS, and share permissions to manage access to company information by employees. Balancing appropriate access to, and security for, network resources is a primary administrative responsibility of a Windows 2000 administrator. This chapter will help you learn to manage and configure appropriate access to local and network resources.

LAB EXERCISE 6.01

Controlling Local Access to Files and Folders

60 Minutes

Working for the Get-It-Right package shipping company, you are quickly becoming a seasoned administrator. Get-It-Right is continuing to make changes to its network infrastructure in an effort to improve efficiency and effectiveness. Because of all the changes that have been implemented, management is now concerned that a number of security holes may exist in the network infrastructure. Management would like you to use Windows 2000 features to control access to local resources on the network servers. The IS manager wants you to create groups that you can use for access control. The management of the resources needs to reflect the organizational design of the company.

Are you ready to provide security for local resources? Can you effectively manage employee access to local resources? Can you handle these additional administrative responsibilities?

Learning Objectives

In this lab, you define the access that a user has to local resources. Get-It-Right has several divisions, whose users require specific resources to adequately perform their jobs. You will configure access to the resources by creating appropriate groups with the required permissions. Applying NTFS permissions controls access to local resources. At the end of the lab, you'll be able to

- Create groups in Windows 2000
- Create a directory and file structure
- Know the six levels of NTFS folder permissions
- Know the five levels of NTFS file permissions
- Know how to apply NTFS permissions to files or folders
- Know how to control permission inheritance
- Determine effective permissions
- Determine NTFS permissions for copied or moved files
- Test access to local files or folders.

Lab Materials and Setup

The lab requires these materials:

- The successful completion of the Chapter 5 lab exercises
- A Windows 2000 domain controller that is configured with two NTFS partitions
- Pen or pencil
- Writing pad (optional)
- Windows 2000 help utility
- Access to the www.microsoft.com web site (optional)

Getting Down to Business

You are going to create a directory and file structure for Get-It-Right. You will then create groups that will you will use to control access to files and folders. Afterward, you will check and document how permissions perform when you copy or move files and folders that are managed by NTFS. In addition, you will document how NTFS permissions react at various levels of the directory structure by testing permission inheritance. Use this procedure:

lab

Warning *These labs should be performed on a Windows 2000 domain controller. You need two NTFS partitions to complete the exercises. The labs assume that the partitions you will use are C and D.*

Step 1. **Plan** for the implementation of local security on the Windows 2000 server.

■ To plan NTFS permissions properly, you must determine

■ the group names to use. You may create new groups or use Windows 2000 built-in groups.

■ the permissions that various users need for particular folders and files.

■ how inheritance will be used. Will inheritance propagate from the parent folder to all child folders? Or will you clear the "Allow inheritable permissions from parent to propagate to this object" check box?

■ To effectively apply NTFS permissions, remember these guidelines:

■ NTFS permissions assigned to a folder are inherited by all of the files and folders within that folder.

■ By clearing the "Allow inheritable permissions from parent to propagate to this object" check box, you can assign more restrictive permissions.

■ Using the Deny Permissions attribute overrides other permissions that have been set for a user or group.

■ When assigning permissions to data or application folders, assign the Read & Execute permission to the Users group and the Administrator's group to prevent accidental deletion and infection of files.

■ When you assign permissions to public data folders, assign the Read & Execute permission and the Write permission to the User Group and the Full Control permission to the Creator Owner user. Users will then be able to read and modify all material, but to delete only the files and folders that they create.

- Give users only the level of access that they require.
- Microsoft recommends assigning permissions to resources at the group level rather than at the user level.

- Your decisions for Get-It-Right should be based on these criteria:

  - The three divisions within Get-It-Right are Admin, Sales, and Accounting.
  - Each division has two managers and two or three users. Some users belong to more than one group.
  - The names of the descriptive groups that represent the managers and users in each division should make determining the group's role within the organization easy.

- Here are the employees and their functions:

  - Admin managers: Joe and Rob
  - Admin users: Markeil, Lynn, and Taylor
  - Sales managers: Melvin, and Wendell
  - Sales users: Lynn, and Tyrese
  - Accounting managers: Godfrey and Chris
  - Accounting users: Lois, Taylor, and Shirley

- No user should have a password. Do not require users to change passwords at next logon.

- All users must be allowed to log on to the local server.

lab
Hint *Whenever you create information for use by network users, remember to keep it simple. Do not get caught up trying to create groups or resource names designed for fellow administrators. Make all resource or group names user-friendly and descriptive.*

- You must create these folders on NTFS volumes:

C:\Microsoft Office	C:\Accounting	C:\Public	C:\Sales
C:\Test	C:\Accounting\Receivables	C:\Public\Benefits	C:\Sales\Customers
D:\Test2	C:\Accounting\Payable	C:\Public\Forms	C:\Sales\Orders

- Administrators of the server, who should be IS staff members, should have full access to all folders and files created.
- Permissions for the Public folder must meet these requirements:
    - Individual users should be able to read, create, and modify the contents, properties, and permissions of the documents that they create in the \Public and \Public\Benefits folders. They should not be able to modify files created by others.
    - Only the Sales users and Sales managers should be able to modify files in the \Public\Forms folder.
- Permissions for the Accounting folder must meet these requirements:
    - Accounting managers should be able to modify files in all Admin folders. They should also be able to delete the folder.
    - Accounting users should be able to run applications, and to read and create new files and folders.
- Permissions for the Sales folder must meet these requirements:
    - Sales managers should be able to modify files in all Sales folders. They can also delete the folder.
    - Sales users should be able to run applications, and to read and create new files and folders.
    - Accounting users should be able to read files in the Sales folders.
- Everyone can read the files in the Test folder.
- Everyone has full control of the Test2 folder.
- All users can run programs in the Microsoft Office folder, but they cannot modify the files found there.

Use Table 6.1 to plan and record the permissions that fulfill the indicated requirements.

Step 2. **Implement** by creating the folders, users, and groups planned in step 1.

- Use the information that you recorded in Table 6-1 to assign the proper permissions to the files and folders.

TABLE 6-1	NTFS Security Information for Get-It-Right		
Path	**User account or group**	**NTFS permissions**	**Inheritance block (yes/no)**
C:\Accounting			
C:\Accounting\Payable			
C:\Accounting\Receivables			
C:\Public			
C:\Public\Benefits			
C:\Public\Forms			
C:\Sales			
C:\Sales\Customers			
C:\Sales\Orders			
C:\Microsoft Office			
C:\Test			
D:\Test2			

lab
ⓘint

Remember to assign permissions to the Creator Owner group for the Public folders.

■ Use the Windows 2000 help utility to review the NTFS folder and file permissions. You may also refer to the Microsoft web site located at www.microsoft.com for additional help in planning and implementing NTFS permissions.

cross
ⓡeference

Chapter 6 of the **Windows 2000 Server Study Guide** *by Tom Shinder and Deb Litttlejohn Shinder (McGraw–Hill/Osborne, 2000).*

Step 3. Test by logging on to the Windows 2000 server.

■ Test the permissions for the Public folders:

    ■ Log on as Wendell. Attempt to create and save a file named Wendell.txt in the \Public\Benefits folder. Were you successful? Why or why not?

    ■ Log off Wendell.

- Log on as Markeil, and attempt to create a file named Markeil.txt in the \Public\Benefits folder. Were you successful? Why or why not?

- Attempt to modify the Wendell.txt file found in the \Public\Benefits folder. Were you successful? Why or why not?

- Attempt to delete the file. Were you successful? Why or why not?

- Test the permissions for the Accounting folders:

  - While still logged on as Markeil, attempt to create a file named Account.txt in the \Accounting\Payable folder. Were you successful? Why or why not?

  - Log off Markeil.

  - Log on as Shirley, and attempt to create a file named Account.txt in the \Accounting\Payable folder. Were you successful? Why or why not?

  - Log off Shirley.

- Test Taylor's effective rights to the Sales folder:

  - Complete Table 6-2 based on the information you obtain by completing the actions that follow.

  - Log on as Administrator, and list the groups that Taylor belongs to. List the groups that have access to the Sales folders.

  - What are the permissions that have been set for the Sales folder for the groups that Taylor is a member of? What are Taylor's effective rights?

  - Taylor's effective rights are equal to the combination of all permissions that are set for the groups of which she is a member. The least restrictive right will determine her "effective rights."

TABLE 6-2   Taylor's Effective Rights to the Sales Folder

Resource	Groups	NTFS permissions	Taylor's groups	Effective rights

- Test how NTFS permissions are applied to moved and copied folders:

  - Record the findings of the test that follows in Table 6.3.

  - Record the group and NTFS permissions for the Accounting folder.

- Copy the Accounting folder to the D:\Test2 folder. Record the NTFS permissions for all groups that have access to the Accounting folder.

- Move the Accounting folder to the C:\Test folder. Record the NTFS permissions for all groups that have access to the folder.

lab
ⓗint
When files or folders are moved or copied to a different NTFS partition, they inherit the NTFS permissions of the destination folder. However, when files or folders are moved to a new folder on the same NTFS partition, the moved files or folders retain their original NTFS permissions.

TABLE 6-3	NTFS Permissions of Moved and Copied Folders			
Resource	**Groups**	**Permissions before move or copy**	**Permissions after copy to D:\Test2**	**Permissions after move to C:\Test**
Accounting				

- Attempt to create, modify, and delete files in the various folders to test the NTFS permissions that you have established.

- Once you are satisfied with your findings, have your instructor or Windows 2000 evaluator check your work.

LAB EXERCISE 6.02

Controlling Access to Distributed File System (DFS) Resources

60 Minutes

The Microsoft Distributed File System (DFS) is a Windows 2000 network component that makes it easier for network administrators to find and manage data more efficiently on their networks. As the Get-It-Right administrator, you must use DFS to present a collection of network resources as a single hierarchical structure.

For Get-It-Right network users to be able to quickly access resources on various servers, you must configure the DFS on a Windows 2000 domain controller. Because the growth of the Get-It-Right network cannot be determined at this time, you must link servers and shares into a simpler, more meaningful name space. You must make files distributed across multiple servers appear to users as if they reside in one place on the network. Network users should not be required to know and specify the actual physical location of files.

Can you help Get-It-Right network users easily access resources on multiple network servers? Can you properly configure the DFS for Get-It-Right?

Learning Objectives

In this lab, you use the DFS snap-in to install a fault-tolerant DFS root on a Windows 2000 domain controller. At the end of the lab, you will be able to

- Install DFS on a Windows 2000 domain controller
- Create and publish a DFS root
- Design a DFS shared folder system
- Create DFS child nodes/links
- Test the distributed file system.

Lab Materials and Setup

The lab requires these materials:

- Access to a computer functioning as a Windows 2000 domain controller
- A computer running Windows 2000 Server or Professional
- Windows 2000 help utility
- Access to the Internet (optional)

Getting Down to Business

You are going to install and configure a domain-based DFS root for Get-It-Right. The managers have asked you to provide access to resources distributed across multiple servers in one convenient location for their network users. They would like you to integrate the DFS into the network so that it can use the features associated with Windows 2000 to help users easily locate network resources. Here's how to proceed:

Step 1.   Plan for the implementation of the DFS service on a Windows 2000 domain controller. The IS staff have provided this information to help you create a domain-based DFS root:

- Host domain for DFS root: Get-It-Right.com
- DFS root share (located on the domain controller): Public

- DFS root name: Get-It-Resources

- DFS root comment: First DFS root for Get-It-Right

- Shares located on Windows 2000 Server or Professional PC: Accounting and Sales

- DFS link names: Accounting and Sales

- DFS link comments: Accounting Link and Sales Link (respectively)

Step 2. **Implement** by configuring the DFS to meet the requirements set forth by the IS staff.

- The Windows 2000 Server help utility or the Microsoft web site (located at www.microsoft.com) can help you configure the domain-based DFS root required to complete this lab.

cross
Reference

Chapter 6 of the **Windows 2000 Server Study Guide** *by Tom Shinder and Deb Litttlejohn Shinder (McGraw–Hill/Osborne, 2000).*

Step 3. **Test** by reviewing the information from the IS staff. Have you met all requirements?

- Log on to the Windows 2000 domain controller, and enter the UNC path to the DFS root.

- Make sure that all shares appear under the Public root share by typing one of the following UNC paths: *server_name***Public** or *domain_name*\ **Get-It-Resources**.

- Once you have completed these tasks have your instructor or evaluator check your work.

LAB EXERCISE 6.03

Controlling Access to Printers

60 Minutes

Print servers are the workhorses of many Windows 2000 networking environments. Microsoft has incorporated the latest technological advances into this fundamental service, making it simpler for both administrators and end users to configure and manage their printing needs. As the Get-It-Right administrator, you must configure a print server to manage printing on the Get-It-Right network.

To successfully accomplish that task, you must familiarize yourself with Windows 2000 printing terms. You must be able to distinguish between a *printer,* a *print device,* a *print server,* and a *printer driver.*

Can you successfully implement network printing for the Get-It-Right network users?

Learning Objectives

In this lab, you use the Add Printer wizard to create and share printers on a Windows 2000 domain controller. You will make it easy for Get-It-Right network users and administrators to locate, configure, and manage their printing needs. At the end of the lab, you'll be able to

- Install a Windows 2000 print server on a Windows 2000 domain controller
- Create and share a printer
- Control access to a network printer
- Configure a printer pool
- Configure priorities between printers
- Connect to a network printer
- Understand the Windows 2000 printer terminology
- Test access to your network printers.

Lab Materials and Setup

The lab requires these materials:

- Access to a computer functioning as a Windows 2000 domain controller
- A computer running Windows 2000 Server or Professional (optional)
- Windows 2000 help utility
- Access to the Internet (optional)

Getting Down to Business

You are going to install and configure a network-based printing solution using a Windows 2000 domain controller as a print server. The Get-It-Right managers have asked you to provide access to printers for various divisions and users within the company. They want you to integrate the Windows 2000 printing services into their network so that users can easily find and control access to print devices on the network. Use this procedure:

Step 1. **Plan** to implement the printing services.

The IS staff have been investigating printing in Windows 2000. They are quite confused about some of the Microsoft terms, particularly *printer,* because they all thought that a printer is a physical device. The IS staff want you to explain the Windows 2000 Server print terminology, because they'll have to explain printing in Windows 2000 to the network users.

The IS staff have also provided information to help you control access to print devices on the network:

- Print server location: Windows 2000 domain.
- All printer share names should easily identify the location and use of the printers.
- Administrators should have full control of all printers.
- Managers of a division must be able to print ahead of users in that division. Users who are not members of the division should always print last.
- In the Sales division, the printers, print locations, and printer permissions are to be set as follows:

  - Two HP 670C color DeskJet printers.
  - Sales managers should always be able to print ahead of sales users and other division users. Sales users should always be able to print ahead of users outside the Sales division.
  - Sales mangers should be able to fully control both printers.
  - Sales users should only be able to print to both printers.
  - All other division managers should be able to manage printers and print.
  - All non-Sales users of the non_Sales_users printers should be able to print to those printers only between 8 and 10 A.M.

- In the Admin division, the printers, print locations, and printer permissions are to be set as follows:

  - Two HP 5SI 17 ppm laser printers.

  - Admin managers should always be able to print ahead of Admin users and users from other divisions. Admin users should always be able to print ahead of users outside the Admin division.

  - Admin printer 2 should automatically accept documents from Admin printer 1 if Admin printer 1 is not available. But Admin printer 1 should not accept documents sent to Admin printer 2.

lab **Hint** *Think about pool printing.*

  - Admin managers should be able to fully control both Admin printers.

  - Admin users should be able to print to both printers.

  - All other division managers should be able to manage printers and print.

  - All non-Admin users of the non_Admin_users printers should be able to print to those printers only between 2 and 3 P.M..

Step 2. **Implement** by configuring the printing services to meet the requirements set forth by the IS staff.

- Use Table 6-4 to give an explanation of the print terminology used in Windows 2000.

- The Windows 2000 Server help utility or the Microsoft web site (located at www.microsoft.com) can help you explain the print terminology and configure printing in this lab.

lab **Hint** *When you establish priority printing, you configure multiple printers that reference the same print device. The print priority is set from 1 to 99, with 99 being the highest priority, and 1 being the lowest priority. Make sure that the names you use to identify your printers easily identify their location and use—for example, Account_manager_printer1.*

TABLE 6-4	Printing terms	Descriptions
	Print device	
Windows 2000 Print Terminology	Print server	
	Print driver	
	Printer	

Step 3. Test by logging on to the Windows 2000 domain controller.

- Log on as Wendell. Select Start | Run. Into the Run box, type the UNC name (*computer_name*) of the Windows 2000 domain controller server where you created the network printers.

Wendell is a Sales user. Will he easily be able to identify the printers to which he has access? Why or why not?

Attempt to connect to one of the Sales user printers. Double-click the printer icon to download the print driver. Were you successful? Why or why not?

Attempt to connect to one of the Sales manager printers. Double-click the Sales manager printer icon to download the print driver. Were you successful? Why or why not?

Verify that Wendell can connect only to the Sales user printers and to the 'all users' printers of each division. (You can also wait until the appropriate times of day to verify that Wendell can print to the Admin 'all users' printer only between 2 and 3 P.M.

Log off Wendell.

- Log on as Markeil. Select Start | Run. Into the Run box, type the UNC name (*computer_name*) of the Windows 2000 domain controller server where you created the network printers.

Markeil is an Admin user. Will she easily be able to identify the printers to which she has access? Why or why not?

Attempt to connect to one of the Admin user printers. Double-click the printer icon to download the print driver. Were you successful? Why or why not?

Attempt to connect to one of the Admin manager printers. Double-click the Admin manager printer icon to download the print driver. Were you successful? Why or why not?

Verify that Markeil can connect only to the Admin user printers and to the 'all users' printers of each division. (You can also wait to the appropriate times of day to verify that Markeil can print to the Sales 'all users' printer only between 8 and 10 A.M. Log off Markeil.

- Review the information that the IS staff provided to ensure that you met all the requirements.

- Log on to the Windows 2000 domain controller and verify that the proper permissions have been set for all users of the Admin and Sales divisions. Make sure that all users who are not members of those divisions can print only during the designated times for non-division users.

- Once you are satisfied with your findings, have your instructor or Windows 2000 Professional evaluator check your work.

LAB ANALYSIS TEST

1. You are the administrator of a Windows 2000 Server computer. A folder named Benefits on the system partition of the server is shared on the network as Corporate_Benefits. The owner of the Benefits folder is Administrators. The share permissions and NTFS permissions are set as follows:

   ■ Everyone: Full Control
   ■ Domain Admins: Read
   ■ Tyrese: Full Control

   Tyrese creates a file in the Benefits folder. He sets the NTFS permissions for the file to list only him on the access control list, with Full Control permission. Tyrese suddenly quits and cannot be contacted. Later, you discover that the file contains personal information and must be removed from the server as soon as possible. You want to delete the file without modifying the permissions of other files in the Benefits folder. You want your actions to have the least possible impact on users who may be using other files in the Benefits folder. You want to use the minimum amount of authority necessary to delete the file. What should you do?

   _____

   _____

2. Robert is the administrator for AJAX printing company. They have a Windows 2000 Server network that runs in mixed mode. Robert has recently installed and shared a new HP LaserJet 4SI printer on a member server. All of his Windows 2000 client computers can print to the new printer successfully. However, when users try to connect to the printer from Windows NT 4.0 workstation clients, they receive a message stating that "The server on which the printer resides does not have a suitable HP LaserJet printer driver installed'.' Robert wants the printer driver to be installed automatically on the Windows NT 4.0 workstations. What should he do?

   _____

   _____

3. Freeda is a new Windows 2000 administrator for the Realty.com company. She would like to create a shared printer for the company's managers so that they do not have to wait for their documents to print when their default printer's queue contains a large number of documents. She configures a new high-priority printer and wants to set permissions for these groups:

   ■ Administrator
   ■ Creator Owner
   ■ Server Operators

■ Everyone

■ Managers

■ Print Operators

She has selected the check box to allow print permissions for the Managers group. She wants only Administrators, Print Operators, Server Operators, and Managers to be able to print. What should she do?

_____

_____

4. Lois is the administrator of a large Windows 2000 network. The network includes a Windows 2000 Server computer that is used as a file server. More than 1200 of your company client computers are connected to that server. A shared folder named "Salaries" is located on one of the server's NTFS partitions. The Salaries folder contains more than 5000 files. The permissions for the Salaries folder are set as shown here:

■ Salaries Share Permissions: Users = Change; Administrators = Full Control

■ Salaries NTFS Permissions: Users = Full Control; Administrators = Full Control

Lois has recently discovered that files within the Salary folder allow employees to modify their own salaries. She needs to immediately prevent five files within the Salary folder from being modified. When she checks the sessions on the server, she discovers that users are connected to the Salaries folder. Lois wants to change permissions on the files, but she wants her actions to have the smallest possible effects on the users who are using other files on the server. Which of the following courses of action should she take?

A. Modify the NTFS permissions for the five files.

B. Modify the NTFS permissions for the Salaries folder.

C. Modify the shared permissions for the Salaries folder.

D. Log the users off the network.

E. Disconnect all users from the Salaries folder.

_____

_____

5. You are the administrator of a Windows 2000 Server computer named GetItOne. You create a DFS root named Accounting. You add a shared folder named NorthEast as a DFS node under the root. The share permissions and NTFS permissions for Accounting and NorthEast are set as shown here:

■ Accounting folder permissions:

Share permissions	NTFS permissions
Everyone: Full Control	Everyone: Full Control
Domain Admins: Full Control	Domain Admins: Full Control

■ NorthEast Folder Permissions:

Share permissions	NTFS permissions
Account users: Read	Account users: Read
Domain Admins: Full Control	Domain Admins: Full Control
Domain users: Full Control	Domain users: Full Control

A user named Jonathan is a member of the Account and Domain user groups. When Jonathan attempts to save the file \\GetItOne\Accounting\NorthEast\Tax.xls, he receives the error message "Access denied." You want Jonathan to be able to change and delete all files in the NorthEast folder. You do not want him to have more access than necessary. What should you do?

_____

_____

KEY TERM QUIZ

Use the following vocabulary terms to complete the sentences below. Not all of the terms will be used.

cross Reference *Chapter 6 of the **Windows 2000 Server Study Guide** by Tom Shinder and Deb Litttlejohn Shinder (McGraw–Hill/Osborne, 2000)*

dedicated

Distributed File System (DFS)

Everyone

inheritance

print device

printer

Read & Execute

1. On a Windows 2000 NTFS partition the _____ group automatically receives Full Control of all folders and subfolders that are created.

2. The _____ is the software interface between the document and the print device. In Windows 2000, this logical interface allows the user to specify a print job's destination and the time that it will be printed.

3. A(n) _____ printer server is a Windows 2000 server whose only role is to provide printing services. The server does not provide directory space for users other than storage for spooled print jobs.

4. The _____ allows system administrators to logically manage a collection of network resources and present those resources to the user as a single, hierarchical structure.

5. In Windows 2000, all parent folder permissions are applied to any files or subfolders in that folder unless _____ has been prevented from propagating from the parent folder to subfolders and files.

LAB SOLUTIONS FOR CHAPTER 6

The sections that follow walk you through the steps to solve the lab exercises. You should avoid looking at these sections unless you are stuck on a particular exercise.

Lab Solution 6.01

The steps required to control access to local resources are outlined on the next few pages. Your answers may vary, but they should resemble those given here.

Step 1. Based on the information supplied, your NTFS security information should resemble that shown in Table 6-5.

TABLE 6-5 NTFS Security Information for Get-It-Right

Path	User account or group	NTFS permissions	Inheritance block (yes/no)
C:\Accounting	Administrators Account_mgr Account_users	Full Control Modify Read &Execute Write	Yes Yes Yes
C:\Accounting\Payable	Administrators Account_mgr Account_users	Full Control Modify Read &Execute Write	No No No
C:\Accounting\Receivables	Administrators Account_mgr Account_users	Full Control Modify Read &Execute Write	No No No
C:\Public	Administrator Creator Owner Users	Full Control Full Control Write	Yes Yes Yes
C:\Public\Benefits	Administrator Creator Owner Users	Full Control Full Control Write	No No No

TABLE 6-5 NTFS Security Information for Get-It-Right *(continued)*

Path	User account or group	NTFS permissions	Inheritance block (yes/no)
C:\Public\Forms	Administrator	Full Control	Yes
	Sales_users	Modify	Yes
	Sales_managers	Modify	Yes
C:\Sales	Administrator	Full Control	Yes
	Sales_users	Modify	Yes
	Sales_managers	Modify	Yes
	Account_users	Read	Yes
	Account_managers	Read	Yes
	Admin_users	Full Control	Yes
	Admin_managers	Full Control	Yes
C:\Sales\Customers	Administrator	Full Control	No
	Sales_users	Modify	No
	Sales_managers	Modify	No
C:\Sales\Orders	Administrator	Full Control	No
	Sales_users	Modify	No
	Sales_managers	Modify	No
C:\Microsoft Office	Administrators	Full Control	Yes
	Users	Read & Execute	Yes
C:\Test	Administrators	Full Control	Yes
	Users	Read	Yes
D:\Test2	Everyone	Full Control	Yes

Step 2. To create the users and groups, log on to the Windows 2000 domain controller with administrative privileges. Select Start | Programs | Administrative Tools | Active Directory Users and Computers. Select Users and right-click New User.

For the Name, type **Wendell**. For the User Logon Name, type **Wendell**. Click Next. There are no passwords. Remove the check mark from "User must change password at next log on." Click Next, and then click Finish. Repeat for each user.

On the menu bar, select Action | New | Group. For the Group Name, type **Admin_Managers**. For the Group Scope, select Global. For the Group Type, select Security. Click OK.

Double-click the Users icon. Find and double-click Admin_Managers. Go to the Members tab, and click Add. Select Joe in the Name box, and press CTRL. Select Rob in the Name box, and click Add. Click OK, and then Apply. Click Close. Repeat step for all groups and group members. Close the Active Directory Users and Computers snap-in when you are done.

To create the directory structure, log on to the Windows 2000 server with administrative privileges. Click Start | Run, and into the Run box, type **cmd**. Press ENTER.

At the Windows 2000 command prompt, type **md C:\Microsoft Office**. Press ENTER. Repeat for each folder. Remember that the Test2 folder should be stored on D:\Test2

To set the NTFS permissions on the Get-It-Right folders, log on to the Windows 2000 domain controller with administrative privileges. Double-click the My Computer icon on the Windows 2000 desktop. Double-click the local disk drive (C:) icon. Select the Accounting folder. Right-click the Accounting folder. Select Properties. Click the Security tab. Clear the "Allow inheritable permissions from parent to propagate to this object" check box. Click Copy. Remove the Everyone group.

Click Add. Select Account_Managers in the Name box. Press CTRL, and select Account Users and Administrators in the Name box. Click OK. Select Account_Managers in the Name window. In the Allow Permissions box, select the Modify check box.

Select Account_users in the Name box. In the Allow Permissions box, select the Read & Execute and the Write check boxes.

Click Add. Select Administrators in the Name box. In the Allow Permissions box, select the Full Control check box. Click Apply, and then click OK. Repeat the entire procedure to set NTFS permissions on the other folders.

To assign permissions to the Creator Owner group for the Public folders, in the Properties dialog box, click Add. In the name list, select Creator Owner. Click Add, and then click OK.

lab
ⓗint   *Remember that, for users to be able to modify the contents, properties, and permissions of the documents they create in the Public folder, the Creator Owner group must be given Full Control over that folder.*

Select Creator Owner in the Properties dialog box. Select the Allow check box next to Full Control. Click Apply, and then click OK.

Step 3.   When you test the permissions to the Public folders, Wendell should be able to create a file in the \Public\Benefits folder because the Sales_managers group of which Wendell is a member has the Read & Execute and Write permissions set.

Markeil should also be able to create a file in the \Public\Benefits folder because the Admin_users group of which Markeil is a member also has the Read & Execute and Write permissions set. However, Markeil will not be able to modify the Wendell.txt file because the Creator Owner permission will allow her to modify only the files that she creates.

When you test the permissions to the Accounting folders, only the Account_managers, Account_users, and Administrators should have access to the accounting folders. Because Markeil is not a member of any of these groups, she will not be able to create the Account.txt file.

Because Shirley is a member of the Account_users group, which has Read & Execute and Write permissions to the Accounting folders, she will be able to create the Account.txt file.

Taylor's effective rights to the Sales folder depend on her membership in her two groups. Her effective NTFS permissions will be the least restrictive of the permissions that have been set for her. Your findings should be similar to those shown in Table 6-6.

TABLE 6-6   Taylor's Effective Rights to the Sales Folder

Resource	Groups	NTFS permissions	Taylor's groups	Effective rights
Sales	Administrators Sales_managers Sales_users Admin_users Account_users	Full Control Modify Read & Execute, Write Full Control Read & Execute	Admin_users Account_users	Full Control

When you determine the NTFS permissions of copied or moved folders, your results for copying and moving the Sales folder to the Test and Test2 folders should resemble those in Table 6-7.

Lab Solution 6.02

Your answers to this exercise may vary, but they should resemble the answers outlined on the next few pages.

		Permissions before move or copy	**Permissions after copy to D:\Test2**	**Permissions after move to C:\Test**
TABLE 6-7	NTFS Permissions of Moved and Copied Folders			
Resource	**Groups**			
Accounting	Administrators	Full Control	Read	Full Control
	Account_users	Read & Execute	Read	Read & Execute
	Account_managers	Modify	Read	Modify

Step 1. Keep the information provided by the IS staff nearby as you carry out the installation.

Step 2. To create a domain DFS root, log on to the Windows 2000 domain controller with administrative privileges. Select Start | Programs | Administrative Tools | Distributed File System.

The Distributed File System console will appear as shown in Figure 6-1.

Right-click Distributed File System. Select New DFS Root. At the opening screen for the New DFS Root wizard, click Next.

FIGURE 6-1

Viewing the Distributed File System console

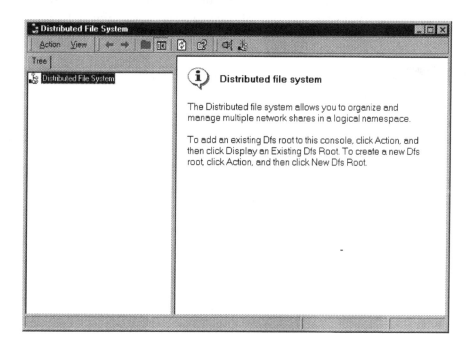

When the Select DFS Root Type dialog opens, select "Create a domain DFS root" and then click Next.

The Select the Host Domain for the DFS Root dialog opens. Into the Domain Name box, type **get-it-right.com**. Click Next.

The Specify the Host Server for the DFS Root dialog opens. Accept the default server name shown. Click Next.

The Specify the DFS Root Share dialog opens. Select "Use an existing share," and type **Public** into the associated text box, as shown in Figure 6-2. Click Next.

The Name the DFS Root dialog opens. Into the DFS Root Name box, type **Get-It-Resources.** Into the Comments box, type **First DFS root for Get-It-Right**. Click Next.

At the Completing the New DFS Root screen that now opens, review the information presented. If all is correct, click Finish.

To create the child nodes/DFS links, log on to your Windows 2000 server or Windows 2000 Professional client with administrative privileges. Double-click My Computer, and then double-click the drive C icon. On the menu bar, click File, and select New | Folder. For the folder name, type **Sales**. Right-click the Sales folder, and choose Sharing. Select the "Share this folder" radio button. Click Apply, and then click OK. Repeat the process for the Accounting folder, and then log off.

On your Windows 2000 domain controller, in the DFS console window, right-click the DFS root, and select New DFS Link.

FIGURE 6-2

Specifying
the share for
the DFS root

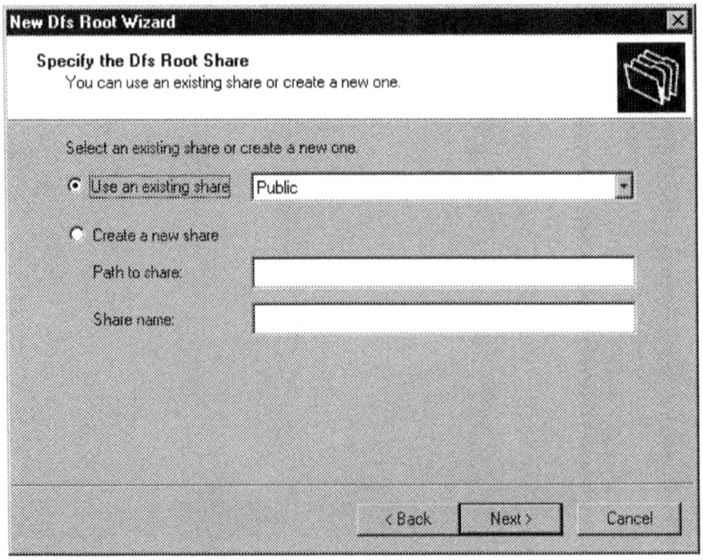

At the resulting Create a New DFS Link screen, type **Sales** into the Link Name box. In the "Send the user to this shared folder" box, type *member_server name*\Sales. Into the Comment box, type **Sales link**. Click OK.

Repeat the process for the Accounting link. When you are done, your DFS console screen should resemble the one in Figure 6-3.

Step 3.   To test the domain DFS root, continue: While still logged on to the Windows 2000 domain controller, click Start | Run. Into the Run box, type the UNC path to your domain controller (*domain controller_name*). Double-click Public. You should see a directory structure similar to that in Figure 6-4.

Lab Solution 6.03

Your answers to this exercise may vary, but they should resemble the description given on the next few pages.

FIGURE 6-3	
Viewing newly created links at the DFS console	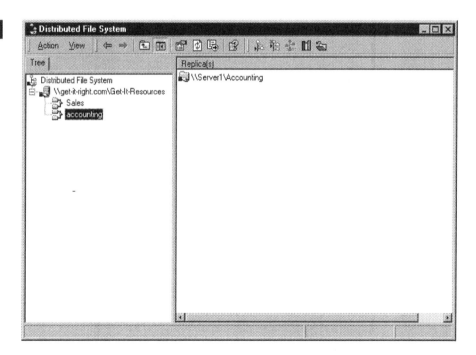

FIGURE 6-4

Checking
the directory
structure of
the DFS root

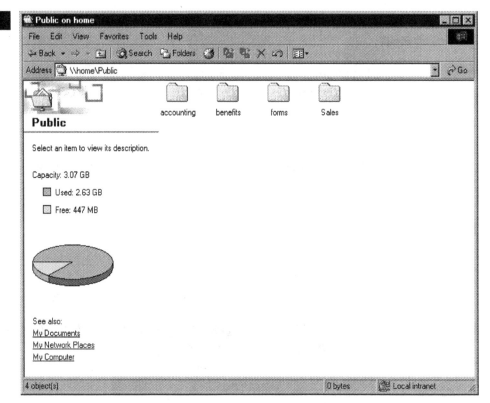

Step 1. Keep the information provided by the IS staff nearby. You'll need the information when configuring the print solutions.

Step 2. To create and share a local print device (HP 670C DeskJet printer) that is directly connected to the print server, and that will be used by the Sales manager, log on to the Windows 2000 domain controller with administrative privileges. Select Start | Settings | Printers. Double-click Add Printer to start the Add Printer wizard. Click Next at the Welcome to the Add Printer Wizard page.

When the Local or Network Printer screen opens, accept the default (Local printer). Clear the "Automatically detect and install my Plug and Play printer." Click Next.

Remember that print devices must be attached to separate physical ports. When the Select the Printer Port screen opens, accept LPT1 as the port for the first printer. (You will select LPT2 for the second physical printer.) Click Next.

In the Manufacturer box, select HP. In the Printer Type box, select HP DeskJet 670C. Click Next.

At the Name Your Printer screen, type a descriptive printer name for the Sales manager's printer, such as **Sales_manager_Color_Printer1**. You do not want your Windows-based programs to use this printer as the default printer, and so select No for that option. Click Next.

At the Printer Sharing window, click Share As, and then type **Sales_manager_Color_Printer1**. Click Next.

Click Yes to ignore the DOS warning message.

At the Location and Comment screen, you should enter the location where the printer will be found and a comment that describes the manufacturer printer type. Click Next.

At the Print Test Page screen, click No, to skip printing a test page. Click Next, and then click Finish.

To create and share a local print device (HP 670C DeskJet printer) that is directly connected to the print server, and that will be used by the Sales users, complete the same process as for the Sales manager's printer, but with these changes:

- For the printer port, select LPT1. (This must be done so that priority printing can be established.)

- Choose to keep the existing driver.

- Name the printer **Sales_users_Color_Printer1**.

- Set printer sharing for Sales_users_Color_Printer1.

To create a printer for users outside of Sales that points to the physical print device of Sales users, complete the same steps as for creating the Sales users printer, but with these changes:

- Select LPT1 as the Printer Port. (This must be done to support priority printing and to allow print scheduling for non-sales users.)

- Choose to keep the existing driver.

- Name the printer **Sales_all_division_users_Color_Printer1**.

- Set printer sharing for Sales_all_division_users_Color_Printer1.

To create the second Sales printer, complete the same procedure as for creating the first Sales printer. But choose LPT2 when you select the printer port.

The same procedures apply to the creation of the two HP 5SI Admin printers. Use a naming convention similar to this one:

Admin_all_division_users_HighSpeed_Printer1
Admin_all_division_users_HighSpeed_Printer2

For the purposes of this lab exercise place these two printers on the ports COM1 and COM2.

To create priority printing for the Sales printers, click Start | Settings | Printers. Right-click the Sales_managers_Color_Printer1 printer. Click Properties. Click the Advanced tab. Into the Priority box, type **50** (leave room for higher priority). Click Apply, and then click OK.

Click Start | Settings | Printers. Right-click the Sales_users_Color_Printer1 printer. Click Properties. Click the Advanced tab. Into the Priority box, type **25** (leave room for higher priority). Click Apply, and then click OK.

Click Start | Settings | Printers. Right-click the Sales_all_division_users_Color_Printer1 printer. Click Properties. Click the Advanced tab. Into the Priority box, type **10** (leave room for higher priority). Click Apply, and then click OK.

To allow printing only during a specified time, click Start | Settings | Printers. Right-click the Sales_all_division_users_Color_Printer1 printer. Click Properties. Click the Advanced tab. Select Available From, and set the time to 8:00 A.M. to 10:00 A.M. Click Apply, and then click OK.

To configure the permissions for the Sales printers, click Start | Settings | Printers. Right-click the Sales_managers_Color_Printer1 printer. Click Properties. Click the Security tab. Select Everyone. Click Remove.

Click Add. Double-click the Admin_managers group. Press the CTRL key, and select Sales_managers and Accounting_managers. Click Add, and then click OK.

Select Sales_managers. Select the Print, Manage Printers, and Manage Documents check boxes, because the division managers must have full control of the printers.

Select Admin_managers, and then select the Print and Manage Printers check boxes. Repeat for the Accounting_managers, so that all other managers can print and manage printers.

Click Start | Settings | Printers. Right-click the Sales_users_Color_Printer1 printer. Click Properties. Click the Security tab. Select Everyone, and then click Remove.

Click Add. Double-click the Admin_managers group. Press the CTRL key and select the Sales_managers, Accounting_managers, and Sales_users. Click Add, and then click OK.

Select Sales_managers. Select the Print, Manage Printers, and Manage Documents check boxes, because the division managers must have full control of the printers.

Select Admin_managers. Select the Print and Manage Printers check boxes. Repeat for the Accounting_managers, so that all other managers can print and manage printers.

Select Sales_users, and then select the Print check box.

Click Start | Settings | Printers. Right-click the Sales_all_division_users_Color_Printer1 printer. Click Properties. Click the Security tab. Select Everyone. Click Remove.

Click Add. Double-click the Admin_managers group. Press the CTRL key, and select the Sales_managers, Accounting_managers, Admin_users, Sales_users, and Accounting_users. Click Add, and then click OK.

Select Sales_managers. Select the Print, Manage Printers, and Manage Documents check boxes, because the division managers must have full control of the printers.

Select Admin_managers. Select the Print and Manage Printers check boxes. Repeat for the Accounting_managers. so that all other managers can print and manage printers.

Select Accounting_users. Select the Print check box. Repeat for the Sales_users and the Admin_users so that all users can print.

Repeat the applicable processes for the second printer in the Sales division and for both printers in the Admin division. When you are done, you should have a total of six printers.

To configure pool printing for the Admin printers, click Start | Settings | Printers. Right-click the Admin_managers_HighSpeed_Printer1 printer, and then click Properties. Click the Ports tab. Click COM2 so that a check mark appears next to Admin_managers_HighSpeed_Printer2. Click Enable Printer Pooling so that a check mark appears next to enable pool printing. Click Apply, and then click OK.

Your description of the Windows 2000 print terminology should resemble that in Table 6-8.

TABLE 6-8	Printing terms	Descriptions
	Print device	The hardware that actually does the printing.
Windows 2000 Print Terminology	Print server	A computer that manages printing on the network.
	Print driver	A software program that translates commands. It is normally supplied by the manufacturer of the print device.
	Printer	The software interface between the document and the print device.

Step 3. When you test access to print resources, Wendell should easily be able to identify the printers to which he has access, because you used a naming convention that identified their uses. Because Wendell is a Sales user, he can access the Sales_users printer and the Sales_not_Sales_users printers. Wendell will not be able to connect to the Sales managers printer, because he does not have permission.

Markeil should easily be able to identify the printers to which she has access, because you used a naming convention that identified their uses. Because Markeil is a Admin user, she can access the Admin_users printer and the Admin_not_Admin_users printers. Markeil will not be able to connect to the Admin managers printer, because she does not have permission.

ANSWERS TO LAB ANALYSIS TEST

1. You should "Take ownership of the file." Then you should grant yourself the permission to modify the file. Once this is complete you should delete the file.

2. Robert should change the sharing options on the printer to install additional print drivers for Windows NT 4.0 or Windows 2000 clients.

3. Freeda should remove the Everyone group or clear all Allow checkboxes for the Everyone group on the manager's printer.

4. Lois should disconnect all Users from the Salaries folder. Once that is done, she should modify the NTFS permissions for the five files in the Salaries folder. (Answers: A, E)

5. Set the share permissions for the NorthEast folder to grant Change permission to Jonathan. This prevents Jonathan from having more permissions than are necessary.

ANSWERS TO KEY TERM QUIZ

1. Everyone

2. printer

3. dedicated

4. Distributed File System

5. inheritance

7

Configuring and Troubleshooting Hardware Devices and Drivers

Windows 2000 retains some Windows NT 4.0 favorites—Device Manager and Hardware Profiles—but it also has a variety of new features that assist administrators in troubleshooting and configuring hardware devices and drivers. Specifically, it offers a troubleshooting wizard that guides you easily through the process of solving common hardware problems.

This chapter focuses on the new utilities provided by Windows 2000 to configure, manage, and troubleshoot hardware devices and drivers. Operating system manufacturers have struggled for years trying to offset the problems caused by poorly written device drivers. During the development process, most software manufacturers test their products with the most popular hardware and device drivers. The cost of such testing has usually fallen primarily on the operating system developer, and not on the manufacturer of the hardware or device driver. As a result, a significant amount of finger-pointing has tended to occur when products fail to work smoothly together. Many companies have lost significant time and money waiting for a resolution to these mini-wars.

To help alleviate some of the issues, Microsoft introduced digital driver signing in Windows 2000. Digital driver signing is designed to assure the user that hardware drivers have been thoroughly tested by their manufacturers. In addition, Microsoft keeps up-to-date listings of the hardware that it recognizes as being compatible with its operating systems. Using the Windows 2000 Hardware Compatibility List (HCL), companies can find out whether the equipment that they plan to use is compatible with a particular Microsoft operating system. Microsoft has also created the Windows Hardware Quality Labs (WHQL), where vendors can have drivers tested and signed.

For an organization to reap the benefits associated with shared network resources, the software on the network must work properly. This chapter introduces you to some of the troubleshooting and configuration aids in Windows 2000. These aids will help you to quickly and successfully configure drivers, or resolve driver-related problems, on your network. These are skills that many IS professionals seek.

LAB EXERCISE 7.01

Configuring Hardware Devices

60 Minutes

Congratulations! You have personally helped to dramatically improve the Get-It-Right network. The managers at the Get-It-Right package shipping company use just one term to describe your Windows 2000 skills—"Awesome." The company would like you to continue to make changes to their network so that their users can efficiently and effectively locate and use company resources.

The rest of the Get-It-Right Information Services staff is also thrilled about the progress that you have made. They are looking forward to sharing the administrative reins of the network with you. For now, however, they are willing to be patient until you complete your initial work on the company's infrastructure. And the IS manager has a new challenge for you.

The company wants you to configure hardware devices on the network servers. You must incorporate Plug and Play and the Advanced Configuration and Power Interface (ACPI) technologies to load hardware drivers and to configure device properties and settings. You also have to troubleshoot failed Plug and Play installations and to incorporate hardware profiles for network users who may use notebook or home computers. In addition, the IS staff want you to manage and update the device drivers that you install.

Can you handle these additional administrative responsibilities? Complete the following exercises and decide.

Learning Objectives

In this lab, you install, configure, manage, and update device drivers on a Windows 2000 server. The Get-It-Right domain controller contains hardware made by several different manufacturers. The Get-It-Right managers want you to remove, and then reinstall hardware devices on the network server. You need to configure Plug and Play and non–Plug and Play devices on the server. You also should create hardware profiles and update device drivers.

At the end of the lab, you'll be able to

- Install and configure Plug and Play devices
- Install and configure non–Plug and Play devices
- Manage device drivers
- Use and locate the Device Manager
- Use and locate the Hardware wizard
- Create hardware profiles
- Use and locate the System Information snap-in
- Test the installation and configuration of device drivers.

Lab Materials and Setup

You need these materials for the lab:

■ A Windows 2000 server that is configured with at least one NIC

■ Pen or pencil

■ Writing pad (optional)

■ Windows 2000 help utility

■ Access to the www.microsoft.com web-site (optional)

Getting Down to Business

You are going to install Plug and Play and non–Plug and Play devices and drivers for Get-It-Right. The device drivers that you use should be updated to the most-recent versions. Also, the IS staff would like you to provide them with information about the company's hardware resources and how to avoid conflicts, including I/O addresses, DMA channels, IRQ priority, and ROM addresses. They would also like to know where to find information regarding the resources and components being used on their Windows 2000 server. Finally, you need to create a hardware profile for users who work from home.

lab
Warning

Do not perform these lab exercises on your Windows 2000 domain controller. The exercises use existing and non-existing equipment. You may receive error messages when dealing with equipment that is not physically installed on your system. The errors may affect the proper functioning of your Windows 2000 domain controller, which is needed for exercises throughout this book. Please ignore any errors that you may receive on your Windows 2000 server.

Step 1. **Plan** to meet the requirements that have been set forth by Get-It-Right. The IS staff have provided this list of tasks:

Task	Details
Install two network interface cards (NICs) into the Windows 2000 domain controller.	One NIC should be on the Windows 2000 HCL. One NIC should be a LinkSys Ether 16 LAN card (IRQ = 10; input/output range = 0300–031F)

Task	Details
Provide definitions and explanations of the hardware resource terms shown in Table 7-1.	
Determine the IRQs used by various devices, so that any non–Plug and Play devices that are added will not cause device conflicts.	Determine if any devices are causing IRQ conflicts.
Locate the input/output addresses assigned to the server.	
Determine which devices have DMA channels.	
Create hardware profiles that users can use at the office and at home.	

TABLE 7-1

Finding Definitions of Hardware Resource Terms

I/O addresses	
DMA channels	
IRQ priority	
ROM addresses	

Step 2. **Implement** the necessary device changes.

- Uninstall your Plug and Play NIC.

- Now, re-install the NIC, and also install and configure your Linksys NIC card according to the parameters set forth by the IS staff.

- Once you have completed the foregoing tasks, you must create hardware profiles that will eventually be used by company employees who work at home and in the office.

lab
Warning

Although this step is normally reserved for notebook computers, more and more businesses are using removable hard drives. A staff member with a bay for a removable hard drive at work and at home can use one physical disk in both machines. The computer at home will probably be non-networked; the office computer normally becomes a member of the company's domain.

■ Use the Windows 2000 help utility to find help on installing, configuring, managing, and understanding hardware devices, resources, and device drivers. You may also refer to the Microsoft web site (located at www.microsoft.com) for additional help.

Step 3.   Test your work by checking the IRQ assignments and looking for IRQ conflicts.

■ Log on to the Windows 2000 server with administrative privileges. Check the System Summary to review the IRQ assignments.

■ Check the Device Manager to see if any devices are not functioning properly.

■ Once you are satisfied with your findings, have your instructor or Windows 2000 evaluator check your work.

LAB EXERCISE 7.02

Updating Device Drivers

30 Minutes

The Windows 2000 operating system uses hardware device drivers to communicate with specific pieces of hardware. If the device drivers are unreliable, the effect on the efficiency and effectiveness of your network can be drastic. Microsoft continually modifies its operating systems to increase functionality and performance. Hardware manufactures must keep in step with Microsoft's modifications, and so they also modify their device drivers to enhance driver performance.

You already provided Get-It-Right with an added level of network security to prevent unauthorized installation of untested device drivers. Although your security fix is a good step in the right direction, it is not the ultimate step.

Many network administrators fail to keep their software up to date. The saying "If it ain't broken, don't fix it" is common among network administrators. Many an administrator has lived for years with nagging network problems, trying to avoid adding new software. Although that approach may have had some validity in the past, it is much less necessary today. Microsoft periodically releases service packs that fix reported OS problems and that add vital enhancements to ease the administrative burden. To ease the process of updating system software, including hardware device drivers, Microsoft has added several wizards that you can use to fix the "unbroken network."

Can you help make sure that Get-It-Right keeps its hardware device drivers up to date? Use the exercise that follows to make that assessment.

Learning Objectives

In this lab, you upgrade hardware device drivers on the Get-It-Right network server. You also make sure that the hardware device drivers are up to date. At the end of the lab, you'll be able to

- Locate a device manufacturer's web site
- Update hardware device drivers
- Use the Upgrade Device Driver wizard
- Verify that your current device drivers are the latest available.

Lab Materials and Setup

The lab requires these materials:

- Access to a computer functioning as a Windows 2000 domain controller
- A computer running Windows 2000 Server or Professional
- Windows 2000 help utility
- Access to the Internet

Getting Down to Business

The IS staff want you to upgrade the network adapter on the Windows 2000 server. The manufacturer of the NIC is known to add enhancements to its products on a regular basis. The IS staff want to take full advantage of any improvements that may contribute to the functionality and reliability of their network services. Use these steps:

Step 1. **Plan** your update of the Windows 2000 server NIC driver.

■ Start by gathering information about the NIC. The IS staff have provided a list of details that you have to know to successfully update the NIC:

Name and model of the NIC	
Date of the NIC driver	
Version of the NIC driver	
Digital signer of the NIC driver	
Manufacturer of the NIC	
Web site of the manufacturer of the NIC	

Step 2. **Implement** by updating the NIC in the Windows 2000 server based on the information that you located in step 1.

■ Unless you have the most recent driver for the NIC, you will probably have to connect to the manufacturer's web site and download the latest version.

■ Use the Upgrade Device Driver wizard from the Windows 2000 Device Manager to simplify the process of updating the device driver.

■ The Windows 2000 Server help utility or the Microsoft web site (located at www.microsoft.com) can help you understand and locate the Upgrade Device Driver wizard.

Step 3. **Test** your work.

■ Review the driver information for the updated driver.

■ Make sure that the new driver has been digitally signed and that the version number of the driver is higher than the current version.

■ You may want to attempt to upgrade other drivers on the server, such as the video adapter. Repeat both step 1 and step 2 before attempting subsequent upgrades so that you can note the changes.

■ Have your instructor or evaluator check your work.

LAB EXERCISE 7.03

Troubleshooting Problems with Hardware

45 Minutes

You have taken steps to protect the Get-It-Right network from improperly installed hardware device drivers. You have updated drivers that you suspect are out of date, and you know how to recognize unsigned device drivers. But even with all of the precautions that you have taken, you are still likely to experience problems with device drivers.

To meet the challenges that arise in diverse networks, IT professionals must have troubleshooting skills. Troubleshooting involves using continual rounds of trial-and-error, combined with large amounts of patience. If you suspect that a hardware device driver is a problem, then you need to investigate and identify the issue. Check the status of suspected devices, and if your findings reveal a problem, take one of four actions:

■ Reinstall the device driver

■ Restart the computer

■ Update the device driver

■ Use the Windows 2000 Troubleshooter

The IS staff at Get-It-Right are most impressed with your ability to deal with hardware issues that may affect the proper functioning of the network. They want you to familiarize yourself with the Windows 2000 Troubleshooter so that you will be able to help other staff members use the utility properly.

Will you be able to teach the IS staff how to properly use the Windows 2000 Troubleshooter?

Learning Objectives

In this lab, you use the Windows 2000 Troubleshooter to find out what is wrong with a hardware device. You will make it easy for the Get-It-Right IS staff to troubleshoot hardware devices because you will be able to show them how to use the Troubleshooter.

At the end of the lab, you'll be able to

- Check the status of a hardware device
- Use the Windows 2000 Troubleshooter wizard.

Lab Materials and Setup

To complete the lab, you need these materials:

- A computer running Windows 2000 Server
- Pen or pencil
- Windows 2000 help utility

Getting Down to Business

Using the Windows 2000 Troubleshooter will give you hints on troubleshooting a problematic hardware device, and your practice will enable you to provide insights and training to IS staff members. Use these steps:

Step 1. **Plan** to check into a problematic hardware device that has been reported to the IS department help desk.

- One of the network servers has recently been configured with a new Linksys Ether16 LAN adapter. The adapter does not appear to be working properly.
- Check the status of the suspect device.
- Use the hardware Troubleshooter to get hints on what might be wrong with the network adapter.
- List several alternative solutions found during your investigation.

Step 2. Implement a "solution" by using the non–Plug and Play adapter that you installed on the Windows 2000 server to simulate a malfunctioning NIC.

■ List, in order of preference, the Troubleshooter solutions that you would try in attempting to resolve your hardware malfunction.

Step 3. Test your selected approach.

■ Discuss your choices with your instructor or evaluator.

■ Ask your instructor or evaluator to explain choices that would have differed from yours.

Remember, troubleshooting is much trial-and-error, liberally mixed with great quantities of patience. Your troubleshooting skills will improve dramatically if you are willing to challenge and critique your technique.

LAB ANALYSIS TEST

1. Melvin has recently been promoted to System Administrator for the Cut-It-All Barber Supply company. The company network comprises several Sales and Shipping divisions being supported by a number of Windows 2000 servers and clients that have recently been upgraded from Windows NT 4.0. The company's computer equipment and peripherals come from several different manufactures. The former administrator had to leave unexpectedly for personal reasons, and Melvin never got a chance to talk to her. Melvin is afraid that the mix of vendor equipment may make his life as an administrator unbearable. What advice can you give Melvin that will help him resolve some of his concerns about managing and troubleshooting devices and device drivers at Cut-It-All Barber Supply?

2. Felecia is administering a Windows 2000 domain consisting of several Windows 2000 domain controllers and Windows 2000 Professional clients. She recently purchased several 3Com network adapters. She needs to configure some settings for the network adapter on one of her domain controllers. To manage that work, she would like to use the tools that Windows 2000 provides. Where would Felecia find the tools?

3. Alexis is an administrator for the Drive-It-Fast Rental Car company. She recently installed Windows 2000 Server on a company computer. She followed all the installation steps, and she successfully logged on to the Windows 2000 server. Alexis made these changes to the new server:

   ■ She created a user account for herself.
   ■ She gave her account administrative privileges, and she changed her workgroup name.

   The system prompted Alexis to restart the computer, and so she did. Now the server fails to start, and she receives a blue screen error. She has no idea what she could have done to cause the error. What advice can you give Alexis so that she can resolve her problem?

4. Dynasty is attempting to install Windows 2000 Server on a Pentium III 650 MHz computer with two bootable CD-ROM drives. She receives a media error every time she starts the installation. This is her third attempt. She decides to change the BIOS settings in the CMOS so that the computer looks at the other CD-ROM drive first for initialization files. However, Dynasty still receives a media error when she attempts to install Windows 2000 Server on the computer. Both of the CD-ROM drives are listed on the Windows 2000 HCL. Which of the following choices will probably resolve her problem?

    a. Contact Microsoft and request a replacement Windows 2000 Server CD.

    b. Replace the CD-ROM drives with ones that are on the Windows 2000 HCL.

    c. Create enough free space for the Windows 2000 installation files on the target partition.

    d. Increase the amount of memory on the server.

5. Lois has recently been hired as the administrator for a Windows 2000 network. The network is running in Windows 2000 Native mode. Lois would like to remove a network adapter from one of the servers and install it into another server. She would like to be sure that the server from which she is removing the NIC is cleaned of unnecessary device driver files. Which two tools should she use for this task?

    a. The Add/Remove Software component

    b. The Add/Remove Hardware component

    c. The Network and Dial-up Connections component

    d. The Disk Cleanup utility

KEY TERM QUIZ

Use the following vocabulary terms to complete the sentences below. Not all of the terms will be used.

ACPI (Advanced Configuration and Power Interface)

DMA (Direct Memory Access)

driver signing

hardware profile

IRQ (Interrupt Request)

Plug and Play

WHQL (Windows Hardware Quality Lab)

1. _____ is Microsoft's way of ensuring that only approved device drivers are used with their Windows 2000 operating systems.

2. Device driver developers can submit their device drivers to Microsoft's _____ to thoroughly test their software with Windows 2000 products. This process increases driver quality and reduces support costs.

3. A _____ is an electronic signal sent to a computer's CPU to indicate that a hardware device requires the processor's attention.

4. A _____ is a set of instructions that tells your computer how to boot the system properly; it is commonly used to support laptop computers.

5. _____ allows Windows 2000 operating systems to automatically detect new hardware, load the necessary drivers, configure the device, allocate the appropriate resources, and update the system.

LAB SOLUTIONS FOR CHAPTER 7

The sections that follow walk you through the steps to solve the lab exercises. You should avoid looking at these sections unless you are stuck on a particular exercise.

Lab Solution 7.01

Here are the steps required to install, configure, manage, and explain hardware devices and device drivers. Your answers may vary, but should be similar to these.

Step 1.   Your completed definitions of hardware resources should resemble Table 7-2.

TABLE 7-2		
Hardware Resource Terms Found	**I/O addresses**	A hexadecimal memory location that identifies the location of registered hardware. Used by the CPU to communicate with the device. Similar to a mailbox.
	DMA (Direct Memory Access) channels	A path for hardware to send data directly to memory without bothering the CPU.
	IRQ priority	There are 16 IRQs in a computer that are answered by the CPU in order of priority. The priority order is 0, 1, 2, 8, 9, 10, 11, 12, 13, 14, 15, 3, 4, 5, 6, 7.
	ROM (Read-Only Memory) addresses	Prepackaged routines and construction sets that are located on the hardware device. The ROM address is where the CPU finds the device ROM.

Step 2.   To remove a Plug and Play NIC, log on to the Windows 2000 server with administrative privileges. Right-click the My Network Places icon on the desktop. Select Properties, and right-click Local Area Connection. Again, select Properties.

At the General tab, look for the label "Connect Using:" Write down the name of the network interface card. Click Cancel.

Click Start | Programs | Settings | Control Panel. Double-click the Add/Remove Hardware icon.

At the welcome screen for the Add/Remove Hardware wizard, click Next.

The Choose a Hardware Task screen opens. Select the "Uninstall/unplug a device" option. Click Next.

At the Choose a Removal Task screen, click Next to accept the default "Uninstall a device."

At the Installed Devices on your Computer screen, select the "Show hidden devices" check box to show devices that may have been hidden by the OS. Select your Plug and Play NIC card in the Devices box. Click Next.

At the Uninstall a Device screen, select "Yes, I want to uninstall this device." Click Next, and then click Finish.

To re-install the Plug and Play NIC, select Start | Programs | Settings | Control Panel. Double-click the Add/Remove Hardware icon.

Click Next to bypass the welcome screen for the Add/Remove Hardware wizard.

At the Choose a Hardware Task screen, click Next to accept the default "Add/Troubleshoot a device."

The New Hardware Detection screen opens. Once your Plug and Play NIC has been found, its name appears in the window. Click Next, and then click Finish.

To install and configure the Linksys NIC, select Start | Programs | Settings | Control Panel. Double-click the Add/Remove Hardware icon.

Click Next to bypass the welcome screen for the Add/Remove Hardware wizard.

The Choose a Hardware Task screen opens. Click Next to accept the default "Add/Troubleshoot a device."

Because the Linksys device is not be found in your computer, the "Choose a Hardware Device" screen opens. In the Devices box, select "Add a device." Click Next.

At the Find New Hardware screen, select "No, I want to select hardware from a list." Click Next.

At the Hardware Type screen, in the Hardware Types list, select Network Adapters. Click Next.

At the Select Network Adapters screen, in the Manufacturer list, select Linksys. In the Network Adapters list, you should see the Linksys Ether16 LAN card. Select it, then click Next.

A Windows 2000 warning message informs you that Windows could not detect the device settings. Click OK.

At the resulting Resources screen, double-click Interrupt Request in the Resource Settings box. Set the Value box to **10**. Click OK.

Double-click Input/Output Range. At the Up tab, set the Value box to **0300-031F.** Make sure that this device causes no conflicts. Click OK, and then click OK again.

The Start Hardware installation screen opens. Click Next, and then Finish. Select Yes to restart the computer.

To check hardware resources using System Information, log on to the Windows 2000 server with administrative privileges.

Right-click the My Computer icon on the desktop. Select Manage. Double-click System Information, and then double-click Hardware Resources. Double-click IRQs. Double-click Conflicts/Sharing, and then DMA, and then I/O. Leave the Computer Management snap-in open.

To check or manage resources using Device Manager, locate and double-click the Device Manager icon in the Computer Management snap-in. All the devices that are part of the computer appear in the right-hand screen. Click a device to expand the snap-in. Verify that no device has a yellow or red indicator next to it.

Right-click the Device Manager icon to view resources by type. If you double-click a resource, you will see additional resource information. Experiment with the other views associated with the Device Manager snap-in. Once you have finished viewing the resources, close the Computer Management snap-in.

To create a hardware profile, select Start | Programs | Settings | Control Panel. Double-click the System icon, and then click the Hardware tab. Choose Hardware Profiles.

At the Hardware Profiles dialog box (Figure 7-1), select the current profile and click Rename. Give the current Profile the name **Office**. Click OK.

Select the Office profile, and click Copy. Type **Home** into the To box. Click OK.

Select the Home profile from the list of available hardware profiles. Click Properties. At the properties page for the profile, select "This is a portable computer." Leave the other settings at their default values, and click OK.

FIGURE 7-1

Establishing up a hardware profile

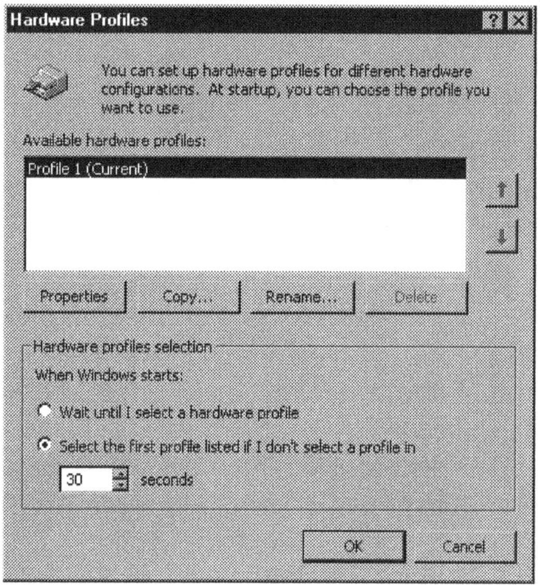

Configure the Hardware Profiles Selection to tell Windows 2000 to "Wait until I select a hardware profile." Click OK.

lab

Warning ***Do not actually perform the next step unless you are working with a notebook computer.***

If you were actually configuring a notebook computer , you would now reboot and select the Home profile. Remove hardware or network connections that would not be found on the home computer.

Lab Solution 7.02

Your answers may vary, but should resemble the steps required to update device drivers on the Windows 2000 server as described here.

Step 1. Here is an example of the information that you require before attempting to update the NIC. (This information changes depending on the NIC and the driver currently installed.)

Name and model of the NIC	NETGEAR FA311 Fast Ethernet PCI Adapter
Date of the NIC driver	11/14/1999
Version of the NIC driver	5.0.2183.1
Digital signer of the NIC driver	Microsoft Windows 2000 Publisher
Manufacturer of the NIC	NETGEAR
Web site of the manufacturer of the NIC	www.netgear.com

To update the network adapter/NIC, log on to the Windows 2000 server with administrative privileges. Right-click the My Computer icon on the desktop, and select Manage from the pop-up menu.

At the Computer Management screen, select System Tools, and then select Device Manager.

The Device Manager snap-in appears. In the right-hand window, double-click the icon for the network adapter that you plan to update.

The Device Properties dialog box opens. Click the Driver tab. At the Driver tab, click the Update Driver button.

The Update Driver wizard starts up. Click Next.

At the Install Hardware Device Driver screen, click Next to accept the default "Search for a suitable driver for my device (recommended)."

At the Locate Driver Files screen, clear all the check boxes. Click "Specify a Location," and click Next.

At the Copy Manufacturers File from: dialog box, browse to the location of the network adapter driver file that you downloaded from the manufacturer's web site. Click OK.

At the Driver File Search Results screen, click Next to accept the new driver. Click Finish.

lab
⚠arning
If you are presented with a "Digital Signature Not Found" screen, you are about to install a driver that has not been digitally signed. If you completed lab exercise 7.03, you will not be able to install the device driver because digital driver signing has been set to block the installation of unsigned device drivers.

Step 3. To verify that the NIC has been updated, log on to the Windows 2000 server with administrative privileges. Right-click the My Computer icon on the desktop, and select Manage from the pop-up menu.

At the Computer Management window, select System Tools, and then select Device Manager.

The Device Manager snap-in opens. In the right-hand pane, double-click the server's network adapter (which you have updated).

The Device Properties dialog box opens. Click the Driver tab. At the Driver tab, compare the driver information on the screen with the driver information that you recorded before the update. The date and version numbers should be different.

Close all windows.

Lab Solution 7.03

The steps required to check the status of a malfunctioning device and to activate and record troubleshooting choices in the Windows 2000 Troubleshooter follow. Your answers should be similar to the ones given here.

Step 1. To check the status of the Linksys Ether16 LAN adapter, log on to the Windows 2000 server with administrative privileges. Right-click the My Computer icon on the desktop, and select Manage from the pop-up menu.

At the Computer Management window, select System Tools and then select Device Manager.

In the right-hand pane of the Device Manager snap-in, double-click the Linksys Ether16 LAN adapter.

At the Linksys Ether 16 LAN Card Properties dialog box, click the General tab. Check the status of this hardware device.

Step 2. Activate the Troubleshooter, and record the choices for resolving the network adapter problem. While still at the General tab of the Linksys Ether16 LAN Properties, click the Troubleshooter button.

Here are some of the choices that you may make as you attempt to resolve the network adapter malfunction:

- Select "My network adapter doesn't work." Click Next.
- Select "I want to skip this step and try something else." Click Next.
- Review the help information displayed, and then select "No, my network adapter doesn't work." Click Next.
- Review the new help information, and then select "No, my network adapter doesn't work" or "I don't need to replace any connection hardware." Click Next.
- Review the further help information, and then select "No, my network adapter still doesn't work" or "I don't have a resource conflict." Click Next.
- Review the help information on the latest screen, choose a course of action, and then proceed or conclude your troubleshooting of the Linksys Ether16 LAN adapter.

ANSWERS TO LAB ANALYSIS TEST

1. Melvin should verify that all of the hardware he is using is listed on Microsoft's Hardware Compatibility List (HCL). Any equipment not listed should be replaced as soon as possible. Once that task is complete, Melvin should run the Windows 2000 File Signature Verification utility to verify that system files have been digitally signed. Finally, Melvin should set the driver signing option on all Windows 2000 computers to prevent installation of unsigned files.

2. Felecia would find these tools on the Hardware tab of the System Properties dialog box. She will find the Hardware wizard, the Device Manager, Driver Signing, and Hardware Profiles, all of which she can use to manage the network adapter.

3. Explain to Alexis that the problem is normally due to an incorrect hardware configuration, primarily owing to hardware that is not compatible with Windows 2000. To resolve the problem, she should verify that all hardware has been properly detected and is on the Microsoft Hardware Compatibility List (HCL).

4. Dynasty should contact Microsoft and request a replacement Windows 2000 Server CD. She is encountering the problem with both CD-ROM drives, even though they are both listed on the Microsoft HCL. The most probable cause, therefore, is that the media itself is bad. (Answer: A)

5. Lois should use the Add/Remove Hardware component to remove the adapter and all drivers from the system. The Disk Cleanup utility helps to free up space on the hard drive. Disk Cleanup searches the drive, and then shows you temporary files, Internet cache files, and unnecessary program files that you can safely delete. Disk Cleanup should be run after the hardware component has been removed. (Answer: B and D)

ANSWERS TO KEY TERM QUIZ

1. driver signing

2. WHQL (Windows Hardware Quality Lab)

3. IRQ (Interrupt Request)

4. hardware profile

5. Plug and Play

8

Managing, Monitoring, and Optimizing System Performance

T he Get-It-Right package shipping company is entering one of its busiest times: the Christmas season. Get-It-Right ships thousands of packages daily. Employees are constantly entering and verifying data in the databases. Any server delay will throw sand into the gears that keep Get-It-Right working smoothly. It is crucial that the network perform at its best.

During a meeting with the Get-It-Right managers, you suggest that the server needs some work before entering "crunch time." The managers, happy with the network as it stands, are reluctant to allow you to work on the server. You suggest that by working on the server now, you can identify potential problems and repair them before the Christmas rush. The managers like your reasoning and allow you to proceed.

LAB EXERCISE 8.01

Creating a Baseline

20 Minutes

The first order of business is to establish a picture of what "normal" is on the Get-It-Right server. That picture is called a *baseline*. The baseline can be used to evaluate future network performance. Having a baseline will help in future meetings with the managers and during the Christmas rush to see if a server is acting strangely.

To create a baseline, you use Performance Monitor. With Performance Monitor, you can view network statistics. *Counters* in Performance Monitor tell you how "busy" a component is. For example, the processor counter can tell you how many processes per second are being handled. You will capture common counters for use in the baseline.

Learning Objectives

In this exercise, you use Performance Monitor to create a baseline for your server. At the end of the lab, you'll be able to

- Start Performance Monitor
- Add counters to Performance Monitor
- Save a baseline image

Lab Materials and Setup

You need these materials:

- Performance Monitor installed on the server
- An administrative account

lab
Hint *Normally Performance Monitor is installed by default on Windows 2000 Server. If your installation does not include Performance Monitor, that component can be installed by using Add/Remove Programs.*

Getting Down to Business

Use these steps to create baselines for the server:

Step 1. **Plan** for your baseline.

- All systems need a baseline; many need several. You will create three baselines: one for "light" activity, one for "normal" activity, and one for "heavy" activity.
- You will use Performance Monitor and add several counters that describe the server.

Step 2. To **implement** your plan, first capture a "normal" baseline:

- Start Performance Monitor about one hour after lunch.
- Add counters that gauge server performance. Include memory, network, disk, and processor counters.
- Save the image as a normal baseline.
- Repeat the process before work to capture a "light" baseline, and about one hour before quitting time to capture a "heavy" baseline.

LAB EXERCISE 8.02

Setting Program Priority

15 Minutes

Ronny, one of the managers at Get-It-Right, sits with you at lunch one day. You are having a pleasant discussion until Ronny asks a network question. He asks why the network seems slower when an administrator is working on the server.

You respond by describing the concept of *priority.* When a server is used as a workstation, the server treats local processes as having a higher priority than remote requests. The network therefore responds slowly to valid and normal requests. When network servers periodically act as workstations, such slowdowns are a necessary fact of life.

Ronny understands the concept, but asks if the priority of applications that need to run on the server can be set lower than a remote request. You like the suggestion, and you tell Ronny that you will advise the administrators to reduce the priority on tasks they are running on the server. With this, your friendly conversation continues.

Learning Objectives

In this lab, you work with Task Manager to set program priorities. At the end of the lab, you'll be able to

- Start Task Manager
- Set program priority

Lab Materials and Setup

You need these materials:

- Administrative account
- Several programs installed on the server

Getting Down to Business

You are going to use the procedure described here to lower the priority of commonly used server programs and thereby speed up the server's response to remote requests.

lab
Hint *If a server is dedicated to a particular task, increasing the priority of that task increases network performance. For example, if a computer is a DNS server, then increasing the priority of DNS speeds up client response time.*

Step 1. **Plan** your approach by creating a list of commonly used server tools.

Step 2. **Implement** your priority changes:

- Start Task Manager.
- Start a program from the list you made in step 1.
- In Task Manager, reduce the priority of that task to "below normal."

Step 3. **Test** to ensure that the given program still runs correctly after the priority change.

LAB EXERCISE 8.03

Setting a Paging File

10 Minutes

You are having lunch with Ronny again. Ronny was reading a magazine article regarding speeding up a home computer. It discussed virtual memory and proper setup. Ronny asks you how virtual memory works, and if the Get-It-Right servers are properly set up.

You respond first by stating that all computers have a finite amount of RAM. If the RAM limit is exceeded, then a tool called *virtual RAM* starts. Virtual RAM uses a file on the hard drive to simulate RAM. Unused applications from RAM are swapped to that file and back to RAM as needed. The constant swapping between RAM and the virtual RAM file causes the file to swell and shrink like an accordion. The continual size variation causes disk fragmentation, which slows network response.

You know that the best solution is to fix the size of the paging file. That change eliminates the chance of disk fragmentation owing to the paging file. In addition, the optimal solution is to place the main paging file on its own disk or partition, and to leave a small paging file on the boot disk for recovery. You will set the paging files properly on the Get-It-Right server.

Learning Objectives

In this lab, you set the paging file options for a server. At the end of the lab, you'll be able to

- Determine an appropriate size for a paging file
- Set two paging files

192 Chapter 8: Managing, Monitoring, and Optimizing System Performance

Lab Materials and Setup

You need these materials:

- Administrative account
- A secondary hard drive with a partition formatted for NTFS (optional)

Getting Down to Business

You are going to set the paging file options for the Get-It-Right servers. Use this procedure:

lab
Hint

If your server has multiple drives, set the larger paging file to reside on a secondary drive. If your server has only one drive, set the paging file on the boot drive as described, and skip the reboot part of the procedure.

Step 1. **Plan** the size and location of the paging file.

- Calculate your paging file requirement using the formula:

  ```
  Server RAM + 12MB
  ```

- Locate a partition with sufficient free space to hold the paging file.

Step 2. **Implement** the changes in the paging file.

- Start Control Panel.
- Start the System applet.
- Using the Performance Button at the Advanced tab, set the minimum and maximum paging file size to the number that you calculated in step 1. Be sure to select a drive other than the boot drive.
- Set a paging file on the boot drive to one half the number calculated in step 1.
- When prompted, reboot the server.

Step 3. **Test** the server to ensure that it works as expected.

LAB EXERCISE 8.04

Cleaning Up a Disk

50 Minutes

Ronny cornered you one day to discuss disk space on the server. One of the other admins requested that additional hard drives be purchased for the server. The admin claimed that the drive was full and more space would be needed soon. Ronny would like you to strip unnecessary files and applications before he makes a decision.

You tell him that Windows 2000 has a clean-up utility that finds files that can be safely removed or compressed. You will use that tool to remove unnecessary files from the computer. When you're finished, you will tell him how much space was freed up, and if the drives are nearing saturation.

Learning Objectives

In this lab, you determine whether files can be removed from the server hard drives. At the end of the lab, you'll be able to

- Run the disk cleanup utility
- Remove unnecessary programs
- Remove unnecessary Windows components

Lab Materials and Setup

You need these materials:

- Administrator account
- Windows 2000 CD
- CD for any program that you want to uninstall (optional)

Getting Down to Business

To free up space on the servers hard drives, use this procedure:

Step 1.   **Plan** your approach by deciding which drives need to be scanned and which programs are the most important to keep.

Step 2. **Implement** your plan.

- Go to the properties for the hard drive to be cleaned.
- Run the cleanup utility and select each option that will reduce disk use. Check the recycle bin for other unneeded files.
- Repeat the process for each drive in the computer.
- Clean up Windows components.
- Clean up installed programs.

LAB EXERCISE 8.05

Defragmenting a Disk

3 Hours

Now that the paging file is set to a fixed size and unnecessary files have been removed, the time has come to defragment the disk. Disks become fragmented over time, causing the system to slow down. Defragmenting the disks improves system performance.

Learning Objectives

At the end of the lab, you will be able to defragment a disk on Windows 2000 Server.

Lab Materials and Setup

For this lab, you need administrative access to the server.

Getting Down to Business

Here's how to defrag the Get-It-Right servers:

Step 1. **Plan** for the defragmentation.

- Go to the tools for a hard drive.
- Analyze the drive to determine if it needs to be defragmented.

Step 2. **Implement** the defragmentation, if necessary.

- Run the defragmentation tool (this will take some time).

Step 3. Test the outcome.

■ Has the disk has been defragmented?

■ Check any errors generated by the system.

LAB EXERCISE 8.06

Creating a Counter Log

20 Minutes

You are working late one evening, and you notice something strange. The server starts spinning the hard drives and acting as if someone were logged on. The behavior is strange, because you are the only person in the office. You are worried that someone is accessing the server remotely, without permission.

You want to solve the mystery before presenting a case to the managers at Get-It-Right. You know that there are two methods of gathering evidence to support your belief: You can stay late every evening for an extended period of time. Or, you can log certain Performance Monitor counters. Because you enjoy having a life, you decide to log the counters for the hard drive, processor, and network attachments (if any). During regular business hours, you will examine the logs for overnight activity.

Learning Objectives

In this lab, you set a counter log to monitor the server overnight. At the end of the lab, you'll be able to

■ Use System Monitor

■ Set a counter log

Lab Materials and Setup

You will need the administrative account to complete this lab.

Getting Down to Business

You want to monitor the server when you are not in the office. Here is what you need to do:

Step 1. **Plan** how best to trap unauthorized activity.

- Determine which counters you should monitor to prove unauthorized remote access.

Step 2. **Implement** your plan by setting the appropriate counters.

- Start Performance Monitor.
- Add the appropriate counters.
- Add and configure a log file for the counters.
- Let your log run for some time.

Step 3. **Test** your results.

- Print the log using Excel or another tool.
- Show it to your instructor.

LAB EXERCISE 8.07

15 Minutes

Setting an Alert

A couple of days after you set up a counter log, the server mysteriously crashes. You reboot the server, and everything seems fine. Curious about the crash, you examine the log and notice that the processor and physical disk were running at 100% usage for several minutes. It looks like a classic denial-of-service attack.

Just before you panic, Caleb, one of the programmers, pokes his head in your door. Caleb says he thinks that he was responsible for the crash. He wrote a program that was to create a series of files on the server. Unfortunately, his code included an infinite loop that inadvertently generated thousands of files. He apologizes profusely, and asks if you need help restoring the server. You shake your head, thank him for being honest, and decide to not let the server crash again for reasons like that.

You know that, if a server processor runs at 100% for more than a minute, the server will typically go down. You therefore decide to have the server alert you when the processor hits 100%. You set an alert in Performance Monitor that will send a message to your computer when processor use spikes.

Learning Objectives

At the end of the lab, you'll be able to use Performance Monitor to set an alert for a counter.

Lab Materials and Setup

You will need the administrative account to complete this lab.

Getting Down to Business

You will set an alert on the Get-It-Right server. Use this procedure:

Step 1. **Plan** the necessary alert.

- Determine the counters that you want to set for the alert.

Step 2. **Implement** your plan by appropriately configuring the alert.

- Start Performance Monitor.
- Add an alert.
- Configure the alert to the counter that you want to track. Have it send a message to your computer.
- Set the threshold and the interval to check.

LAB ANALYSIS TEST

The questions that follow will help you apply your knowledge in a business setting.

1. Why is it so important to increase disk performance on a file server?

2. What is a problem with running too many alerts and logs on a server?

3. You notice that the server hard drive has become a bottleneck on your network. What can you do to alleviate the problem?

4. How does defragmenting a hard drive speed up file access on that drive?

5. In creating a log file, what are the differences between a circular trace file and a sequential trace file?

KEY TERM QUIZ

Use these vocabulary terms to complete the sentences below. Not all of the terms will be used.

        alert

        baseline

        bottleneck

        counter

        fragment

        log

        paging file

        priority

        Performance Monitor

        threshold

1. You should establish a(n) _____ to determine what "normal" is for your server.

2. Virtual memory writes applications in RAM to the _____ as more space in RAM is needed.

3. A phenomenon that slows a network down is often called a(n) _____ .

4. An application's _____ determines how much of the CPU time is allocated.

5. When setting an alert, you must set the _____ for the alert.

LAB SOLUTIONS FOR CHAPTER 8

The sections that follow walk you through the steps to solve the lab exercises. You should avoid looking at these sections unless you are stuck on a particular exercise.

Lab Solution 8.01

Your work to capture several baselines for your server should have used a process similar to the one described here.

Step 1. Table 8-1 lists a selection of counters commonly recorded for a baseline.

TABLE 8-1	Object	Counter	Instance
	DNS	Total query received	—
Commonly Tracked Performance Monitor Counters	FileReplicaConn	Packets sent in bytes	—
	Memory	Pages/sec	—
	NTDS	DRA inbound properties total/sec	—
	NTDS	DRA outbound properties total/sec	—
	NTDS	DS % searches from LDAP	—
	NTDS	DS directory reads/sec	—
	Paging file	% Usage	Total
	Server	Bytes total/sec	—
	System	File data operations/sec	—

Step 2. During a normal load on the server, log on and select Start | Administrative Tools | Performance. Click the Add ➕ button.

You will add several counters to the baseline. For example, add the DNS counter as shown in Figure 8-1.

Repeat the process for every counter that you want to record.

When you are finished, let the counters run for a few minutes. The screen will look something like Figure 8-2.

When you are confident that the screen represents a "typical" server session, right-click the graph, and select Save. Name the file **normal_*todaysdate***, and save it as an HTML file.

Repeat the counter setup and capture for a light load and a heavy load, changing the file name accordingly.

FIGURE 8-1

Adding
the DNS counter

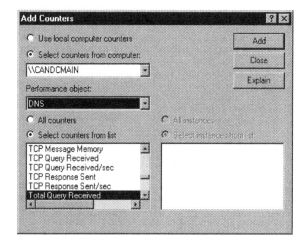

FIGURE 8-2   Viewing a typical baseline performance graph

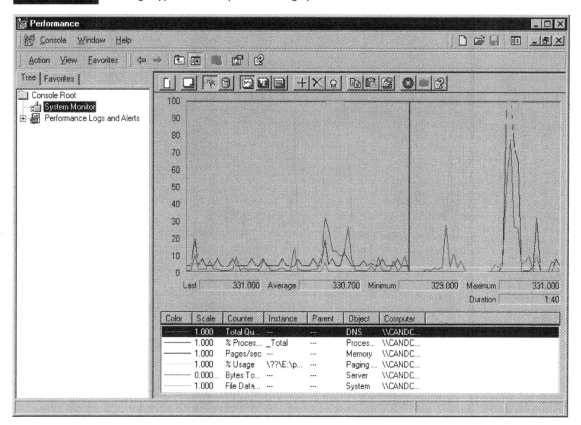

Lab Solution 8.02

Changing program priorities to speed service for users involves the steps described here.

Step 1. To generate a list of common tools, press CTRL-ALT-DEL to start Task Manager, and then click the Task Manager button. The Task Manager list of processes opens:

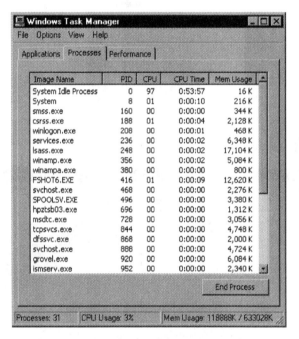

If the Processes tab is not currently selected, select it now. Next, start any program that you use often on the server. Then, scroll to the bottom of the list and find the name of the application. The Microsoft Management Console (MMC) is running whenever Active Directory Sites and Services is selected.

Table 8-2 lists some common applications and the image names associated with them.

Step 2. Now that you have a list of commonly used applications, you can set priorities. During off-hours for your organization, start Task Manager, if it is not already running. Open Windows Explorer or My Computer. Right-click mdm.exe in Task Manager and select Set Priority | BelowNormal from the pop-up menu as shown in Figure 8-3.

Program name	Image name
Active Directory Sites and Services	mmc.exe
Active Directory Users and Computers	mmc.exe
Notepad	notepad.exe
Performance Monitor	mmc.exe
Windows Explorer	mdm.exe
Windows Task Manager	Taskmgr.exe

TABLE 8-2

Image Names for Some Commonly Used Applications

You will receive a warning about system instability:

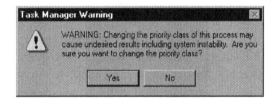

Click Yes to set the priority, then test the system to ensure that all is running well.

FIGURE 8-3

Setting the Priority Class for Mmc.exe

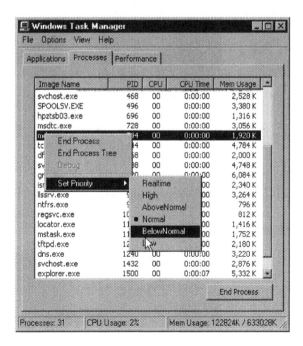

Lab Solution 8.03

Setting the paging file options for the Get-It-Right servers should be done as explained here.

Step 1. Calculate the minimum paging file requirement for your server. For example, a server with 256MB RAM would require a minimum of 268MB in the paging file. The paging file should be located on a drive separate from the boot drive. Devoting a partition to the paging file is a good idea. Remember to leave some free space to add additional virtual RAM in the future!

lab
ⓗint *The additional 12MB paging file space is used to hold a copy of the system registry kept in server RAM.*

Step 2. Now that you have calculated the space required for the paging file, select Start | Settings | Control Panel.
  Open the System applet, and select the Advanced tab.
  Click Performance, and then Change to open the Virtual Memory dialog.
  Set the options using either your numbers or the numbers suggested by Microsoft, whichever are larger. Keep clicking OK until you are prompted to reboot. Close all open programs and reboot the server.

Lab Solution 8.04

When a server runs out of storage space, the problem typically occurs on user and shared data drives. Those drives should have priority.

Step 1. If a server is running out of system room, the scanning should include the main boot drives. If in doubt, scan all drives.

Step 2. Open My Computer from the desktop. Right-click the drive that you want to scan, and select Properties.
  Click the Disk Cleanup button. An information message shows progress as the program scans your drive for unneeded files:

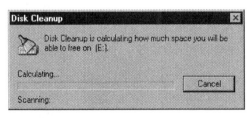

When the scan is complete, the Disk Cleanup dialog box opens (Figure 8-4). (Naturally, the numbers for your server will be different than those shown in the figure.)

Select the options that you want to use, and click OK. Read any warnings, and then click Yes to continue with the cleanup. A message shows the progress of the cleanup:

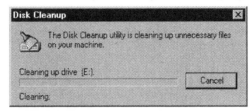

lab
Hint   *Cleanup took 21 minutes on an AMD Athlon 1.2 with 256MB RAM and a 7200 RPM EIDE Ultra ATA-100 hard drive.*

Now that unneeded files have been removed from the system, you want to look for unnecessary Windows components and programs.

Return to the hard drive properties. Again, click the Disk Cleanup button. (This time, the analysis will be much faster.)

Click the More Options tab.

In the Windows Components frame, click Clean Up. Many unnecessary components can be found under Accessories and Utilities. Select Accessories and Utilities, and then click Details (Figure 8-5).

FIGURE 8-4

Choosing disk
cleanup options

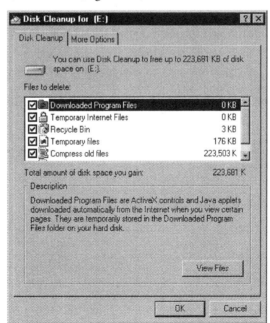

FIGURE 8-5

Deselecting
the games
from among
the system
accessories

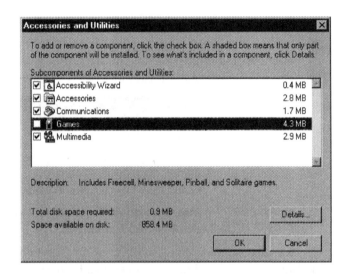

As shown in Figure 8-5, clear the Games check box to free 4.3MB disk space. Remove other components that you are sure are unnecessary on the server. When you are finished, click OK to return to the Windows Component wizard.

Click Next to remove the unneeded components. The wizard shows you the progress as files are deleted.

When the wizard is done, click Finish to return to the More Options tab of the Disk Cleanup dialog box.

To remove extraneous application programs, click the Clean Up button in the Installed Programs frame. Select each program, and check its frequency of use.

As Figure 8-6 shows, the payroll program is rarely used. Click Remove to uninstall it.

lab
ⓗint *Add/Remove Programs and Windows Components are both available from the Control Panel.*

Report back to your instructor regarding the services, programs, and size of files removed from the server.

Lab Solution 8.05

Defragmenting a disk takes a long time. It is best performed overnight.

Step 1.   Open My Computer, and then open the Properties dialog box for the disk that you want to defragment. Click the Tools tab, and select Defragment Now.

In the Disk Defragmenter dialog box (Figure 8-7), select the drive to defrag, and then click Analyze.

FIGURE 8-6

Removing
an unneeded
application program

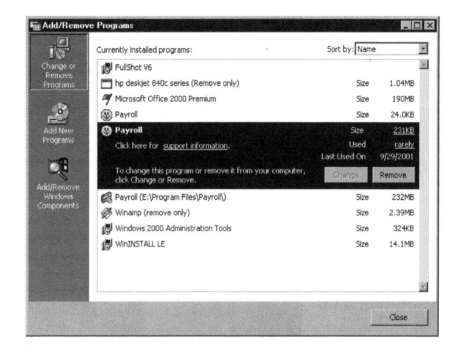

FIGURE 8-7

Selecting
the hard drive
to defragment

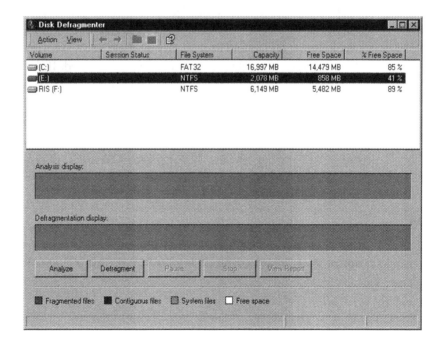

When the Analyze tool finishes its work, it gives you a recommendation. The recommendation for a system that needs to be defragged looks like this:

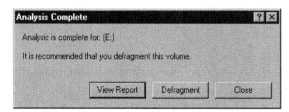

Click View Report to see how badly the drive is fragmented. The white section at the bottom of the screen lists files that are fragmented.

Step 2.   When you are done reading the report, click Defragment.
While the drive is being defragged, you can watch the progress of the operation.

Lab Solution 8.06

Appropriately monitoring the server can trapping unauthorized access. Your solution should be similar to the one used here.

Step 1.   Because you are worried about a remote hacker accessing your system, you decide to watch the physical disk, the server object, and the TCP object. An overnight hacker has an effect on each of these items. Theoretically, server usage should be low overnight, because no users are attached. If the log shows usage, you know that someone is accessing the system.

Step 2.   Choose Performance from the Start button. Expand the Performance Logs and Alerts. Click the Counter Logs icon. Right-click in the right-hand pane, and select New Log Settings. Name the log **Overnight** (Figure 8-8).
Click the Add button to add counters to the log. Configure the Add Counters dialog as shown in Figure 8-9.

lab
(i)int   *The screen shots in this and the following chapters were generated on a server that is configured differently than the one in Chapters 1 through 7. You will notice that the server name here is "CandCMain" instead of "GetItRight."*

Repeat the process to add "bytes total/sec" for the server object and "segments/sec" for the TCP object. When you are finished, the screen will look like Figure 8-10.

FIGURE 8-8

Creating a log file

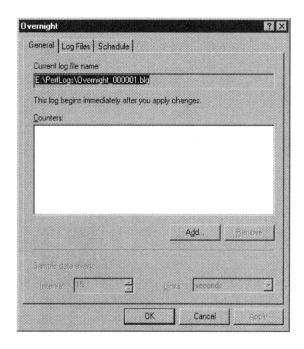

Click Apply, and then OK to set up the log. Click Yes if a warning appears. Close Performance Monitor. The log remains active in the background.

FIGURE 8-9

Adding a counter
to a log file

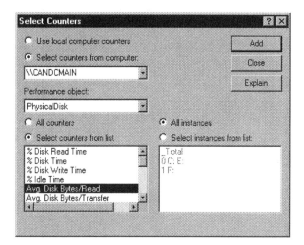

FIGURE 8-10

Reviewing
the counters that
are to be logged

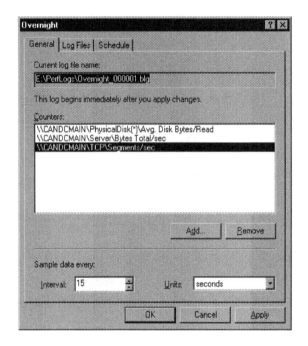

Lab Solution 8.07

You can monitor many conditions and arrange for alerts to bring the problems to
your attention. In this case you want to watch for processor overuse.

Step 1. You are worried that a wayward program will bring the server down
again, and so you decide to watch the processor objects. If the counter reaches 85%
or higher, the server could be in trouble.

Step 2. Choose Performance from the Start button. Expand the Performance
Logs and Alerts. Select the Alerts icon. Right-click the white area in the right-hand
pane and select New Alert Settings. Name the alert **Denial**.

   Click the Add button to add the "total" counter for the processor object. Configure
the interval, value, and comment as shown in Figure 8-11.

   The alert must alert somebody. Double-click the alert, and configure it as shown
in Figure 8-12, placing your workstation name in the text box.

   Click Apply, and then OK to set the alert. The alert should appear in
Performance. Close Performance. The alert continues to run even when no one is
logged into the server.

FIGURE 8-11

Configuring
a counter

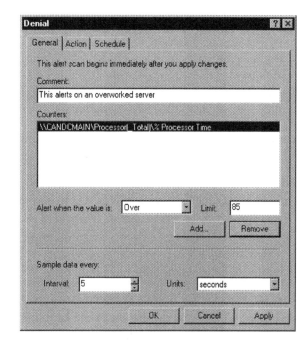

FIGURE 8-12

Configuring
an alert

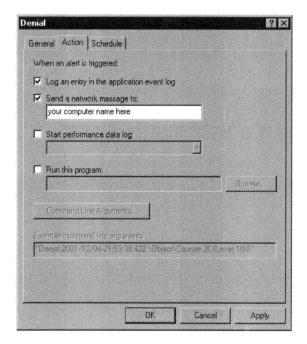

ANSWERS TO LAB ANALYSIS TEST

1. Disk performance is the most crucial aspect of a file server. With several users accessing the disk of one server, the disk must perform at its peak all of the time. A 1% reduction in disk performance produces a drop in performance for every user on the network. That drop in performance affects the entire organization, because work takes longer to get done.

2. Alerts and logs run as a service in Windows 2000. They are therefore running at all times. Too many logs will take system resources away from the server, resulting in increased network lag.

3. Several methods are available to reduce disk bottlenecks. One simple method is to ensure that the disks are the fastest available. Another method is to employ striping across several disks (RAID 0 or 5). Striping distributes data across many hard drives, providing several disk heads the chance to find the desired data. In theory, striping across three disks should cut read time by one third. A final method is to employ a "server farm" with data replicated to several servers. Many servers then have a chance to find the desired data.

4. When a drive is fragmented, the files are scattered all over the drive. Reading a fragmented file requires several seeks. (A "seek" is the process of the hard drive head finding the required data.) Seeks take time. A file requiring three seeks opens three times slower than a file requiring one seek. Defragmenting the disk reduces most file access operations to one seek, reducing the time it takes to read the data.

5. The difference occurs when the maximum size of the log is reached. A circular trace file starts writing new data at the beginning of the file, overwriting existing data. A sequential trace file creates a new file, preserving old data. The circular trace file results in a constant log file size; the sequential trace file can have an infinite size.

ANSWERS TO KEY TERM QUIZ

1. baseline

2. paging file

3. bottleneck

4. priority

5. threshold

9

Protecting and Restoring Systems

Thehe managers at Get-It-Right are happy with the work you have performed to date. Your ability to monitor the server and to provide management with a server baseline will make their jobs easier. You are not so happy, though. You know that, despite the planning and maintenance that have gone into the server, things still happen to computers. When things happen, data and functionality are often lost. You corner Ronny one Monday and express your misgivings.

Ronny shares your concern; a dead server would disrupt business and reduce profits. He asks if you know a way to completely protect the server from damage. You of course reply that nothing can completely protect the server, but that taking certain steps can reduce the chance of lost data. You describe the concept of backup and recovery to Ronny, and you suggest immediately implementing a backup and recovery scheme. Ronny admires your initiative. He suggests that you begin working on your plan immediately, reporting back to him as soon as you have finished.

LAB EXERCISE 9.01

Backing Up Server Data

20 Minutes

The first step in protecting the data on the server is to make a backup of the server. The best time for making backups is after hours, when users are logged off. Because you are worried about data integrity, you decide to create a backup now. When backing up data, you must take care to select, at a minimum, the system data and all the files that cannot be reproduced. These are what make your network unique from every other network.

lab Hint *To reduce the time needed for this lab, select only a small number of files for backup. Be sure to include a file that can be safely deleted so that you can later complete lab exercise 9.02.*

Learning Objectives

In this lab, you back up the Get-It-Right server. By the end of the lab, you'll be able to

- Start ntbackup.exe
- Select files for a backup

- Select system data for a backup
- Select a backup location.

Lab Materials and Setup

The lab requires these materials:

- Administrative account
- High capacity tape drive and tape (optional)
- Sufficient room on a volume to store the backup (optional)

lab
(i)int *In the workplace, backups are typically sent to tape. If your machine lacks a tape unit, then backing up to a hard disk will provide sufficient practice in creating a backup.*

Getting Down to Business

To back up the Get-It-Right server data, complete these tasks:

Step 1. **Plan** for the backup.

- Decide which files need to be protected.
- Locate the medium on which to store the backup.

Step 2. **Implement** your plan by backing up the chosen files to the selected medium.

- Go to the properties of a hard drive. Start the backup application.
- Select the files to back up.
- Select the location to store the backup.
- Start the backup.

cross
(C)eference *Exercise 9-4 in the Study Guide suggests starting backups with the Run command.*

Step 3. Test the success of the backup.

- Read all or part of the contents list from the backup medium.

LAB EXERCISE 9.02

Restoring a File from the Backup

15 Minutes

You are pleased that the server data is now backed up to tape. You know that a backup is good only if the data can be recovered from it. You also know that a need for data recovery may be due to a server failure. In that case, emotions will be running high, and your bosses will be breathing down your neck to get the data back. If your first attempt to recover a file occurs under those conditions, you might make a mistake and lose the data forever. Thus, you decide to practice recovery on a nonessential file or folder. You will rename a file, and then try to recover the original from the backup.

Learning Objectives

In this lab, you practice restoring data from a backup set. At the end of the lab, you'll be able to

- Start the Restore wizard
- Restore a file from the backup set.

Lab Materials and Setup

You need these materials:

- A backup set containing the files to recover
- Administrative account
- A nonessential file to practice with.

lab
Hint   *Be absolutely sure that the file you pick is nonessential.*

Getting Down to Business

By practicing recovery of a file from a backup set, you be more confident in recovering files in an emergency. Use these steps:

Step 1.   **Plan** your approach to the recovery.

- Pick a nonessential file or folder to recover. Be sure that it is included in the backup set that you created in lab exercise 9.01.

Step 2. **Implement** your recovery plan.

■ Go to the server location of the file that you have chosen to recover, and rename that file.

■ Start Backup, and go to the Restore tab.

■ Select the backup set.

■ Select the file to restore.

■ Restore the file.

Step 3. **Test** the success of the recovery.

Compare the restored file with the renamed file. Be sure that they are exactly the same.

LAB EXERCISE 9.03

Scheduling a Daily Backup

20 Minutes

Later in the day, Ronny stops by to see how your project is going. You describe the full backup and the successful restore that you have performed. Ronny is pleased, but wants to know who will run the backup each day. You tell him that backups can be scheduled to run every day, every week, or every month. In fact, your next task will be to configure the backup to run daily at 10:00 P.M. Because Get-It-Right has people working 7 days per week, backing up daily is a very good idea.

Learning Objectives

In this lab, you create a backup job and schedule it to run every day. By the end of the lab, you'll be able to

■ Create a backup job

■ Set a daily schedule for the backup.

Lab Materials and Setup

You need these materials:

- Administrative account
- High capacity tape drive and tape (optional)
- Sufficient room on a volume to store the backup (optional)

Getting Down to Business

Use this procedure to implement a daily backup scheme for Get-It-Right:

Step 1. **Plan** for the daily backup.

- Decide which files need to be protected.
- Locate media to store the backup.
- Determine the best time to run the backup.

Step 2. **Implement** your plan by scheduling the backup.

- Start the backup program.
- Using the wizard, select the files to back up and location for the backup set.
- Set the backup schedule: run the backup later at 10:00 P.M., and every day thereafter.

Step 3. **Test** your scheduled backup.

- Stay in the classroom and ensure that the first scheduled backup starts as implemented.

lab Hint *If 10:00 P.M. is too late to stay in the classroom, then schedule the backup for a more convenient time.*

LAB EXERCISE 9.04

Installing Recovery Console

15 Minutes

You feel better knowing that the server data is protected. However, you are still worried that the server could become unusable. Viruses, worms, Trojan horses, and simple hardware failures can lead to corrupted files and dead servers. You know that one of the new features of Windows 2000 is its Recovery Console. Recovery Console is a command-line tool that you can use to recover corrupt or lost files.

Learning Objectives

In this lab, you learn how to install Recovery Console as a menu option at boot-up.

Lab Materials and Setup

You need these materials to complete the lab:

- Windows 2000 Server CD
- Administrator account

Getting Down to Business

To install Recovery Console for Windows 2000 Server, use these steps:

Step 1.   Your **plan** is to make Recovery Console a boot option.

Step 2.   To **implement** Recovery Console, you must start by inserting the Windows 2000 Server CD into the computer. Then,

- Run the command to install Recovery Console.

See Exercise 9-1 in the Study Guide for the necessary command.

- Run MMC. Add the Group Policy snap-in.
- Set the local policies to allow use of the Set command in Recovery Console. If a domain-level policy is present, set its value as well.

Exercise 9-3 demonstrates the policies as they should be set at both the local and the domain level.

Step 3.   To **test** your implementation of Recovery Console, reboot the server.

- Verify that Recovery Console is now an option in the boot menu.

LAB EXERCISE 9.05

Using Recovery Console

30 Minutes

Recovery Console, like all emergency tools, is something you should be familiar with before you have to use it. You therefore decide to practice using the features of Recovery Console. Skills that you should practice include recovering a lost file, running fixmbr, setting environment variables, and starting a service. Practicing those skills requires downing the server. You should schedule time for this lab after your users have gone home.

lab

Warning *Oddly enough, Recovery Console can damage a server. You should make a backup of your files before using this tool.*

Learning Objectives

In this lab, you become skilled at using Recovery Console. At the end of the lab, you'll be able to

- Start Recovery Console
- Run fixmbr
- Set environment variables
- Recover a file from removable media
- Start a service.

Lab Materials and Setup

You need these items to complete the lab:

- Floppy disk
- Nonessential file to practice recovery
- Administrative account

Getting Down to Business

You should be very familiar with the workings of Recovery Console before an emergency forces you to use it. Here is what you need to do:

Step 1. **Plan** your practice by setting up situations that might typically call for the use of Recovery Console.

- Copy a nonessential file to a floppy disk. (The file does not have to be big, but look for files with names of 8 characters or fewer.) Delete the chosen file from the server.
- Choose a service that you will attempt to start in Recovery Console.
- Determine the environment variables that you will need set to obtain access to the floppy disk and CD drive and to restore a file to its original location.

Step 2. To begin **implementing** your plan, start a server reboot.

- Enter Recovery Console.
- Set the necessary environment variables.
- Restore the deleted file.
- Start a service. Stop the service.
- Learn the options of fixmbr.

Step 3. To **test** that all is well with the server, reboot again, and verify that the boot proceeds properly.

LAB ANALYSIS TEST

The following questions will help you to apply your knowledge in a business setting.

1. You are in Recovery Console, and you cannot copy from a disk to the c:\My Documents folder. What are the most likely problems?

   _____

   _____

2. What is the difference between a full backup and an incremental backup?

   _____

   _____

3. Create a good backup schedule for your network.

   _____

   _____

4. In troubleshooting a server problem, when is using safe mode with networking not a good idea?

   _____

   _____

5. Your network performs a full backup on Fridays and incremental backups during the week. On Wednesday, the server RAID system was hit by a large electrical spike and was destroyed. After you replace the damaged equipment, what steps do you need to perform to recover all the backed up data from the backup tapes?

   _____

   _____

KEY TERM QUIZ

Use the following vocabulary terms to complete the sentences below. Not all of the terms will be used.

AVBoot

boot record

differential

environment variables

fixmbr

full

incremental

Recovery Console

restore

safe mode

1. Fixmbr fixes the _____ on a downed Windows 2000 server.

2. _____ is a GUI interface for fixing Windows.

3. Backing up without resetting the archive attribute of files that have changed is the function of the _____ backup.

4. Getting files back from a backup set is the job of the _____ wizard.

5. In Recovery Console, you set _____ to be either enabled or disabled.

LAB SOLUTIONS FOR CHAPTER 9

The sections that follow walk you through the steps to solve the lab exercises. You should avoid looking at these sections unless you are stuck on a particular exercise.

Lab Solution 9.01

Here's how to complete the server file backup exercise.

Step 1.   You will back up files on the Get-It-Right server. For the purposes of learning how to use ntbackup, you will back up some of the data files on your server. You will also include data about the system state. If the server is equipped with a tape drive, you should back up to tape; otherwise, back up to a hard drive on the system.

Step 2.   Open My Computer. Right-click the drive that you want to back up, and select Properties. Click the Tools tab.
   As shown in Figure 9-1, click Backup Now to start the wizard.
   Now click the Backup Wizard button to start backing up the files.
   Click Next to bypass the splash screen.
   Configure the What to Back Up dialog box as shown in Figure 9-2.

FIGURE 9-1

Starting Backup
from the Tools
dialog box

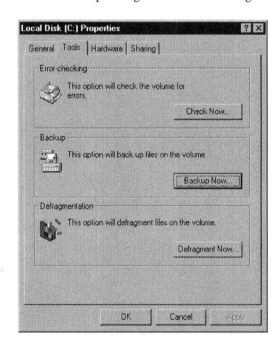

FIGURE 9-2

Choosing
file options

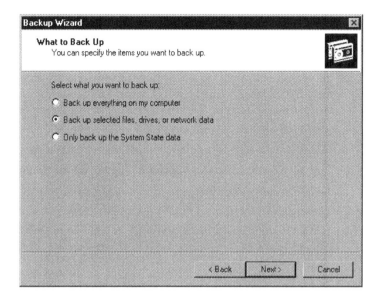

At the Items to Back Up dialog box, select the files that you want to back up. Be sure you include the data under System State (Figure 9-3).

Browse to the location where the backup set is to be stored. Name the set **backup** *todaysdate*, where *todaysdate* is expressed in digits.

FIGURE 9-3

Selecting
the data under
System State

At the final dialog box, click Finish to start the backup. While the files are being backed up, you will see the analysis and progress messages.

Step 3.   After the backup is finished, view the directories and files backed up by clicking the Restore tab and selecting your backup set.

Lab Solution 9.02

The file restore exercise is much like the file backup exercise and makes use of another option within the same tool.

Step 1.   From among the directories that you backed up in lab exercise 9.01, select a file or folder that contains nonessential data. Rename it **olddata**.

Step 2.   Start Backup, and choose the Restore wizard. Click Next to bypass the splash screen.

Select the file that you want to restore (Figure 9-4). If the right-hand pane lists multiple backup sets, select the set that you just created in lab exercise 9.01.

FIGURE 9-4

Selecting files
to restore

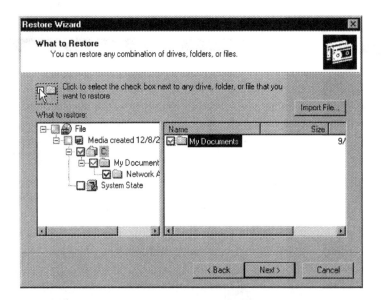

Click Next, and then Finish. When the Enter Backup File Name dialog box opens, type the name of the location where the backup set is stored:

When the restore finishes, you should see a summary screen something like this:

Step 3.   The data is back, but you should verify that the data is correct. The DOS command fc can be used to compare files and report differences between them. Select Start | Run, then enter **cmd**.

A DOS window opens. Enter the commands that will take you to the location of the newly restored file. The example in Figure 9-5 demonstrates changing to the C:\My Documents\Network Administration folder, which is the folder that I restored.

To compare a restored file with a file in another folder, you can use the fc command as shown in Figure 9-6 (which also demonstrates entering a relative path name to the old file).

FIGURE 9-5

Changing
to a newly
restored folder

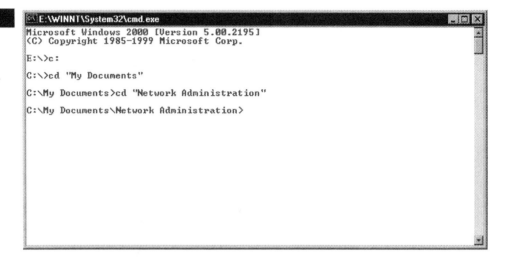

The output of fc being run on two identical files is shown in Figure 9-7.

lab
ⓗint

In Windows 2000, DOS mode supports spaces in file names by allowing you to place quotation marks around the filename or pathname containing the spaces. You could also use the DOS file name for speed. For example, the DOS name for My Documents is MYDOCU~1.

FIGURE 9-6

Using the fc
command

FIGURE 9-7

Viewing
the results
of an fc command

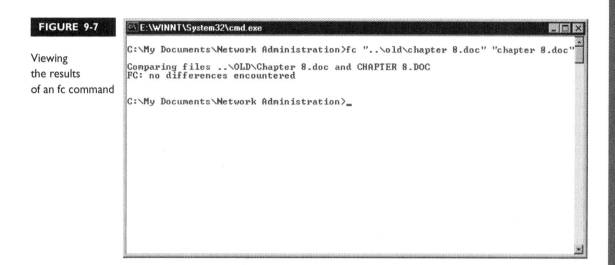

```
E:\WINNT\System32\cmd.exe

C:\My Documents\Network Administration>fc "..\old\chapter 8.doc" "chapter 8.doc"

Comparing files ..\OLD\Chapter 8.doc and CHAPTER 8.DOC
FC: no differences encountered


C:\My Documents\Network Administration>_
```

Lab Solution 9.03

Yet another option of the Backup tool handles your need for scheduled backups.

Step 1. Because the backup that you want to schedule is for the entire server, you will back up all files and folders. You should have a tape drive available to handle a load that large. If you have no tape drive available, then back up just a subset of the hard drive.

Step 2. Start Backup, and click the Schedule Jobs tab.
Click Add Job (Figure 9-8) to start the Backup wizard. Click Next to bypass the startup screen.
At the What to Back Up dialog, select Backup Entire Computer. Click Next.
Name the job and specify its storage location as shown in Figure 9-9.
At the next two screens, accept the default options. At the Media Options screen, select the Replace option.
Label the backup appropriately.
When prompted, enter the administrative password. At the When to Back Up screen, name the backup job, and click Set Schedule.
Configure the Schedule Job dialog box as shown in Figure 9-10.
Click OK, and then Next to reach the summary screen.

The Schedule Jobs tab should contain a backup image in every day of the month, as Figure 9-11 shows. Exit the backup wizard.

FIGURE 9-10

Setting the
options for a
daily backup

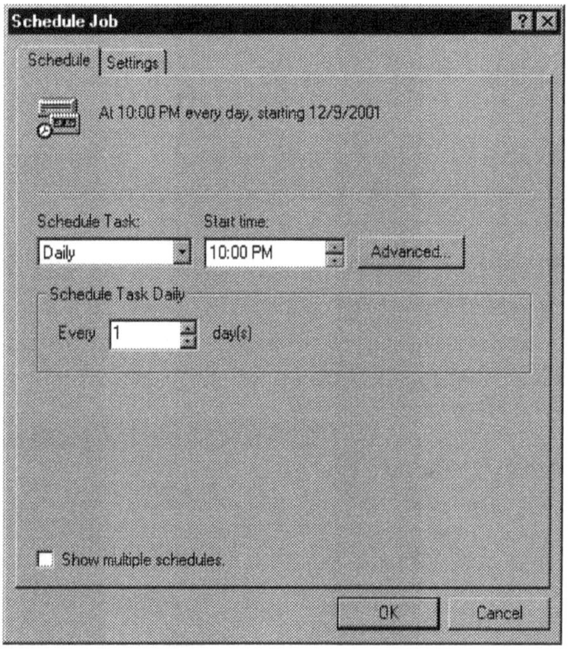

FIGURE 9-11

Reviewing
the calendar
of scheduled
backups

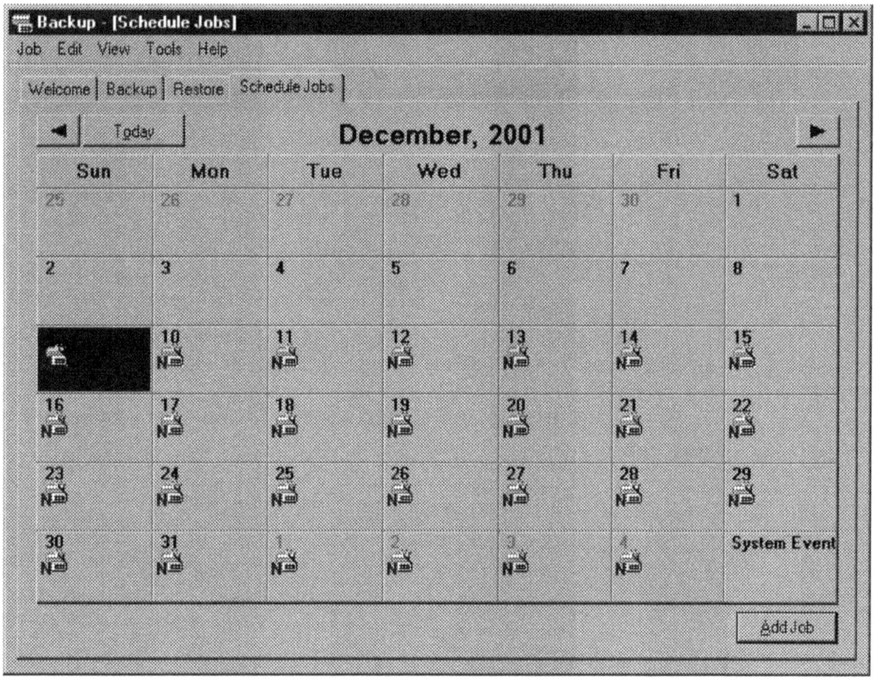

Lab Solution 9.04

Installing Recovery Console is a fairly quick process.

Step 1. As the exercise indicated, your first step is simply the decision to have Recovery Console available at boot-up time.

Step 2. Insert the Windows 2000 Server CD. To avoid CD autorun, press and hold SHIFT until the disk stops spinning. Select Start | Run.

Enter the winnt32 command as shown here, substituting the drive letter of your CD-ROM for **D:** if necessary:

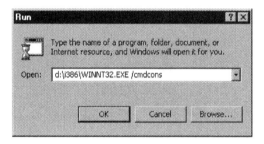

Click OK.

After a pause, a message asks you to confirm your choice:

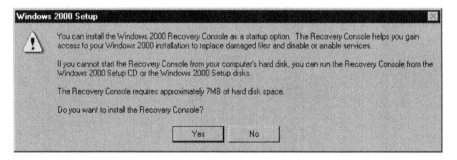

Read the warning, and then click Yes. During the install, several screens will open and close.

When the install is finished, another message box confirms the installation:

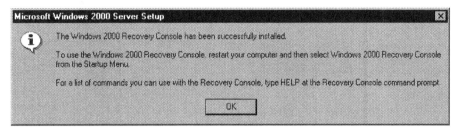

Click OK to end the install. Reboot the server during a period of inactivity. You should see Recovery Console as a menu option.

Select Start | Run. Type **mmc**. From the console's menu, select Add/Remove Snap In. Click the Add button.

At the Add Standalone Snap-in dialog box, select the Group Policy entry (Figure 9-12).

Click Add. Accept the default (Local Computer) in the Select Group Policy dialog box. Click Finish, and then Close, and then OK to return to the MMC screen.

Expand the tree as shown in Figure 9-13. Enable both Recovery Console policies, as shown in the figure.

FIGURE 9-12

Adding the
Group Policy
snap-in

FIGURE 9-13 Setting the policies for Recovery Console

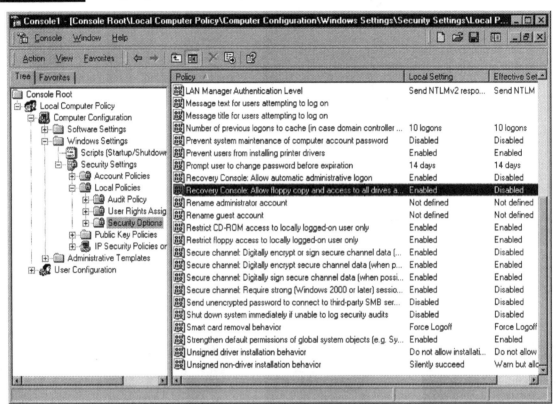

Lab Solution 9.05

To test Recovery Console, you first have to set up a situation that requires a recovery.

Step 1. On the server, locate a file that is nonessential. Copy that file to a clean, formatted floppy disk. A quick way to copy is to browse to the file in My Computer, right-click it, and select Send to 3 ½ Floppy A:. (I chose c:\My Documents\ourhouse.jpg for this exercise.) Now delete that file from the server.

Step 2. Restart the computer. At the black screen with the bar running across the bottom, press F8 to see the menu choices. Select Recovery Console.

To restore the file that you copied and deleted, start by enabling the environment variables.

Enter these commands:

```
Set AllowAllPaths = true
Set AllowRemoveableMedia = true
```

Now, change to the folder that held the original file. For example, enter a command something like this one:

```
cd "my documents"
```

Use quotes around folders that have spaces in their names. Once you have reached the correct location, type this command, substituting the name of your restore file for ourhouse.jpg:

```
copy a:\ourhouse.jpg
```

Reply "yes" to the overwrite prompt.

I chose to start the udfs service with a manual startup option. Begin by entering the command:

```
listsvc
```

The list of available services is shown. To enable the udfs service, you would use the command:

```
udfs service_demand_start
```

To disable a service, simply enter "disable" and the service name. For example:

```
disable udfs
```

Finally, if the server will not boot, running fixmbr may solve the problem. At any Recovery Console prompt, enter **fixmbr**. Read the warnings, and type **y** if you want to continue. For the purposes of this lab, feel free to type **n**.

ANSWERS TO LAB ANALYSIS TEST

1. Several problems could exist. One problem could be a bad floppy disk. More likely, you did not set the environment variables AllowAllPaths and AllowRemovableMedia.

2. A full backup copies all files specified in the Backup wizard. An incremental backup copies only the files that have been changed.

3. Answers to this question can vary. One possible answer is a full backup once weekly, with incremental backups on the other days of the week.

4. Safe mode is used when a server will not boot. Servers often fail to boot because of faulty drivers or services. If the network card or other network service is not working properly, you will be unable to boot in safe mode with network services. That situation may lead you to believe that the network is the problem. However, another driver related to the network services (PCI for example) may be at fault. In such a case, you may be falsely blaming the network card when you still cannot boot to safe mode with network support.

5. After restoring the equipment, you need to restore the files. Assuming that the server crashed before you ran the Wednesday backup, you will need to recover from three backup sets. Restore the complete backup first. Afterward, restore from the Monday backup. Finally, restore from the Tuesday backup. That sequence will restore the server to a Tuesday state. Any work done on Wednesday is most likely lost, but there is nothing you can do about that.

ANSWERS TO KEY TERM QUIZ

1. boot record

2. Safe mode

3. differential

4. Restore

5. environment variables

10

Managing Storage Use

LAB EXERCISES

I n Lab 8, you cleaned up much of the server hard drive. After you reported your findings to Ronny, he decided to add another disk to the server. He is having the hardware technician, Steve, physically install the drive on Saturday. Ronny is leaving the configuration of the drive in your hands.

You know that Windows 2000 includes a new type of disk management called *dynamic disks.* The new technology allows you to use every feature of Windows 2000 disk protection and fault tolerance. To allow for future growth, you will extend the size of the Active Directory partition. To provide for fault tolerance, you will mirror the drive that contains the company's information database.

You are excited to be managing the storage options for Get-It-Right. You know that the hard drives in a server are among the most important parts of a network. Being trusted to work with those drives is a distinct honor.

LAB EXERCISE 10.01

Converting a Disk into a Dynamic Disk

10 Minutes

Saturday evening has come, and Steve has finished installing the new hard drive. Now you have to start working. Before Get-It-Right can use the disk, you have to convert it into a dynamic disk. The conversion will allow you to use all of the Windows 2000 disk and storage features. You know that, because the drives will be mirrored and spanned, both disks in the system have to be converted.

Learning Objectives

In this lab, you learn how to convert a basic disk into a dynamic disk.

Lab Materials and Setup

You need these materials to complete the lab:

- Administrative account
- Secondary hard drive

Getting Down to Business

To convert the disks in the Get-It-Right server, use these steps:

Step 1. To **implement** dynamic disk, begin by starting Computer Management.

■ Run the Upgrade wizard, and select both disks.

■ Restart the computer when prompted.

LAB EXERCISE 10.02

Extending a Volume

5 Minutes

Despite the cleanup that you performed on the data drive of the server (Chapter 8), you feel that it is in the company's best interest to add 1GB to the Active Directory partition (F: in my case). Future upgrades and installations will consume more disk space. Increasing the size of the partition provides a buffer against future growth needs.

The task that you will perform is called a *span*. It allows partitions on separate hard drives to be combined into one volume set. The resulting volume set looks like one hard drive to users of the computer. Only you will know that the volume set is actually spanned.

lab
Hint

To extend the volume, the volume must have been created on the dynamic disk, not upgraded from a basic disk. If your server has not been set up that way, skip this lab or practice using a different volume.

Learning Objectives

In this lab, you build a span between two hard drives. At the end of the lab, you'll be able to

■ Run disk management

■ Create a span between partitions.

Lab Materials and Setup

You need these items to complete the lab:

- Administrative account
- Secondary hard drive

Getting Down to Business

Increasing the size of the Active Directory partition on the Get-It-Right's server involves these steps:

Step 1. **Plan** for the change.

- Ensure that the partition you wish to add is healthy and of the same type (basic or dynamic) as the Active Directory (AD) partition.
- Check the free space on the drive.

Step 2. To begin **implementing** the change, start Disk Management. Then, span the AD partition to the new partition.

Step 3. **Test** your change by ensuring that the free space on the drive is now 1GB larger.

LAB EXERCISE 10.03

Mirroring a Partition

30 Minutes

Thanks to your efforts, the data at Get-It-Right is well protected using a backup scheme. However, you know that backups will not prevent data loss if a hard drive crashes during the middle of the day. A mirror set, on the other hand, will copy the contents from one drive to another automatically. The mirror set provides an up-to-the-minute backup of critical files. You decide to mirror the partition that holds Get-It-Right's information database.

You know that a side benefit to a mirror set is increased read response from the server. Because the data is kept on two disks at one time, two disk read/write heads are looking for the data. Whichever head finds the data first reads it into RAM. Theoretically, network read times are halved.

lab
Ⓗint

Other candidates for mirroring are the home folders belonging to users.

Learning Objectives

In this lab, you provide fault tolerance for a partition. At the end of the lab, you'll be able to

- Use Disk Management
- Create a mirror of an existing partition.

Lab Materials and Setup

You need these materials to complete the lab:

- Administrative account
- Secondary hard drive

Getting Down to Business

You will mirror an existing partition for Get-It-Right's server. Here is what you need to do:

Step 1. **Plan** for the change.

- Ensure that the unallocated space is larger than the data partition.

Step 2. To begin **implementing** the change, start Disk Management.

- Mirror the data partition to unallocated space on the new drive.

Step 3. **Test** your work by ensuring that the drive and mirror status are healthy.

Compressing a Folder

5 Minutes

You notice that a folder on the Get-It-Right server contains rarely used data. The users occasionally need that data, but seldom. You therefore decide to compress the folder to save disk space.

Learning Objectives

In this lab, you compress a folder containing rarely used files. At the end of the lab, you'll be able to

- Create a folder
- Copy files into the folder
- Compress a folder.

Lab Materials and Setup

You need these items to complete the lab:

- A folder containing nonessential files
- Administrative account

Getting Down to Business

To reduce the storage needs for Get-It-Right, you'll compress a folder. Here's how:

Step I. **Plan** your approach.

- Decide which files and folders should be compressed.
- Determine the total size of those files and folders.

Step 2. **Implement** your change:

- Create the folder to be compressed and place the files into that folder.
- Compress the folder.

Step 3. **Test** your change by comparing the new size of the folder to its original size.

LAB ANALYSIS TEST

The following questions will help you to apply your knowledge in a business setting.

1. What are the differences between a striped set and a striped set with parity?

   _____

   _____

2. What advantages does dynamic storage offer to an administrator?

   _____

   _____

3. In lab exercise 10.02, you increased the size of the data partition by spanning to another drive. What are two other methods that could have worked?

   _____

   _____

4. What are some of the problems or dangers associated with using NTFS disk compression?

   _____

   _____

5. Why is neither mirroring nor RAID 5 ("redundant arrays of independent disks") secure enough to stand as the only fault tolerance scheme?

   _____

   _____

KEY TERM QUIZ

Use the following vocabulary terms to complete the sentences below. Not all of the terms will be used.

    basic

    dynamic

    encryption

    exabytes

    mirroring

    quota

    RAID

    span

    striping

    terabytes

1. In Windows 2000 Server, to enable encryption, you must have your disks configured using _____ disk storage.

2. NTFS 5.0 supports up to 16 _____ of disk storage.

3. Restricting the size of user directories is an example of a disk _____ .

4. Copying the contents of a partition or volume to another partition or volume is considered _____ .

5. Interleaving portions of files across drives is considered _____ .

LAB SOLUTIONS FOR CHAPTER 10

The sections that follow walk you through the steps to solve the lab exercises. You should avoid looking at these sections unless you are stuck on a particular exercise.

lab
Hint
For lab solutions 10.01 through 10.03, do not close Computer Management.

Lab Solution 10.01

The only planning in a boot partition upgrade is to make sure that the partition is upgradeable. After that, you can simply carry out the task.

lab
Hint
If your computer's boot partition is upgradeable, be sure to upgrade to dynamic disk. I am unable to upgrade my boot disk because it lives on a drive with a FAT32 partition.

Step 1. Select Start | Programs | Administrative Tools | Computer Management. Expand Storage, and then click Disk Management (Figure 10-1). (If the wizard starts, close it.)

On the example screen, disk 2 is the new secondary drive. The new disk is currently unavailable. Right-click your new drive, and select Write Signature. That option converts the drive to a basic drive.

Now right-click drive 1 or 2, and select Upgrade to Dynamic Disk. In the Upgrade to Dynamic Disk dialog box that opens, select all of the drives that you want to upgrade. For example:

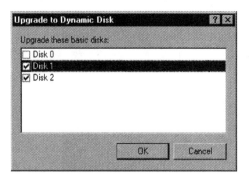

FIGURE 10-1   Viewing disk drives in Computer Management

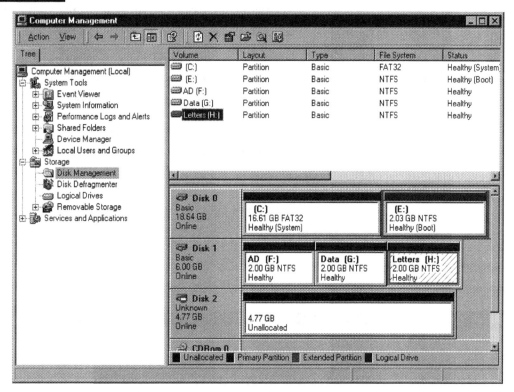

Remember that, for a drive to be upgraded, it must have at least 1MB unallocated space.

When you are finished, the bar on the volumes on drive 1 should change to yellow, indicating that they are now volumes.

Lab Solution 10.02

Unlike the partition upgrade, which can simply proceed if the partition is upgradeable, a partition size increase requires that you do a little checking into the size and health of the partition space that you're going to add.

Step 1.   In Computer Management, scroll the top left-hand window to the right until you can see the free space on the drive. Write that number down for future reference. In my case, the drive has 1.99GB free. If you complete the lab correctly, the free space should increase.

Step 2.   Right-click the volume that you want to span, and select Extend Volume. Click Next to bypass the splash screen, and reach the Select Disks dialog of the Extend Volume wizard (Figure 10-2).
   Click Remove All to eliminate the free space on drive 1 from the span possibilities. Add drive 2 and configure for 1024 bytes as shown in Figure 10-3.
   Notice that the volume size is now more than 3GB.
   Click Next, and then Finish.

Step 3.   The two purple F: volumes show the successful span (Figure 10-4). Free space is now 2.99GB.

Setting the initial
span properties

FIGURE 10-3

Configuring
the span

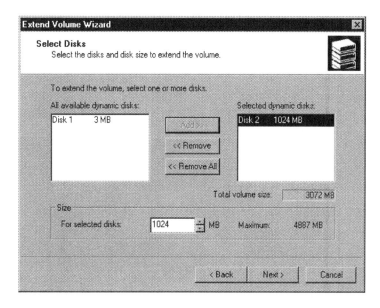

FIGURE 10-4   Verifying the span

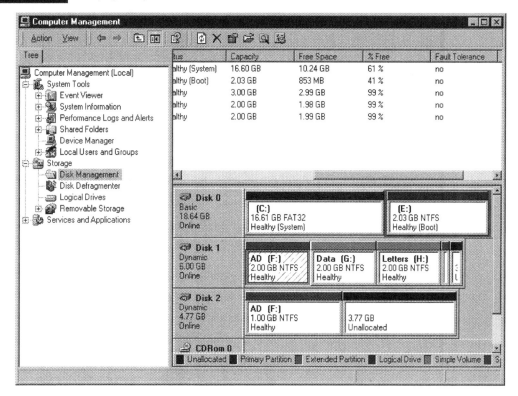

Lab Solution 10.03

Partition mirroring also requires that a couple of quick checks be carried out before proceeding.

Step 1. Right-click the data volume, and select Add Mirror. A list opens, showing all possible drives to mirror to:

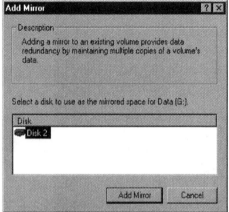

Step 2. Select disk 2, and click Add Mirror. While the mirror is being built, the screen will look something like Figure 10-5. Notice the mirror volumes are now red and show the message "Regenerating" in the status area. Building the mirror takes some time. When the mirror is finished, close Computer Management.

Lab Solution 10.04

Use My Computer or Windows Explorer to browse to the folder that you want to compress. The example shows the compression of a folder called Letter Templates.

Step 1. Right-click your chosen folder, and check its size. As shown in Figure 10-6, Letter Templates is 43.8MB.

Step 2. Click Advanced, and then select the check box next to "Compress contents to save disk space," as shown in Figure 10-7.

FIGURE 10-5   Verifying mirror status

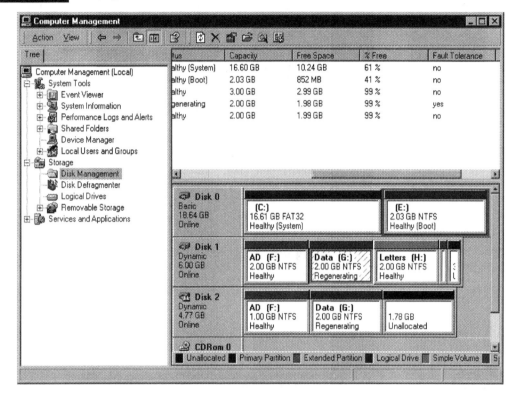

Click OK, and then Apply. When given the choice, be sure to compress files and subfolders as well:

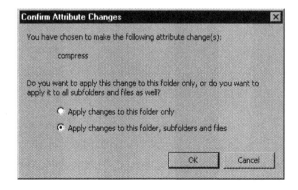

FIGURE 10-6

Checking the
current size of
Letter Templates

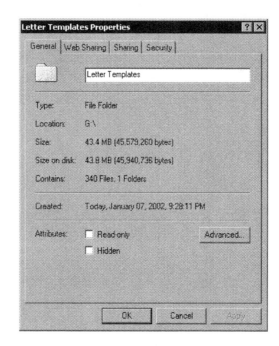

FIGURE 10-7

Choosing to
compress a
folder

A message shows the progress of the file compression:

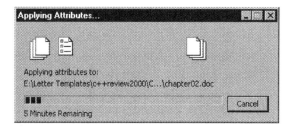

Step 3. Figure 10-8 shows the new folder size. Your results may not be as dramatic as those shown in the figure. I placed mostly .tif files into the Letter Templates folder. TIF files compress well.

Letter Templates Properties

General | Web Sharing | Sharing | Security |

Letter Templates

Type: File Folder
Location: G:\
Size: 43.4 MB (45,579,260 bytes)
Size on disk: 8.47 MB (8,885,576 bytes)
Contains: 340 Files, 1 Folders

Created: Today, January 07, 2002, 9:28:11 PM

Attributes: ☐ Read-only   [Advanced...]
               ☐ Hidden

[OK] [Cancel] [Apply]

ANSWERS TO LAB ANALYSIS TEST

1. Striping and striping with parity both provide faster access to the data stored on a server. They differ in a few important aspects. Striping with parity interleaves sections of files and repeats the sections on multiple disks. Striping simply interleaves sections of files across hard drives. The repetition of files, of course, implies that striping with parity uses more disk space than striping. But, by repeating sections of files, striping with parity provides a level of fault tolerance; plain striping provides no disk protection. Finally, striping with parity requires a minimum of three disks; striping requires a minimum of two disks.

2. Dynamic disks provide several advantages to the administrator. The first advantage is the ability to resize volumes (partitions) without losing data. A second advantage is the ability to set disk quotas on user folders. Encryption is a third advantage of dynamic disks.

3. The span method to increase the available size is one very good way to increase the size of a partition. An alternate method would be to install a larger—and faster—hard drive, and then to transfer the partitions to that drive. A second alternate requires some available space on another partition on the data drive. If that drive had been converted to dynamic, then the partition could have been resized.

4. Using compression is a nice way to increase available space on a drive. Two problems arise when using compression, however. The first problem is a reduction in network response time. NTFS has to decompress the file before serving it to a user, and then must compress the file again for storage. If the file is very large, then a second problem can arise. If the decompressed size of the file is larger than the available free space, then decompression will fail, and the user will be unable to get the file.

5. Mirroring and RAID 5 (striping with parity) both depend on additional drives stored on the same server. If that server is damaged, then those drives are also likely to be damaged. If those methods are the only backup of the server data, then all data could be lost. A better strategy is to employ one of the above options, *and* a regular backup scheme.

ANSWERS TO KEY TERM QUIZ

1. dynamic

2. exabytes

3. quota

4. mirroring

5. striping

MCSE
MICROSOFT CERTIFIED SYSTEMS ENGINEER

11

Configuring Remote Connections in Windows 2000

LAB EXERCISES

G et-It-Right is in the process of modernizing its entire organization. One of the steps toward modernization is equipping its drivers with a device that sends delivery information to a central server. Your server is going to fill that role.

Ronny explains the new process to you over one of your Friday lunches. Apparently a device has been approved that will connect to a Windows 2000 server using TCP/IP over a virtual private network (VPN). The device is pre-configured by the manufacturer. You will have to set up the server to permit the remote connection. Ronny asks what is involved in permitting such connections and how the Get-It-Right data will be protected.

Immediately, you know that this project is a big can of worms. You tell Ronny that configuring the server as a VPN is fairly easy. You then go on to inform him that protecting the data is very difficult and will require software that is not included with Windows 2000 Server. Specifically, a firewall and strong antivirus software is needed to protect the server. Once those items are procured, setting the necessary local security policies is relatively easy. In addition to the policies, Dynamic Host Configuration Protocol (DHCP) and TCP/IP must be installed to support the devices carried by the drivers.

Ronny tells you that he will get a budget approved for you to order the necessary software. In the meantime, he wants you to get to work on the VPN setup. Get-It-Right would like the new process up and running ASAP. The drivers are scheduled to train on the new equipment next week.

LAB EXERCISE 11.01

10 Minutes

Creating a Dialup Connection to the Internet

lab
Hint   *Your lab may be set up with a different Internet connection. In that case, consult your instructor or lab technician for instructions.*

After lunch, you get right to work. Your first step is to connect the server to the Internet. Until you get the firewall and antivirus software, you decide to use a dialup connection. A dialup allows you to limit the time spent on the Internet and possibly to minimize the risk of infection or intrusion. Once the firewall is in place, you will switch to the company's high-speed connection.

Learning Objectives

In this lab, you connect the computer to the Internet. At the end of the lab, you'll be able to run the Internet Connection wizard.

Lab Materials and Setup

To complete this lab as written, you need these materials:

- Administrative account
- Windows 2000 Server–compatible modem installed
- Working telephone line
- Working telephone cord

Getting Down to Business

To connect the server to the Internet through a modem, here is what you need to do:

Step 1. **Plan** the dialup connection.

- Gather all the information necessary to connect to Get-It-Right's Internet service provider (ISP). Important information includes number to dial, valid account logon information, and the addresses of the DNS and mail servers.

Step 2. **Implement** the dialup connection by running inetwiz, the Internet Connection wizard.

Step 3. **Test** your work by connecting to the Internet and visiting a couple of well-known sites.

LAB EXERCISE 11.02

Verifying TCP/IP and DHCP

15 Minutes

The devices that Get-It-Right's drivers have received use TCP/IP as the primary protocol. You need to verify that TCP/IP is working on the server. In addition, each device is configured to accept an IP address from the server upon connection. You plan to use DHCP to configure those clients. You need to verify that your DHCP scope has enough room for 45 internal computers and 120 drivers.

Learning Objectives

Verification of settings is an important part of network management. At the end of the lab, you'll be able to

- Configure TCP/IP and verify that it is working
- Verify that DHCP is working.

Lab Materials and Setup

You need the administrative account to complete the lab.

Getting Down to Business

To verify that the local server has the appropriate protocols installed to allow remote access over TCP/IP, follow these steps:

Step 1. **Plan** your work so that you can verify all options and settings at the same time.

- Determine a valid range of IP addresses that can be included in the scope. Be sure to provide for future growth. The devices used by the drivers prefer to receive private IP addresses.

- Determine what the proper IP address should be for the server. It most likely should be a private IP address in the same network assigned to the driver devices.

- Create a list of valid IP addresses in the organization.

Step 2. **Implement** your plan by carrying out the verification process in an orderly manner:

- ■ Go to the properties of TCP/IP. Change the IP address if necessary.
- ■ Start the DCHP snap-in.
- ■ Ensure that the scope is active and serving the appropriate addresses. Change it if necessary.

Step 3. **Test** your work by opening a command-prompt window, and then using ping to check the connection from the server to other valid IP addresses.

LAB EXERCISE 11.03

Creating a Virtual Private Network Server

15 Minutes

Now it's time to implement the VPN on the Get-It-Right server. You have laid the groundwork for a successful installation. You are confident that VPN will work as advertised, allowing the drivers to send delivery and pickup information securely to the Windows 2000 Server. The TCP/IP protocol will be used to send and receive the information.

Learning Objectives

In this lab, you set up a VPN for Get-It-Right. At the end of the lab, you'll be able to

- ■ Start the Routing and Remote Access snap-in
- ■ Enable remote access
- ■ Configure the VPN.

Lab Materials and Setup

You need these materials to complete the lab:

- Administrative account
- Connection to the Internet
- TCP/IP installed and working
- DHCP installed and working

Getting Down to Business

Using these steps, you set up the VPN for Get-It-Right:

Step 1. **Plan** the VPN setup.

- Decide on the protocols that are needed, the Internet connection, and the location from which the clients receive an IP address.

Step 2. **Implement** the VPN setup. Begin by starting the Routing and Remote Access snap-in.

- In the Common Configurations dialog box, select Virtual Private Network.
- Configure the appropriate protocols, connection, and address assignment settings.

LAB EXERCISE 11.04

Creating a Remote Access Policy

20 Minutes

Before you enable remote access, you plan to create a policy that limits what remote users can do while logged on. Such a policy is a start toward protecting the server and its data. The device that the drivers will be using is very fast—able to transfer the necessary data in under 1 minute—and supports high encryption. Given those capabilities, you set a maximum logon time and days and times for remote access, and you force strong encryption.

Learning Objectives

In this lab, you configure a policy for remote access. At the end of the lab, you'll be able to

- Start the Routing and Remote Access Service (RRAS)
- Create a default remote access policy
- Edit the policy.

Lab Materials and Setup

You need the administrative account to complete the lab.

Getting Down to Business

Creating a remote access policy is a necessary step toward protecting the data on the Get-It-Right servers. Here is what you need to do:

Step 1. **Plan** your policy needs before proceeding.

- Determine the policies that you need to set to protect the server.
- Decide on the settings for the chosen policies.

Step 2. **Implement** the selected policies.

- Start the RRAS tool from the Start button.
- Add a remote access policy.
- Add the attributes that you require on the remote access policy.
- If other policies exist, then add the same attributes to those policies.

LAB ANALYSIS TEST

The following questions will help you to apply your knowledge in a business setting.

I. You are trying to use "access by policy" to configure remote access on your server but it is not working. What is a likely source for the problem?

_____

_____

2. All computers have ports. Provide a list of three common ports and their uses.

_____

_____

3. Windows 2000 Server can share an Internet connection among clients on the network. Why is it a bad idea to use the primary server on a large network to perform this task?

_____

_____

4. You have established a dial-in connection for remote clients. Initially, when usage was low, the modem connection worked well. Now, usage is climbing, and users are complaining that it takes too long to connect. How can you increase the number of users that can connect, but still use a dial-in option?

_____

_____

5. You have enabled Internet connection sharing and DHCP. Your clients can access the server (192.168.100.1) via TCP, but they cannot access the Internet. What is the problem?

_____

_____

KEY TERM QUIZ

Use the following vocabulary terms to complete the sentences below. Not all of the terms will be used.

    DHCP

    L2TP

    NWLink

    ping

    PPTP

    private

    public

    strong

    strongest

    subnet mask

    telnet

1. The _____ protocol allows Windows 2000 Server to connect to Novell servers.

2. The protocols _____ and _____ can both be used to build a VPN.

3. Addresses in the range 192.168 are said to be _____ addresses.

4. The _____ encryption level provides a 56-bit key.

5. A program that verifies that an IP address is up and running is _____ .

LAB SOLUTIONS FOR CHAPTER 11

The sections that follow walk you through the steps to solve the lab exercises. You should avoid looking at these sections unless you are stuck on a particular exercise.

Lab Solution 11.01

The connection setup wizard makes this work simple; just be sure to have all the necessary information on hand before you begin.

Step 1. Your connection information will be unique to your setting. If you are unsure of what you need, consult with your instructor or evaluator.

Step 2. Select Start | Run, and enter **inetwiz** in the Run box.

When the Internet Connection wizard opens (Figure 11-1), select "Connect using my phone line."

Into the wizard's Step 1 dialog box, enter the telephone number to dial. (See Figure 11-2 for an example.)

The wizard's Step 2 dialog box asks for a valid account and password, and Step 3 requires a name for the connection. Provide a name as indicated in Figure 11-3, but use the name of your own ISP.

FIGURE 11-1

Selecting
the type
of Internet
connection

Internet Connection Wizard

Set Up Your Internet Connection

If you already have an account with an Internet service provider and have obtained all the necessary connection information, you can connect to your account using your phone line. If you are connected to a local area network (LAN) that is connected to the Internet, you can access the Internet over the LAN.

Which method do you want to use to connect to the

○ Connect using my phone line

○ Connect using my local area network (LAN)

< Back | Next > | Cancel | Help

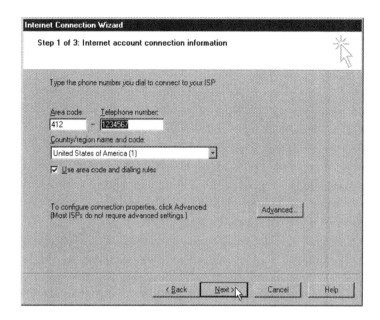

FIGURE 11-2

Entering
the telephone
number

Using a server to send and receive e-mail is not advisable, and so you select No when asked if you want to configure an Internet mail account.

Step 3. Test your new connection by double-clicking the Explorer icon on the desktop.

FIGURE 11-3

Naming the
dialup connection

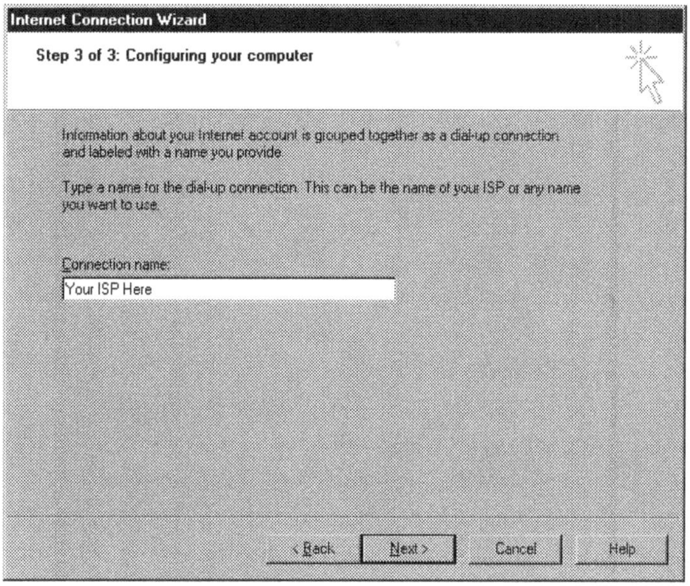

Lab Exercise 11.02

Checking the remote access protocols is simply a matter of being well-organized and methodical.

Step 1. A valid range of IP addresses would be any private range that uses a netmask of 255.255.255.0. That netmask provides addresses for 255 computers on your network, leaving plenty of space for the 165 computers described in the scenario. A valid range is 192.168.1.2 to 192.168.1.254. The "1" is reserved for the server.

Step 2. Right-click Network Neighborhood on the desktop, and select Properties. When the Network and Dial Up settings open, right-click Local Area Connection. Select Properties.

In the Local Area Connection Properties dialog box, select Internet Protocol as shown in Figure 11-4.

Click the Properties button. Set the server's IP properties as shown in Figure 11-5. Click OK twice in succession to apply the changes.

From the Start button, select Programs | Administrative Tools | DHCP. Verify that the DHCP settings are active (Figure 11-6).

Double-click Address Pool to verify that the range of addresses is correct (Figure 11-7).

If a range is invalid, right-click Scope, and select Properties. Configure as show in Figure 11-8.

FIGURE 11-4

Accessing
the properties
for the local area

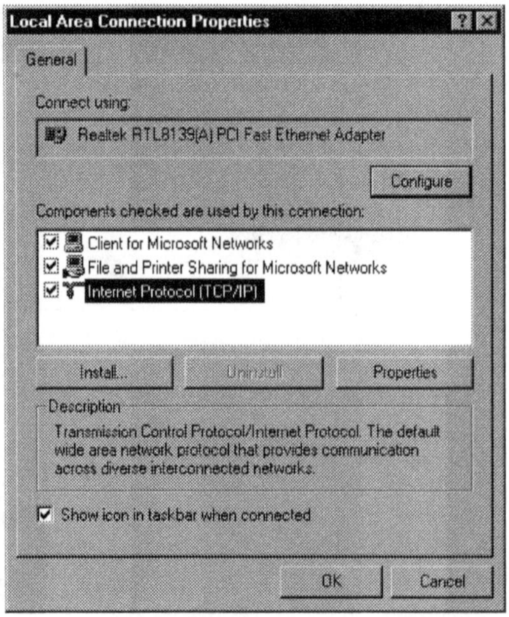

FIGURE 11-5

FIGURE 11-5

Setting the Internet
Protocol properties

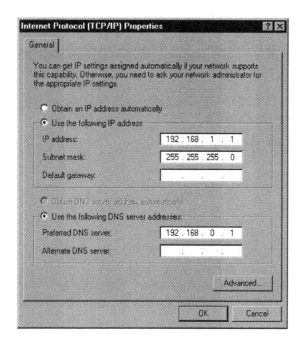

Step 3. To test that the IP settings are correct, run **cmd** from Start | Run. Enter **ping 127.0.0.1** to verify that your loopback address is working. Ping other known addresses. If a problem exists, you'll see messages something like those shown in Figure 11-9.

FIGURE 11-6   Verifying that DHCP is active

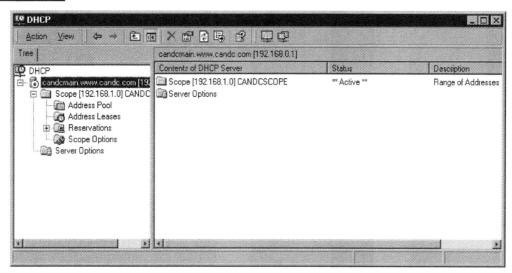

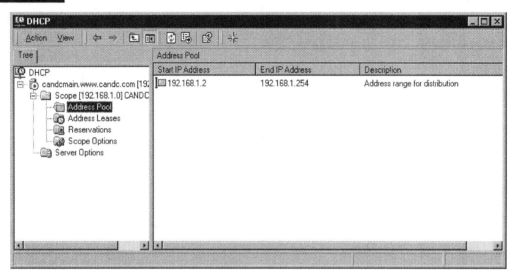

FIGURE 11-7 Verifying the DHCP lease pool

FIGURE 11-8

Setting a
DHCP scope

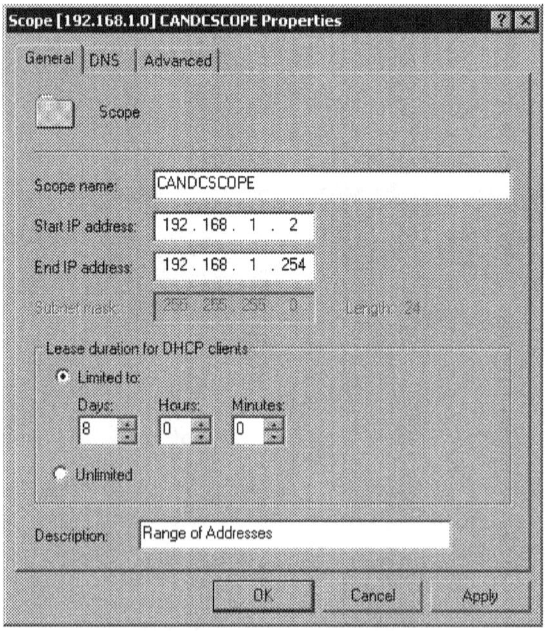

FIGURE 11-9

Finding an
IP problem
using ping

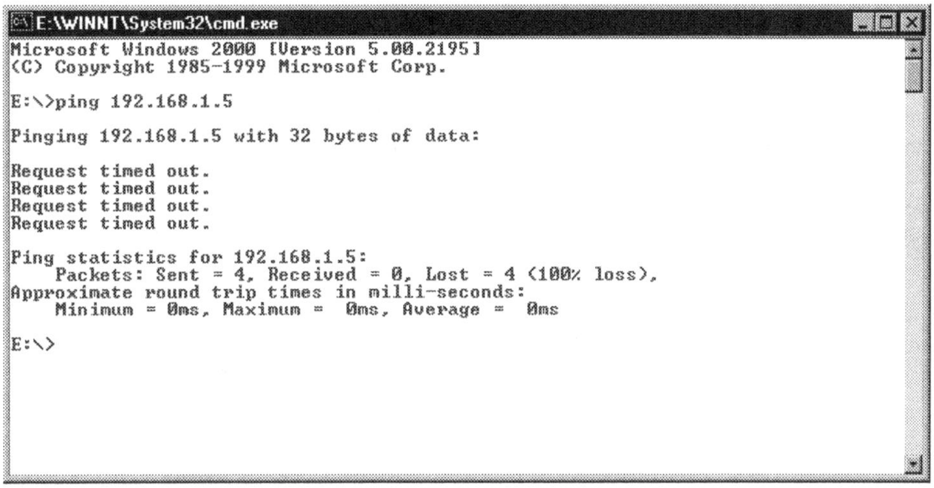

```
E:\WINNT\System32\cmd.exe
Microsoft Windows 2000 [Version 5.00.2195]
(C) Copyright 1985-1999 Microsoft Corp.

E:\>ping 192.168.1.5

Pinging 192.168.1.5 with 32 bytes of data:

Request timed out.
Request timed out.
Request timed out.
Request timed out.

Ping statistics for 192.168.1.5:
    Packets: Sent = 4, Received = 0, Lost = 4 (100% loss),
Approximate round trip times in milli-seconds:
    Minimum = 0ms, Maximum =  0ms, Average =  0ms

E:\>
```

Lab Solution 11.03

Setting up a virtual private network is quick work, if well organized in advance.

Step 1.   The VPN requires TCP/IP and DHCP. You verified those services in lab exercise 11.02.

Step 2.   Select Start | Programs | Administrative Tools | Routing and Remote Access. Right-click the server object, and select Configure and Enable Routing and Remote Access. After you pass the splash screen, select the VPN option (Figure 11-10).

At the Remote Client Protocols screen (Figure 11-11), verify that TCP/IP is present. Click Next.

At the Internet Connection screen, select the available Internet connection. If no connection is currently available, configure as shown (Figure 11-12).

Allow DHCP to automatically assign IP addresses, and click Next. You will not be using a RADIUS server, so click Next, and then Finish.

After the service starts, you receive a message regarding DHCP and a relay agent. You must set the DHCP relay agent to the local DHCP server.

Right-click DHCP relay agent, and select Properties. As shown in Figure 11-13, enter the server IP address, and click Add.

Leave RRAS open for the next lab exercise.

FIGURE 11-10

Configuring
the Routing and
Remote Access
Service for virtual
private network
(VPN)

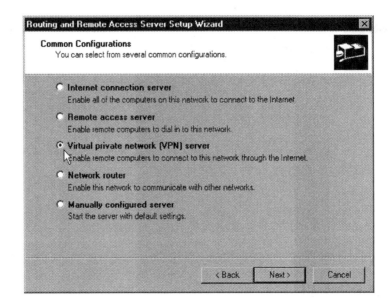

FIGURE 11-11

Verifying
that TCP/IP
is present

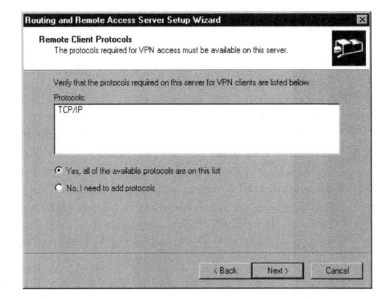

FIGURE 11-12

Configuring
the Internet
Connection
screen

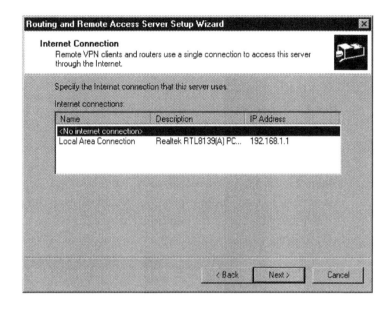

FIGURE 11-13

Specifying the
DHCP server

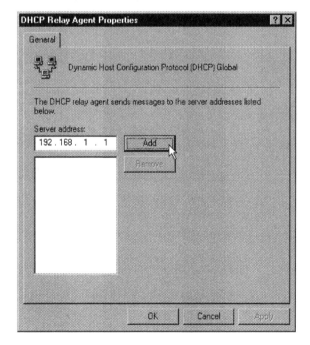

Lab Exercise 11.04

Remember that you choices are based on the device that the drivers will be using: fast and able to support high encryption.

Step 1. In designing the remote policy, you decide to limit the permitted times and the length of time for a connection. You also decide to enforce a strong level of encryption.

Step 2. In RRAS, select Remote Access Policy. As shown in Figure 11-14, right-click the "Allow access if dial-in permission is enabled" icon, and select Properties.

Remove the time restriction from the main text box. Click Add to add new restrictions:

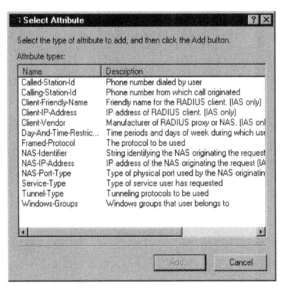

Add the Day and Time restriction. A "Time of day constraint" dialog box opens. Configure it as shown in Figure 11-15.

Click Add to see the policy Properties screen (Figure 11-16).

FIGURE 11-14

Accessing
the properties of
the default policy

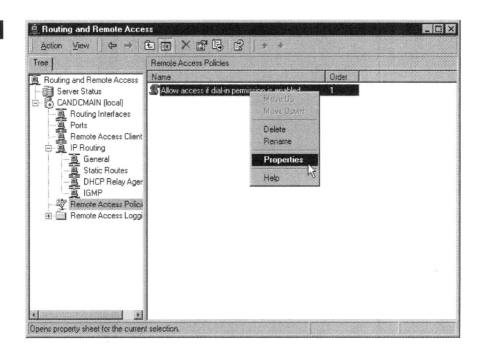

FIGURE 11-15

Restricting time
of day to connect

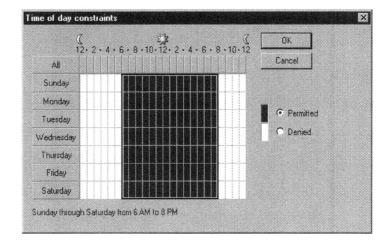

FIGURE 11-16

New properties
of the default
policy

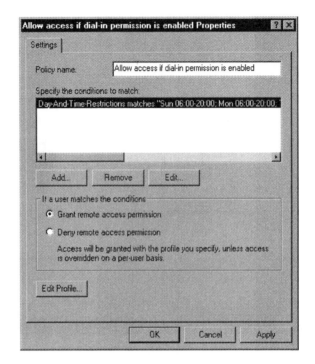

Click Add again, and add the attribute NAS-Port-Type. Configure it as shown here:

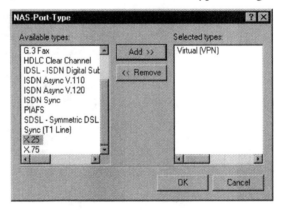

Click OK to return to the Properties dialog box.

Click Edit Profile to continue modifying the default settings. Set the dial-in constraints as shown in Figure 11-17.

Select the Encryption tab, and configure strong encryption as shown in Figure 11-18.

lab ⓗint *Leaving the server open to any connection is dangerous. You will configure a group for remote access in the next chapter.*

FIGURE 11-17

Configuring
the dial-in
constraints

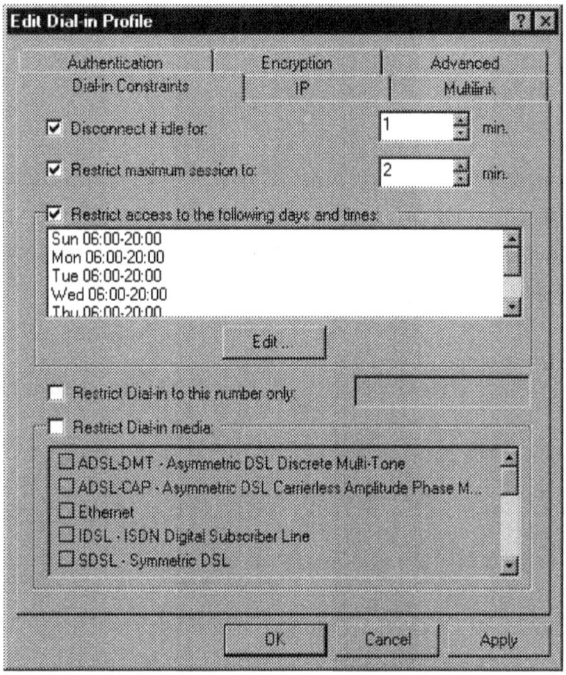

FIGURE 11-18

Enabling strong
encryption

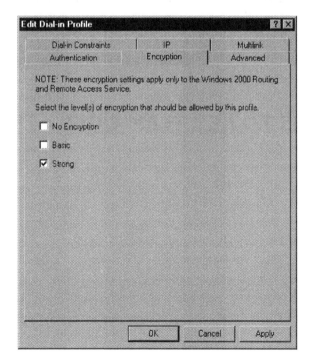

ANSWERS TO LAB ANALYSIS TEST

1. To use "access by policy," your network must contain only Windows 2000 servers. If your network contains Windows NT servers, you will not be able to enforce access by policy.

2. Computers have 65,535 ports. Most of the "well-known ports" are defined under 1023. Three very common ports are 21, 23, and 80. Port 21 is used for ftp programs to upload and download files. The telnet program, which can control remote computers, uses port 23. Finally, HTTP and browsers use port 80.

cross
Reference *See www.networksorcery.com/enp/ for a complete listing of well-known ports.*

3. Sharing an Internet connection is fine for a small office or a home setup. The drain on the server for a few Internet shares has little effect on the network at large. However, as the number of clients grows, performance on the server can degrade severely. That reduction in server efficiency will slow the entire network. A better solution here is to set up a separate server running Internet connection sharing.

4. One option is to use a modem pool. With a pool, the server can use a number of modems, thus allowing one dial-in connection per modem. The only downside is that you may need to increase the number of telephone lines. Those additional lines may drive the monthly cost beyond that for a dedicated option.

5. The problem lies with a limitation of the Internet connection share software. ICS requires the server to use the private IP address 192.168.0.1.

ANSWERS TO KEY TERM QUIZ

1. NWLink

2. PPTP, L2TP

3. private

4. strong

5. ping

MICROSOFT CERTIFIED SYSTEMS ENGINEER

12

Implementing User Security with Policies, Profiles, and Encryption

Ronny pokes his head into your office. He tells you that the drivers are very pleased with the new devices. The remote access is working well. However, the managers at Get-It-Right are concerned with data security. They understand that once remote access is enabled, nearly anyone with the will can access the server remotely. That means that a hacker could get in and take over the network. Ronny asks what security measures you intend to implement to protect the server.

You think for a few minutes, and then come up with some solutions. The first step will be to disable remote access for users who do not need it. You will then use group policies to protect the server and workstations. Those changes will take some time, and will need to be carried out when the server is inactive. You tell Ronny that you will stay late tonight to implement the security changes.

LAB EXERCISE 12.01

Limiting Remote Access

20 Minutes

You know that remote access is a two-edged sword. Your users need it to allow them to work off site. However, with remote access enabled, your server has a partially opened door that a dedicated hacker could exploit. The default in Windows 2000 is to allow all users remote access. You will limit access to the drivers only.

Learning Objectives

In this lab, you limit remote access to drivers only. At the end of the lab, you'll be able to

- Start Active Directory Users and Computers
- Create a security group
- Create a user
- Add a user to a security group
- Modify a remote access policy.

Lab Materials and Setup

You need these materials to complete the lab:

- Windows 2000 Server with VPN installed
- Administrative account

Getting Down to Business

To enable remote access for the drivers and disable it for other users, here is what you need to do:

Step 1. **Plan** the security carefully: make a list of all the drivers.

Step 2. **Implement** your plan by restricting access to the people on your list.

- Start Active Directory Users and Computers.
- Create a security group called "drivers" under the Users tab.
- Create a user for each driver. Be sure to grant remote access. Make each driver a member of the "drivers" security group.
- Start Routing and Remote Access.
- Deny remote access to other users.

LAB EXERCISE 12.02

Securing the Server and Workstations with a Group Policy

15 Minutes

As an experienced administrator, you know that most security breaches are effected by internal users. The breach may be accidental or intentional; but, in either event, the damage is done.

You will use the policies provided by Microsoft to secure the server and the workstations alike. Windows 2000 includes security templates that apply rules to the computer to make it more secure.

Learning Objectives

In this lab, you make Get-It-Right's network more secure by applying security templates. At the end of the lab, you'll be able to

■ Start Group Policy Editor

■ Create a group policy

■ Apply a security template to the server and workstations.

Lab Materials and Setup

You need these items to complete the lab:

■ Administrative account

■ Windows 2000 Server that has been promoted to domain controller

cross
Reference

If your server does not have Active Directory installed, see Exercise 4-3 in the Study Guide.

Getting Down to Business

Use this procedure to secure the server and workstations for Get-It-Right:

Step 1. **Plan** the level of security that you intend to implement.

■ Windows 2000 includes three security templates: basic, secure, and highly secure. Choose the desired level.

Step 2. **Implement** your chosen security option.

■ Using Start | Run, start the MMC program.

■ Add the Group Policy snap-in.

■ Add the local computer.

■ Create a new policy called "users."

■ Add the snap-in for Security Configuration and Analysis.

■ Apply the desired template to each group policy object.

■ Save the console screen as **users.msc**.

LAB EXERCISE 12.03

Linking Policies to the Domain

5 Minutes

Now that the security policies are built, you need to link them to your domain. By linking, you apply the policies to the users as they log onto the server. If you fail to set up the links, the user workstations will remain insecure.

Learning Objectives

In this lab, you link the policy to the domain for your server. At the end of the lab, you'll be able to

- Start Active Directory Users and Computers
- Apply a group policy to the network.

Lab Materials and Setup

You need these materials to complete the lab:

- Administrative account
- Policies created in lab exercise 12.02

Getting Down to Business

The policies won't be effective until linked to the domain. Use these steps:

Step 1. Continue **implementing** the security that you started in the previous lab exercise:

- Start Active Directory Users and Computers.
- Go to the properties of the domain. Select Group Policy. Remove current policies, if any.
- Add the "users" policy created in lab exercise 12.02.

Step 2. Test your security set-up by logging onto the network, and verifying that the settings are applied.

LAB EXERCISE 12.04

Verifying Roaming Profile

5 Minutes

You receive an e-mail from Brenda, a user in Shipping. She had to move from one computer to another computer, and she claimed that her settings did not follow her. You want her to verify that her account is properly set up.

Learning Objectives

In this lab, you learn how to view a computer's profiles.

Lab Materials and Setup

You need the administrative account for this lab.

Getting Down to Business

To check whether Brenda's profile is set to "roaming," here is what you need to do:

Step 1. **Implement** your verification routine.

- Log in as administrator.
- Start the Control Panel, then the System icon.
- Check the profiles, and verify that all profiles are roaming.

LAB EXERCISE 12.05

Switching Off Control Panel

20 Minutes

To further assist the help-desk staff, you decide to switch off access to the Control Panel. That action will limit a user's ability to modify the workstation. By disabling

Control Panel, you ensure that users will not be able to change their screen settings or otherwise customize computers.

Learning Objectives

In this lab, you use Group Policy to disable access to the Control Panel. At the end of the lab, you'll be able to

- Start Group Policy Editor
- Edit an existing policy.

Lab Materials and Setup

You need these materials to complete the lab:

- Administrative account
- Users.msc file created in lab exercise 12.02

Getting Down to Business

Here's how you create a group policy to disable the Control Panel:

Step 1. **Plan** how much of Control Panel to disable.

- Decide which aspects of the Control Panel are "safe" to be left on.

Step 2. **Implement** your plan by disabling selected features.

- Open the users.msc file in Microsoft Management Console (MMC).
- Expand the User Configuration tab to see Control Panel.
- Disable the policies that you believe are unsafe.

Step 3. **Test** your work by logging onto the network as a regular user. Verify that Control Panel is indeed disabled.

LAB EXERCISE 12.06

Encrypting a Folder

10 Minutes

Ronny stops in one day with a simple question. He is working on employee reviews, and would like to encrypt the folder holding the reviews. He asks what he should purchase to allow him to encrypt his folder.

You tell him that Windows 2000 supports encryption. You start to tell him how to do it, but he stops you and says, "Show me. I will forget everything you say unless I see it." You log onto the server to demonstrate.

Learning Objectives

At the end of the lab, you'll be able to encrypt a folder or file.

Lab Materials and Setup

You need these materials to complete the lab:

- User account for the server
- A folder to encrypt and decrypt

Getting Down to Business

You will use a feature of NTFS 5 to encrypt a folder. Here's how:

Step 1. **Plan** by deciding which files or folders you want to encrypt.

Step 2. **Implement** your plan by organizing the files and folders into a single folder, and then encrypting the folder.

LAB ANALYSIS TEST

The following questions will help you to apply your knowledge in a business setting.

1. Other than annoyed users, what are some of the potential ramifications of disabling access to the Control Panel?

2. What is the difference between roaming mandatory profiles and roaming profiles?

3. Who are the two users capable of decrypting a file, and why do two users have that authority?

4. A user is copying personal encrypted files to a floppy disk that was formatted in a home Windows 98 machine. How is that user creating a security hole?

5. Why is using a local profile for users that move throughout the network considered inefficient?

KEY TERM QUIZ

Use the following vocabulary terms to complete the sentences below. Not all of the terms will be used.

      Active Directory

      cipher

      encrypt

      GPO

      inheritance

      mandatory

      MMC

      policy

      roaming

      template

1. A profile that follows the user from computer to computer is said to be a(n) _____ profile.

2. The command line tool that encrypts files is _____ .

3. _____ is the tool needed to modify group policies.

4. One policy passing down to another policy is a definition of _____ .

5. The easiest way to secure a server is to apply a _____ to the policies.

LAB SOLUTIONS FOR CHAPTER 12

The sections that follow walk you through the steps to solve the lab exercises. You should avoid looking at these sections unless you are stuck on a particular exercise.

Lab Solution 12.01

Get-It-Right has many drivers. For this lab, limit your driver list to four drivers.

Step 1.   In the solution that follows, I've named the drivers Shawneka Gayles, Luke Redd, Linsday Russell, and Misty Walker. For the usernames, follow the standard convention of "first letter of first name, full last name."

Step 2.   Select Start | Programs | Administrative Tools | Active Directory Users and Computers. Expand the domain, and then the Users folder to see its contents (Figure 12-1).

Right-click the white area in the right-hand pane, and select New | Group. Configure the new group object as shown in Figure 12-2.

Click OK to return to Users and Computers. You will see that the "drivers" group has been added.

FIGURE 12-1

Viewing the Users folder

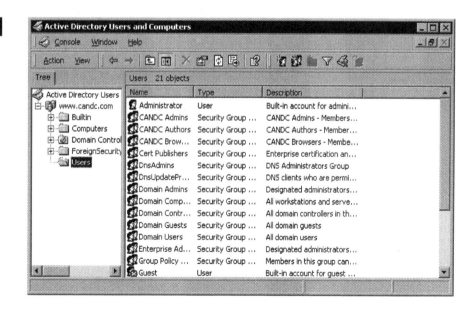

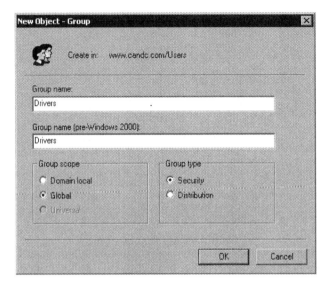

Right-click the white area, and select New | User. Begin to create Shawneka's
account (Figure 12-3).

Click Next to configure the password options. Set no password, but force
Shawneka to create a password on the next logon (Figure 12-4).

Click Next, and then Finish to add "sgayles" to the Users folder.

Go to the Properties for the user. Select the Dial-in tab. Set the dial-in access as
shown in Figure 12-5.

Repeat the foregoing process for every user to be added.

FIGURE 12-3

Creating
a user account

FIGURE 12-4

Setting password
options on a
user account

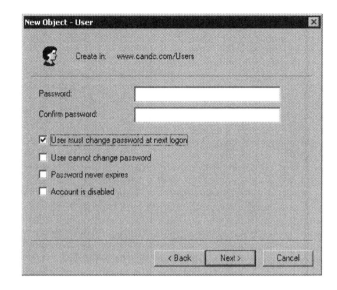

Now, add the users to the Drivers group. Right-click the group, and select
Properties. Select the Members tab. Click Add, and then double-click each user to
add him or her to the group (Figure 12-6).

FIGURE 12-5

Enabling
dial-in access

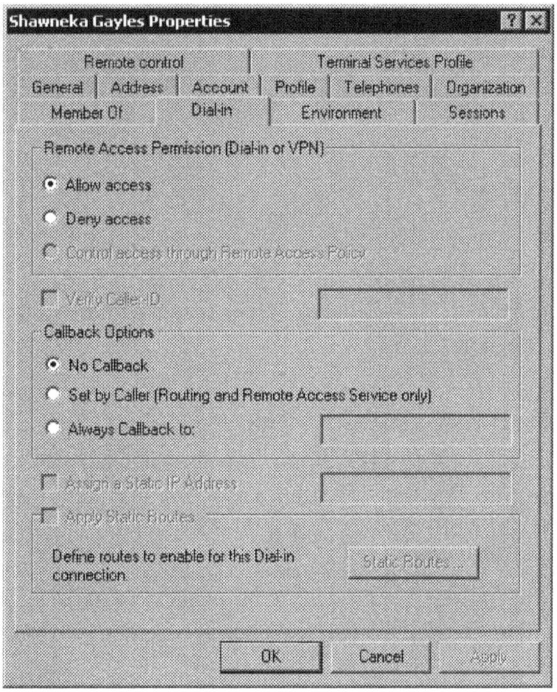

FIGURE 12-6

Adding members
to a security
group

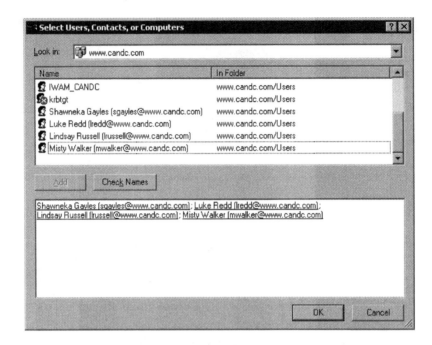

Close all open windows. Select Start | Programs | Administrative Tools | Routing and Remote Access. Select Remote Access Policies in the left-hand pane. Double-click the Allow Access policy in the right-hand pane. Deny access to users by selecting the Deny Access radio button (Figure 12-7).

Lab Solution 12.02

Preventing internal security breaches is the main focus of this lab.

Step 1.   Get-It-Right values its data highly, and so you are going to choose the highest level of security.

Step 2.   Select Start | Run, and in the Run box, enter **mmc**. At the console screen, select Console | Add/Remove Snap-in. The Add/Remove Snap-in dialog opens (Figure 12-8).
Click the Add button to see a list of available snap-ins. As shown in Figure 12-9, select the Group Policy snap-in.
Click Add to start the Select Group Policy Object wizard (Figure 12-10).
Click Browse to begin creating a new policy. In the Browse for a Group Policy Object dialog box (Figure 12-11), right-click the white area, and select New.

FIGURE 12-7

Denying remote
access to users

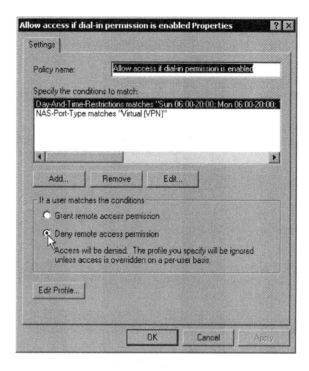

FIGURE 12-8

Preparing
to add a policy

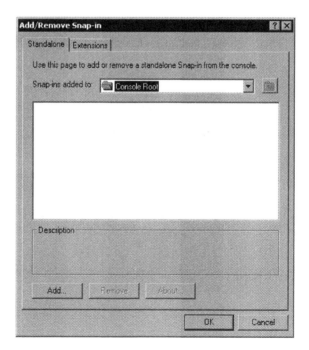

FIGURE 12-9

Selecting the
Group Policy
snap-in

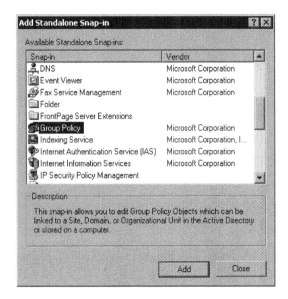

Give the policy the name **users**. Again, add the Group Policy snap-in. This time, do not click Browse; simply add Local Computer.

You are done adding snap-ins.

Click Close, and then OK to return to the MMC. Save the current console as **users.msc**.

FIGURE 12-10

Opening
the Select Group
Policy Object
wizard

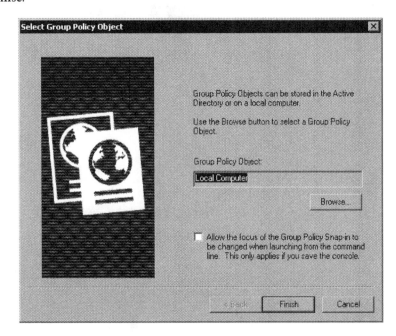

FIGURE 12-11

Browsing for
a group policy
object

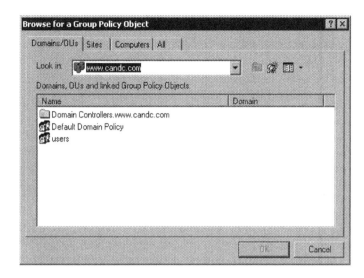

From the console menu, create a new window. Add the snap-in for Security Configuration and Analysis, just as you added the Group Policy snap-in. You also need to add all group policies currently on the computer. These include Local Policy, users, and Default Policy. When you are finished, the Add/Remove dialog box should look something like Figure 12-12.

FIGURE 12-12

Preparing
to configure
security

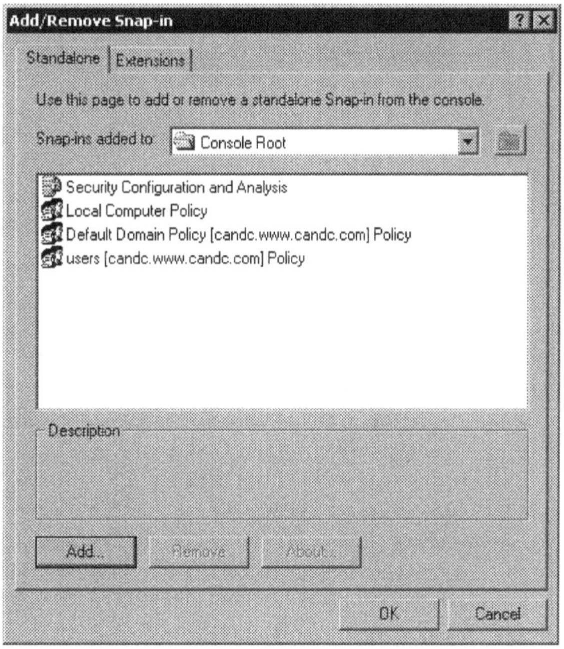

Click OK to return to the MMC.

As shown in Figure 12-13, right-click the Security Analysis icon and select Open Database.

Give the database the name **secure** (Figure 12-14). Click Open.

At the Import Template screen, select hisecdc. Click Open to open the template.

Expand the local policy to see the security settings (Figure 12-15).

Right-click the Security Settings icon, and choose Import Policy. Because you're working with the local server, you will import the hisecdc policy. Select it as shown in Figure 12-16.

For users and Default Policy, repeat the foregoing steps, but import hisecws. That file protects the users' computers. Close and save as **allpolicies.msc**.

Configuring the security analysis tool

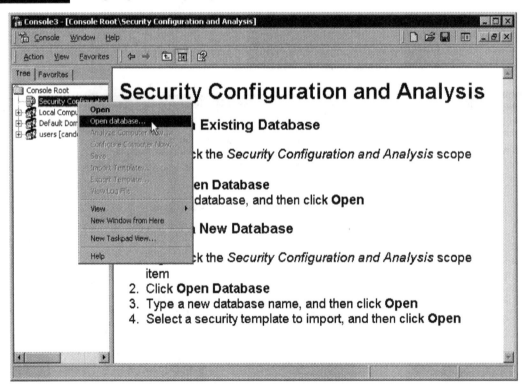

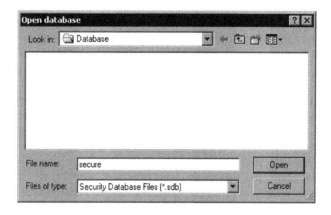

FIGURE 12-14

Creating
the security
database

Lab Solution 12.03

Policies are not effective until linked to the domain, and linking was the focus of this lab
exercise.

Step 1.   Select Start | Programs | Administrative Tools | Active Directory Users
and Computers. Right-click the domain, and choose Properties, as shown in
Figure 12-17.

Click the Group Policy tab. Ensure that the policies are listed in the Group Policy
Object Links box as shown in Figure 12-18.

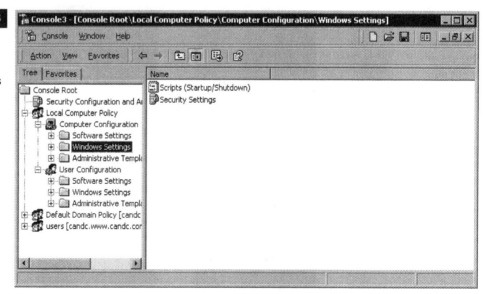

FIGURE 12-15

Browsing to
local computer
security settings

FIGURE 12-16

Choosing
a security
template

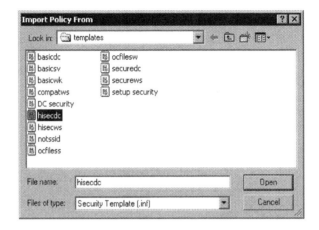

If a policy is missing, click Add, and then select the missing policy as shown in
Figure 12-19.

Lab Solution 12.04

Verifying a roaming profile is a simple job.

Step 1. Log on to the computer as administrator. Select Start | Settings | Control
Panel | System. Click the User Profiles tab. Verify that the user profile is "roaming."

FIGURE 12-17

Accessing
the properties
of the domain
object

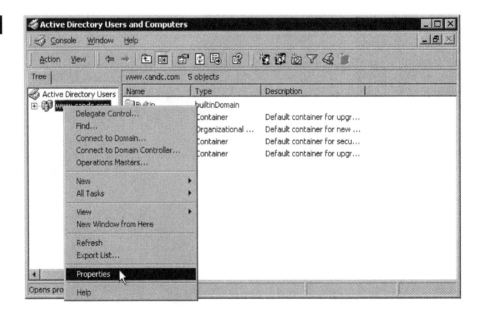

FIGURE 12-18

Verifying that
policies are linked
to the domain

Figure 12-20 shows two user profiles (testprofile and buildprofile) that are "roaming" (the administrator account is "local"). Those settings are correct. If Brenda's account is set to "roaming," then it should follow her from computer to computer.

FIGURE 12-19

Adding a
missing policy

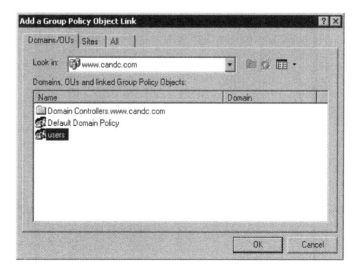

FIGURE 12-20

Verifying
roaming access

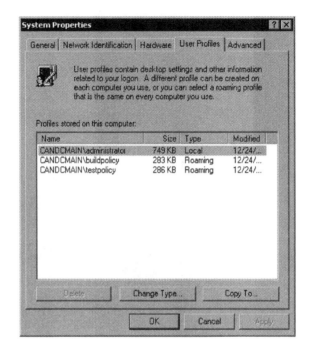

Lab Solution 12.05

Always remember that some Control Panel functions are crucial to user comfort.

Step I. Get-It-Right would like to disable all Control Panel entries except the mouse. One of the managers is left-handed and appreciates the ability to swap buttons. (The necessary file is main.cpl.)

Step 2. Start the MMC, and open the users.msc file that you created earlier. Expand the folders under the Users tab as shown in Figure 12-21.

Double-click "Show only specified control panel applets." Click the enabled radio button, and then click Show. Add main.cpl as shown here:

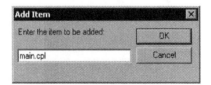

FIGURE 12-21

Finding Control
Panel options

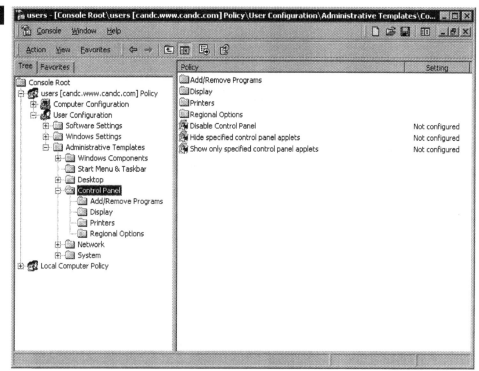

You still have more to do, though. A user who knows that files ending with .cpl are control panel files can still run Control Panel. You need to disable every policy under the Control Panel settings. Figure 12-22 shows one sample: security for printer options. Addition and deletion of printers is disabled, but users can find existing printers.

Lab Solution 12.06

Practice folder encryption on non-critical documents at first.

Step 1.   On an NTFS drive, create a folder containing some data.

Step 2.   Right-click your chosen folder, and select Properties. In the Properties dialog box, select Advanced. Configure the folder as shown in Figure 12-23.

FIGURE 12-22 Securing printer options

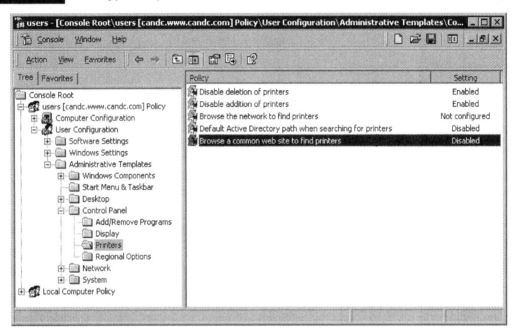

FIGURE 12-23

Setting encryption
on a folder

Click OK, and then Apply. When you are prompted (Figure 12-24), choose to encrypt the current folder and all its children. The files can now be read only by you and the administrator.

FIGURE 12-24

Applying encryption to child objects

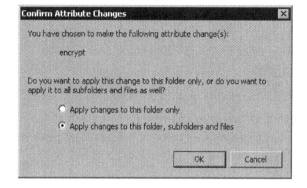

ANSWERS TO LAB ANALYSIS TEST

1. Occasionally, a user has a legitimate need to access the Control Panel. One example is users with poor eyesight. Such users would like to be able to change the computer's accessibility options. With the Control Panel switched off, they would be stuck with the resolution and colors provided by the network. Accessibility is a serious issue. If a person is physically challenged, the Americans with Disabilities Act (ADA) requires that that person be able to work on the computer. Entirely disabling the Control Panel in that circumstance is in violation of the ADA.

2. Both profiles follow a user from computer to computer, but the profile types have two major differences. The first difference is the ability to change the profile. Roaming profiles allow the user to change the settings; mandatory profiles are read-only. The second difference occurs in the absence of a profile. If a roaming profile is absent, the user can still log on. A mandatory profile must be present for the user to be able to log on.

3. The two users are the user who encrypted the file and the data recovery agent—typically the administrator of the computer. Having two users with this authority is a failsafe. If the original user is unable to decrypt a file for any reason, the administrator can access the file.

4. This copy operation is a classic security hole. EFS is supported only on Windows 2000–formatted NTFS 5 disks. The disk in question is formatted using FAT32. FAT32 does not support Windows 2000 encryption. When the files are copied, the encryption is lost on the copied files. If the disk is lost or stolen, the files can easily be read.

5. The approach is inefficient because the user or administrator would need to edit the profile on each machine that the user intends to use. That chore is both tedious and error-prone. Local profiles should be used only when a user never changes computers.

ANSWERS TO KEY TERM QUIZ

1. roaming

2. cipher

3. MMC

4. inheritance

5. template

13

Auditing Folders, Simplifying User Creation, and Modifying Security Settings

LAB EXERCISES

During one of your lunches with Ronny, he mentions a problem in Personnel. The company is having a hard time keeping drivers. A driver will work for a few weeks, and then quit. The problem is not the turnover itself, but the computer work associated with the turnover. For each driver, a new user must be created and an old user deactivated. While the process is rather simple, it is tedious and error-prone. Ronny would like to know if there is a way to simplify the user creation task.

An additional problem is the password policies. The security settings require the password to be changed every 42 days. That's fine for an in-house user, who is warned for several days about the need to change. The drivers, owing to a problem with the shipping unit, are not notified. When a password expires, the driver is unable to access the server. Ronny wants "maximum days" removed from the password policy.

Finally, the managers of the drivers think that a lag is noticeable between the time that the drivers' device sends confirmation of a delivery and the time that the delivery is actually recorded in the database. The database programmers are looking into the problem from their end, but they suggested auditing the folder for changes.

"Whew!" you say. Normally, your lunches with Ronny are not quite this productive. You assure Ronny that you can solve his problems. In fact, the problems can be solved before the end of the day.

LAB EXERCISE 13.01

Auditing a Folder

20 Minutes

You get back from lunch and immediately start to work on the problems raised by Personnel. Because deliveries are the most important transactions at Get-It-Right, you decide to set up the audits first. You know that you will have to enable auditing, and then switch auditing on for the appropriate folder.

Learning Objectives

In this lab, you audit folder usage. At the end of the lab, you'll be able to

- ▓ Modify a security policy
- ▓ Enable object auditing
- ▓ Switch on auditing for a folder.

Lab Materials and Setup

You need these items to complete the lab:

- Administrative account
- Shared folder named "deliveries"

cross
Reference   *See Exercise 6-1 in the Study Guide for help on sharing a folder.*

Getting Down to Business

To enable auditing for the Get-It-Right deliveries folder, here is what you need to do:

Step 1.   **Plan** your approach by determining which folder and which events should be audited. Also, decide on the size of the audit file.

Step 2.   **Implement** you audit plan:

- Start the local computer policies.
- Expand Computer Configuration, Windows Settings, and then Local Policies.
- Enable the appropriate policies in each group policy.
- Repeat for each group policy linked to the domain.
- Using My Computer or Windows Explorer, browse to the folder to be audited. Switch auditing on.

lab
Hint   *The audit policy may already be enabled, depending on the security template that you applied in Chapter 12.*

LAB EXERCISE 13.02

Creating a User Template

15 Minutes

The next task that you tackle is creating a user template.

The user template is set up as a typical user would be. The template is then copied when a new user needs to be built. All the administrator has to do is enter the user's personal information; the template takes care of the other details. This approach eliminates the need to enter repetitive data or site-specific data for each new user. It also reduces the time required to create a user and the possibility of user errors.

Learning Objectives

In this lab, you create a user template. At the end of the lab, you'll be able to

- Create a user
- Specify user account settings.

Lab Materials and Setup

You need these materials to complete the lab:

- Shared folder named "home"
- Administrative account

Getting Down to Business

Here's how to create a user template for Get-It-Right:

Step 1. **Plan** the contents of the template.

- Study the existing driver accounts to determine the "typical" settings for the template.
- Watch for remote access and home folder settings.

Step 2. **Implement** a user template that encompasses all the typical settings for drivers.

- Start Active Directory Users and Computers.
- Create a user called "#DRIVER_TEMPLATE".
- Set the appropriate rights.

Step 3. **Test** your new template by copying it to create an account for Alfred Kerfonta.

LAB EXERCISE 13.03

Changing Password Policies

10 Minutes

The requirement to change passwords every 42 days is a security setting that looks good on paper. However, you know that users who are required to change passwords frequently will often write their passwords down, creating a huge security breach. Conversely, keeping the same passwords indefinitely also invites a security breach: someone may learn and exploit a user's password. But because there is a problem with the driver devices, you must remove the maximum password age policy.

Learning Objectives

In this lab, you modify a security policy. At the end of the lab, you'll be able to

- Open the Group Policy snap-in
- Modify a policy setting.

Lab Materials and Setup

You need these materials to complete the lab:

- Administrative account
- Users.msc file created in Chapter 12

Getting Down to Business

Changing the password policies for Get-It-Right involves these steps:

Step 1. **Implement** the change in the appropriate location:

- Start MMC and open Users.msc

lab
Hint
If you don't have users.msc, add the Group Policy snap-in for MMC, and add all policies on the server, including Local Computer.

■ Expand Computer Configuration, Windows Settings, Security Settings, and then Password Policies.

■ Disable Maximum Age.

■ Repeat the process for every Maximum Age setting contained in a Group Policy.

LAB EXERCISE 13.04

Analyzing the Security Settings

5 Minutes

Ronny pops his head into your office before the end of the day. One of his supervisors has asked him a question regarding the security settings on the server. The supervisor was afraid that the settings were too low. Ronny came to you to check that the server is indeed as secure as possible.

You remind Ronny that the server is set up using the High Security Domain Controller template. Just to calm Ronny's boss's nerves, you run a security analysis of the server.

lab
Warning
No server that is attached to a network is 100% secure. Anyone that wants in badly enough will find a way. To help combat breaches, you should always install service packs as soon as they are available. In addition, pay attention to news from Microsoft and CERT regarding security breaches in software. Many infamous security breaches, such as Code Red, were made possible by server administrators who failed to install the newest security patches.

Learning Objectives

In this lab, you analyze your server and verify that it indeed complies with Microsoft's high security standards. Upon completing the lab, you'll be able to run a security analysis of your computer.

Lab Materials and Setup

You need the administrative account to complete the lab.

Getting Down to Business

Use this procedure to analyze the security settings for the Get-It-Right server:

Step 1. **Implement** by running an analysis and checking the results:

- Start MMC, and add the Security Configuration and Analysis snap-in.
- Build a new database.
- Apply the hisecdc.inf template.
- Right-click the Security Configuration, and select "Analyze computer now."
- Expand every tab and look for failed policies.

LAB ANALYSIS TEST

The following questions will help you to apply your knowledge in a business setting.

1. You want to map the network drive h: to \\server\home. What is the net use command that you would put in the login script?

   _____

   _____

2. You set a policy on the local machine for no password age. However, users are still being told that their passwords are about to expire. What is the most likely problem?

   _____

   _____

3. How can security groups simplify the assignment of rights and permissions?

   _____

   _____

4. What is the difference between rights and permissions? Provide an example of each.

   _____

   _____

5. Why is it important to keep current with Microsoft service packs?

   _____

   _____

KEY TERM QUIZ

Use the following vocabulary terms to complete the sentences below. Not all of the terms will be used.

audit

computer accounts

group

Kerberos

logon script

permission

policy

right

templates

user accounts

1. A(n) _____ is run whenever a user logs on to the server.

2. The primary authentication protocol for Windows 2000 is _____ .

3. You can set the _____ of remote access to a(n) _____ .

4. The application of security _____ makes writing a security _____ much easier.

5. A(n) _____ contains users having the same rights or job descriptions.

LAB SOLUTIONS FOR CHAPTER 13

The sections that follow walk you through the steps to solve the lab exercises. You should avoid looking at these sections unless you are stuck on a particular exercise.

Lab Solution 13.01

When establishing any policy, remember that you have to both set up the policy and apply it.

Step 1. You know that you're going to audit the Deliveries folder. Make your own choice of the particular events that you will audit (or just follow the suggestions in the solution).

Step 2. Select Start | Programs | Administrative Tools | Local Security Policy. Expand to see the Audit Policy under Local Policies (Figure 13-1). As shown in the figure, switch on "success" for Audit Object Access.

Close Local Security Settings.

Select Start | Programs | Administrative Tools | Active Directory Users and Computers. Right-click the domain object, and select Properties (Figure 13-2).

Click the Group Policy tab. Choose to edit the Default Domain Policy (Figure 13-3).

Expand and configure as shown in Figure 13-4. Repeat the process for every Group Policy object shown in Figure 13-3.

Close Active Directory Users and Computers.

Select Start | Run, and enter **cmd**. Refresh the security policies by entering the command shown here:

```
D:\WINNT\System32\cmd.exe

Microsoft Windows 2000 [Version 5.00.2195]
(C) Copyright 1985-1999 Microsoft Corp.

D:\>secedit /refreshpolicy machine_policy_
```

Wait for a minute, for the policy to be updated.

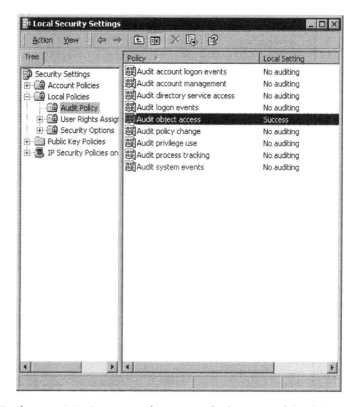

Using Explorer or My Computer, browse to the location of the folder that you
want to audit. Right-click the folder, and select Properties. Click the Security tab,
and then click the Advanced button.

In the Access Control dialog box, select the Auditing tab. As shown in Figure 13-5,
select the Add button.

Add the audit for the drivers group:

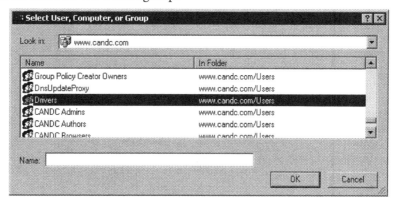

FIGURE 13-2 Opening the properties of a domain object

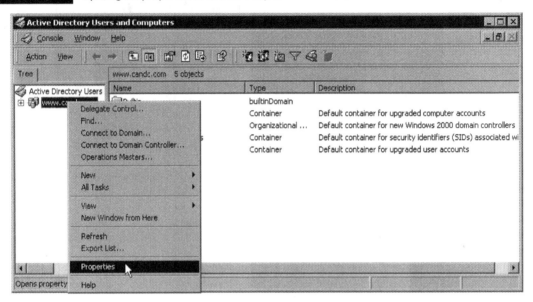

FIGURE 13-3

Choosing
to edit linked
group policies

FIGURE 13-4

Setting domain
audit policies

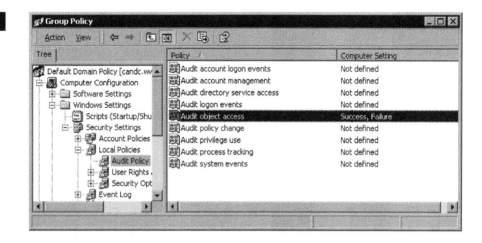

Configure the audit as shown in Figure 13-6.

FIGURE 13-5

Adding an
audit entry

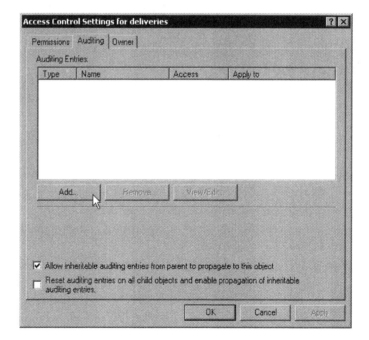

FIGURE 13-6

Picking audit
events

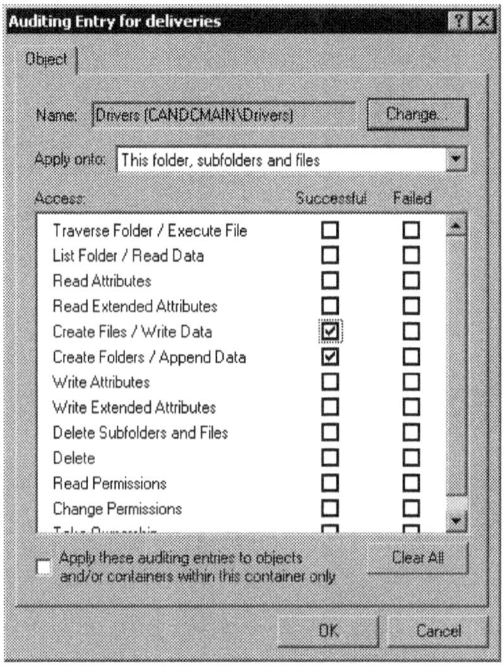

Lab Solution 13.02

If you have a user that is "typical" of a group, setting up a user template is a quick job.

Step 1.   Choose one of the drivers that you set up in Chapter 12 and that has all of the "typical" settings.

Step 2.   Select Start | Programs | Administrative Tools | Active Directory Users and Computers. Select your "typical" driver.

From the Action menu, select Copy. Configure the user template as shown in Figure 13-7. Click Next.

At the password dialog box, select a complex password, and configure so that the password must be changed at the next logon (Figure 13-8). I chose **pftDsoTm73** for the password. Click Next.

Right-click DRIVER_TEMPLATE, and select Properties. Verify that the Dial-in permission is set as shown in Figure 13-9.

FIGURE 13-7

Creating a user
template for
Get-It-Right
drivers

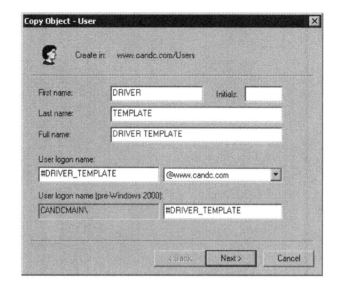

Map the home folder as shown in Figure 13-10. Be sure to replace *server* with the
name of your server. Click OK to close the Properties dialog.

Step 3.   Test the template by copying the account, and creating a new user.
Verify that the home folder was properly created. Unfortunately, Windows 2000
does not carry over the remote access; you will need to set that option manually.

FIGURE 13-8

Setting the
template
password

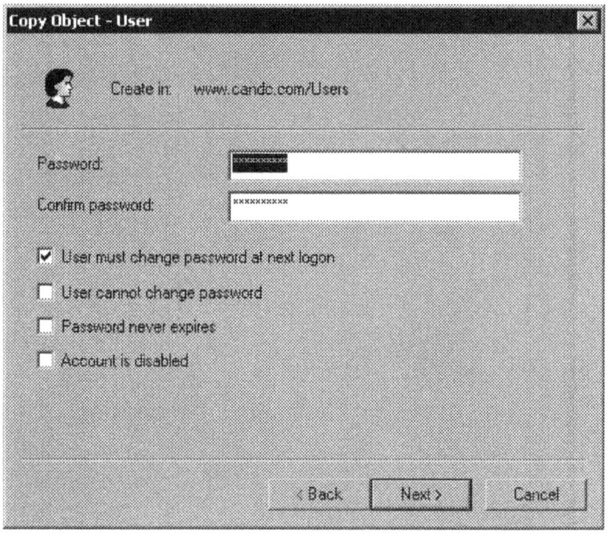

FIGURE 13-9

Setting the right to dial in

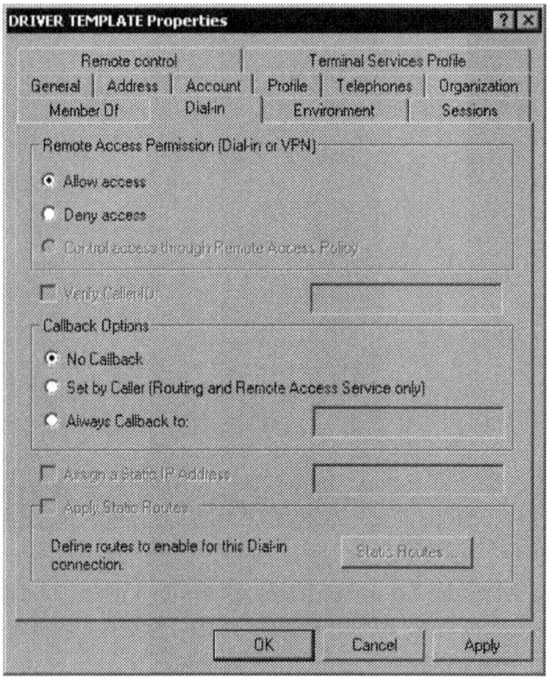

FIGURE 13-10

Mapping the home folder

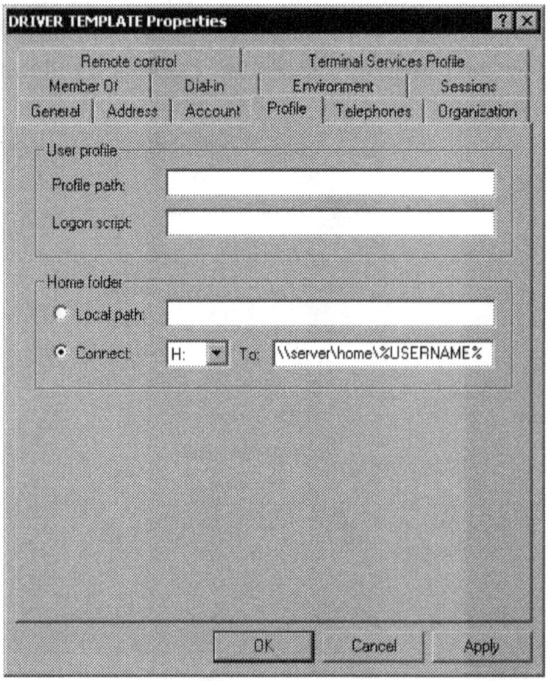

Lab Solution 13.03

Remember that password policies may exist in several locations.

Step I. Select Start | Programs | Administrative Tools | Users.msc. Browse to the Password Policy as shown in Figure 13-11.

Double-click Maximum Password Age. Switch off the policy as shown here:

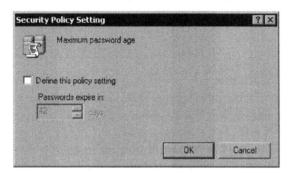

FIGURE 13-11 Expanding to see password policies

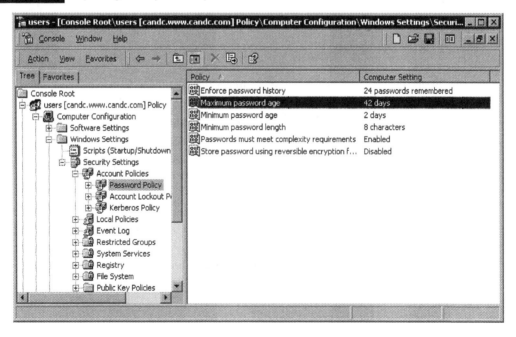

Click OK. You will receive this notification:

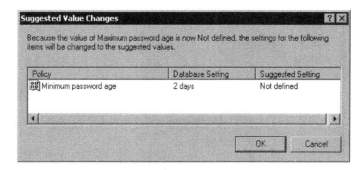

Click OK.

If other policies exist, make the same change in each of those policies. As you did in lab exercise 13.01, refresh the machine policy.

lab

⒣int

Changing the password policies in each policy object may be overkill. The inheritance rules should allow the change to take affect. However, applying the change to every policy guarantees its effectiveness.

Lab Solution 13.04

Running a security analysis from time to time—and every time you change your policies—can help to keep your server secure.

Step 1. Select Start | Run, and enter **mmc**. From the Console menu, select Add/Remove Snap-In.

Click the Add button, and pick Security Configuration and Analysis (Figure 13-12).

Click Add, and then Close, and then OK to return to the MMC. Click the Security Configuration icon once to see the directions for using Security Configuration and Analysis.

Right-click the Security Configuration icon, and select Open Database. Create a new database named **verify** as shown in Figure 13-13. (The server used in the figure already has two databases; you will not see them on your computer.)

Click Open. At the Import Template dialog box (Figure 13-14), select the hisecdc.inf template, and click Open. You are returned to the MMC.

FIGURE 13-12

Adding the Security
Configuration
and Analysis snap-in

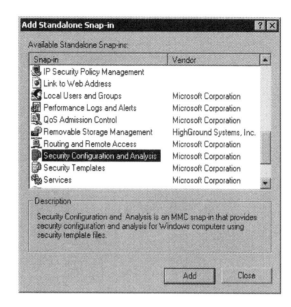

Right-click the Security Configuration icon again, and select Analyze Computer Now. Click OK to accept the default log selection. When the wizard finishes, you are returned to the MMC.

Expand the lockout policy. A passing policy gets a green check mark as shown in Figure 13-15.

Verify that the other policies agree with the template.

FIGURE 13-13

Creating a
new database

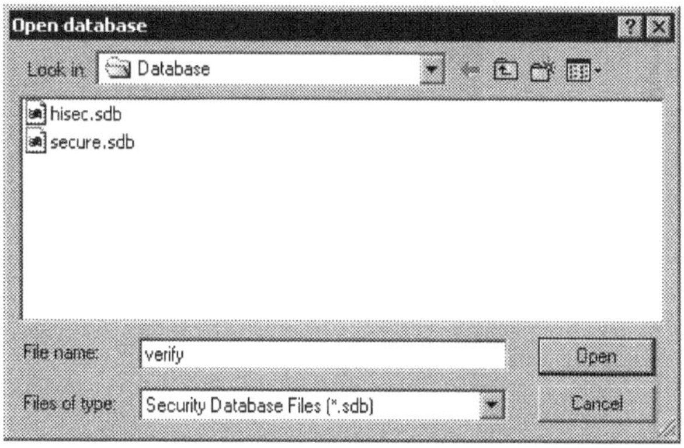

FIGURE 13-14

Opening
the hisecdc.inf
template

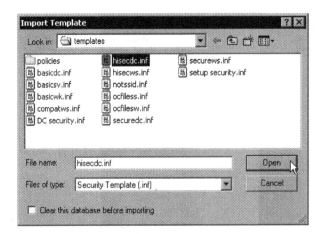

FIGURE 13-15   Reviewing a passing policy

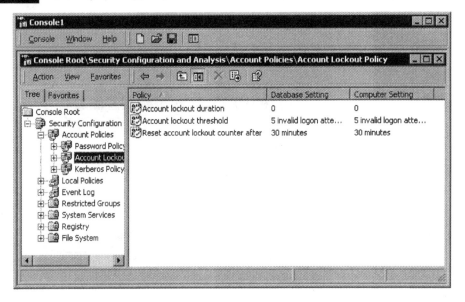

ANSWERS TO LAB ANALYSIS TEST

1. The command is:

```
net use h: \\server\home
```

2. The most likely problem is other policies on the machine. Any domain-level policy overrides local policies. You should look at the Group Policy objects that are linked to the domain. Use Active Directory Users and Computers to find the information. Disable the policy in each policy object.

3. Security groups, as the name implies, allow you to group similar users into containers. In the Get-It-Right scenario, a group of drivers could hold specific rights applicable only to drivers. That group can be given exclusive permission to access certain objects. By grouping the drivers, the administrator does not need to add each user to the specific object.

4. Rights are assigned to user accounts or groups. Permissions are given to users or security groups on particular objects. For example, a user has rights in regard to permissible logon hours. A user might have the right to log on between 8:00 A.M. and 6:00 P.M. Monday through Friday. An example of a permission on a printer object is "able to print." If a user lacks that permission in regard to a printer object, then that user cannot print to that printer.

5. Microsoft is aware that their software has problems. By their good grace, they provide solutions to these problems as they come to light. While your server might not suffer from a particular problem now, there is no guarantee that, tomorrow, your server will not encounter the problem. In addition, as Microsoft releases new software to run on servers, that software will most likely require the prior installation of the most up-to-date service pack for the software being upgraded. If your server is up-to-date on service packs, installing new software will take less time. Finally, service packs fix identified security holes. Often, the holes are located before hackers or script kiddies can exploit them.

> **lab ⓗint** *A "script kiddie" is a hacker-wannabe who steals code that "real" hackers wrote and applies it for his/her own devices. The recent Goner virus was written by a group of script kiddies.*

ANSWERS TO KEY TERM QUIZ

1. logon script
2. Kerberos
3. right, user accounts
4. templates, policy
5. group

14

Using Terminal and Internet Information Services

Things are looking up at Get-It-Right. They recently purchased their biggest competitor, Timely Delivery. Get-It-Right will mold Timely Delivery's assets and organization into the Get-It-Right model. Luckily, Timely has used Windows 2000 Server for its network servers. You will need to be able to control your server and access files whenever you are working at the Timely site. To solve this problem, you will install Terminal Services and an FTP server on the Get-It-Right server. These features will allow you to access Get-It-Right's server and provide files for Timely employees to download.

LAB EXERCISE 14.01

Installing Terminal Services in Remote Administration Mode

15 Minutes

You have no desire to set up thin clients on the network, but you would like to remotely administer the server if necessary. Terminal Services in the remote administration mode provides that functionality. Terminal Services Client will need to be installed on the Timely server. You have asked Ronny to send an appropriate directive to the Timely administrator.

Learning Objectives

In this lab, you install Terminal Services. At the end of the lab, you'll be able to install Terminal Services in remote administration mode.

Lab Materials and Setup

You need these items to complete the lab:

- PC with Windows 2000 Server installed and configured
- Administrative account
- Windows 2000 Server CD

Getting Down to Business

To set up the remote administration mode for Get-It-Right, here is what you need to do:

Step 1   **Plan** the installation by deciding whether Remote Administration or Terminal Services mode is appropriate.

Step 2.   **Implement** the installation.

- First, start the Add/Remove Programs applet in Control Panel.
- Add Terminal Services.
- Select the appropriate mode.
- Reboot when prompted.

Step 3.   **Test** the installation. Is Terminal Services Manager installed?

LAB EXERCISE 14.02

Monitoring Terminal Services

10 Minutes

You will be spending a lot of time at the new site. Local staff at Get-It-Right will have to cover your job. One new job that has been added is the need to monitor Terminal Services. Terminal Services can place a strain on a server. In cases of any network lag, a local admin has to be able to determine if that lag is a result of your remote logon. You decide to train the local administrators to monitor Terminal Services.

Learning Objectives

In this lab, you monitor the terminal service. Upon completion of the lab, you'll be able to

- Use Terminal Services Manager
- Use Performance Monitor.

Lab Materials and Setup

You need these materials to complete the lab:

- Administrative account
- Terminal Services installed as described in lab exercise 14.01

Getting Down to Business

You have gathered your staff around the main computer to train them how to monitor Terminal Services usage. Use this procedure:

Step 1. **Plan** how to deal with server strain.

- Remind the staff that Terminal Services can cause strain on the server.
- If they notice strain, they should check Terminal Services before worrying about other causes.

Step 2. **Implement** a process for checking out the problem.

- Start Terminal Services Manager.
- Start Performance.
- Add the counters for Terminal Service.

LAB EXERCISE 14.03

Installing Internet Information Services

5 Minutes

Get-It-Right eventually wants to have a web site devoted to the merger. Ronny has promised to hire a web programmer, Jamie-Lynn, to build the site. To prepare for Jamie-Lynn's arrival, you plan to install Internet Information Services (IIS). IIS allows Get-It-Right to host web pages.

Learning Objectives

At the end of the lab, you will be able to install IIS.

Lab Materials and Setup

You need these materials to complete the lab:

- Administrative account
- Windows 2000 Server CD

Getting Down to Business

Here's how to install IIS for Get-It-Right:

Step 1. **Implement** the web hosting capability in two quick steps:

- Start the Add/Remove Programs applet in Control Panel.
- Select IIS and finish.

LAB EXERCISE 14.04

Configuring an FTP Site

10 Minutes

You will need to provide the workers at Timely Delivery with patches and programs to match their equipment to Get-It-Right's specifications. Jamie-Lynn cannot start until next week, and the files need to be distributed now. One way to accomplish that distribution is to provide an FTP site. Users can then access the files that they need, before their computers are added to the Get-It-Right network. In addition, home users will be able to get the files they need for laptops and other home computers.

Learning Objectives

In this lab, you set up and configure an FTP site for Get-It-Right. At the end of the lab, you'll be able to

- Start IIS
- Configure an FTP server.

Lab Materials and Setup

You need these items to complete the lab:

- Administrative account
- IIS installed on the server

Getting Down to Business

Configuring the FTP server so that employees of Timely Delivery can access the patches and programs necessary to conform to Get-It-Right's specifications involves these steps:

Step 1. **Plan** the installation by listing the user accounts that will be allowed to access the FTP server.

Step 2. **Implement** your plan for the FTP server this way:

- Start IIS.
- Configure the FTP server, including number of connections and duration of connection.
- Set up anonymous logon for specified user accounts.

LAB ANALYSIS TEST

The following questions will help you to apply your knowledge in a business setting.

1. When would application server mode be appropriate for an organization?

   _____

   _____

2. Other than FTP, what are some services that IIS offers?

   _____

   _____

3. Application server offers remote control. How could remote control be used in an educational environment?

   _____

   _____

4. What is the primary difference between a thin and a fat client?

   _____

   _____

5. What is the preferred manner of shutting down the Terminal Service?

   _____

   _____

KEY TERM QUIZ

Use the following vocabulary terms to complete the sentences below. Not all of the terms will be used.

bandwidth throttling

fat

HTTP

IIS

IPX

RDP

remote control

TCP/IP

Terminal Service

thin

TS CAL

1. A typical computer (but missing a sound card) can be said to be a(n) _____ client.

2. The protocols necessary for Terminal Services Client to work are _____ and _____ .

3. _____ allows an administrator to take over a remote session in Terminal Services.

4. A Terminal Services client needs a(n) _____ to legally connect to the terminal server.

5. The primary protocol for sending and receiving web pages is _____ .

LAB SOLUTIONS FOR CHAPTER 14

The sections that follow walk you through the steps to solve the lab exercises. You should avoid looking at these sections unless you are stuck on a particular exercise.

Lab Solution 14.01

Being able to remotely manage a server can be very useful in many situations.

Step 1.   You decide that Terminal Services is the best mode for this particular situation.

Step 2.   Select Start | Settings | Control Panel | Add/Remove Programs. Click Add/Remove Windows Components. As shown in Figure 14-1, select Terminal Services, and click Next.

Configure Terminal Services for remote administration mode as shown in Figure 14-2. When prompted, insert the Windows 2000 Server CD, or enter a path to the CD location. Click OK to continue. Wait while Windows copies the necessary files and enables terminal services. That process takes a few minutes.

Click Finish when the install is complete. When prompted to reboot, remove the Windows 2000 Server CD from the drive, and then click Yes to reboot.

FIGURE 14-1

Adding Terminal
Services to
the server

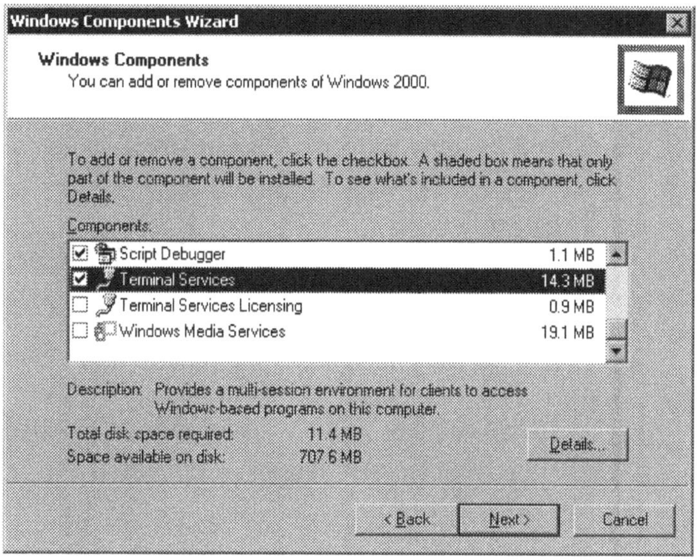

FIGURE 14-2

Configuring
for remote
administration
mode

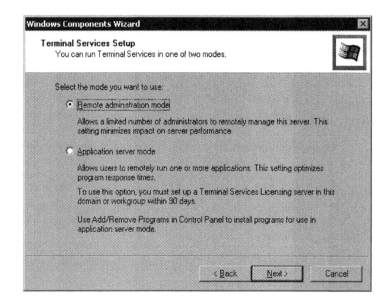

Lab Solution 14.02

When Terminal Services is in use, checking it first in cases of server strain is practical.

Step 1. You warn the staff about checking Terminal Services first when server strain appears.

Step 2. Select Start | Programs | Administrative Tools | Terminal Services Manager (TSM). All current users are listed on the Users tab in the right-hand pane of the TSM display (Figure 14-3).

Click the Sessions tab to see all current sessions on the server. In Figure 14-4, two sessions are in progress.

Close TSM.

Select Start | Programs | Administrative Tools | Performance. As shown in Figure 14-5, click the + button (Add) to add a counter.

Now, select the Terminal Services counter, and add Inactive Sessions (Figure 14-6).

Change the counter object to Terminal Services Sessions, and configure the counter as shown in Figure 14-7.

Watch the monitor. A high number of inactive sessions or a session that is taking a large amount of processor time signals a problem.

FIGURE 14-3

Showing
the current users
in Terminal
Services Manager

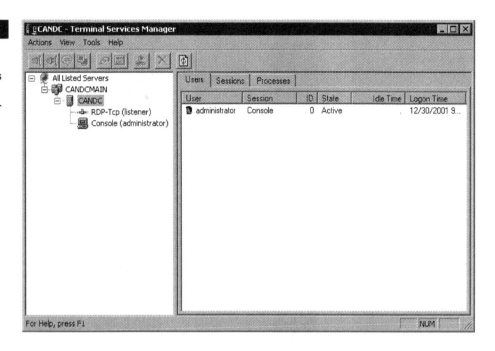

FIGURE 14-4

Viewing the
current sessions
in Terminal
Services Manager

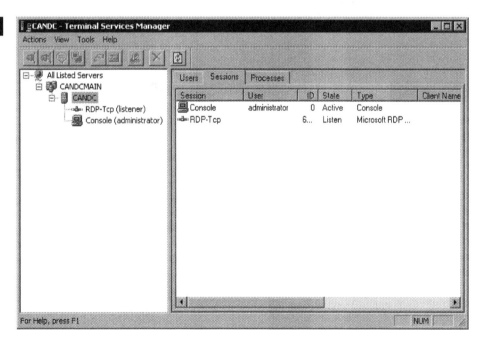

FIGURE 14-5

Adding a counter
to Performance

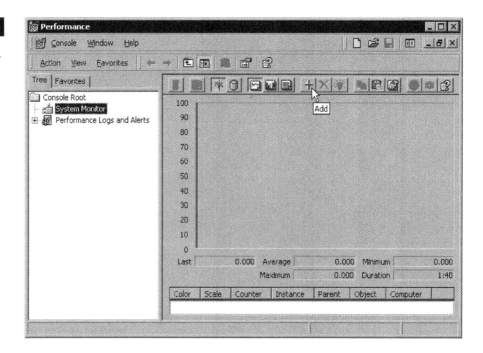

FIGURE 14-6

Adding the
Terminal Services
counter

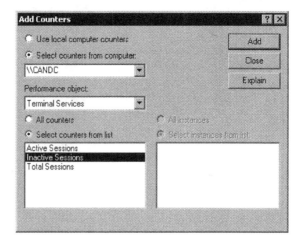

FIGURE 14-7

FIGURE 14-7

Adding the
Session counter

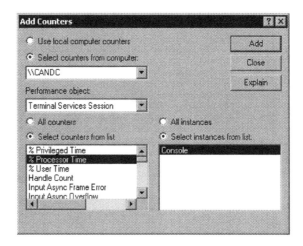

Lab Solution 14.03

Adding IIS is a very simple procedure.

lab
ⓗint

If the check box next to IIS is gray, then IIS is partially installed. Clear and then re-select the check box so that its background is white.

Step 1. Select Start | Settings | Control Panel | Add/Remove Programs. Click Add/Remove Windows Components.

As shown in Figure 14-8, place a check mark next to Internet Information Services. Click Next. Click Next to bypass any other dialog boxes. When prompted, insert the Windows 2000 Server CD.

Lab Solution 14.04

An FTP server provides functionality that can make work go very smoothly for remote users.

Step 1. Decide which of Get-It-Right's users will be allowed to access the FTP server.

Step 2. Select Start | Programs | Administrative Tools | Internet Services Manager. Right-click Default FTP Site. Select Properties.

Set the FTP site properties as shown in Figure 14-9. If your server has a public IP address, use that address instead of the private address.

FIGURE 14-8

Adding Internet
Information
Services

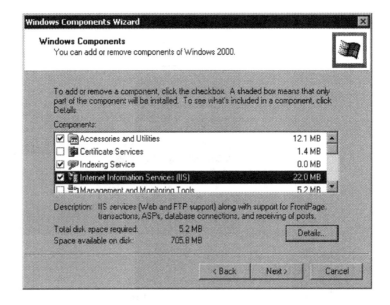

Configure the Security Accounts tab as shown in Figure 14-10.

Figure 14-11 shows sample messages for use on the Messages tab. Feel free to change the messages, but be sure to keep them polite.

FIGURE 14-9

Setting
the properties
for File Transfer
Protocol

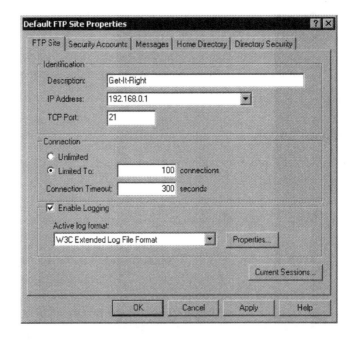

FIGURE 14-10

Configuring
anonymous access
under File
Transfer Protocol

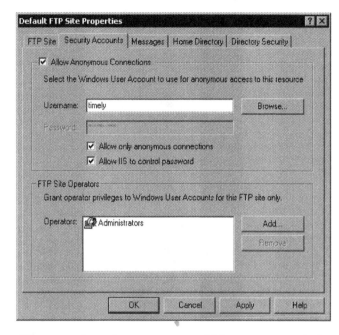

The Home Directory tab can be set to use any folder you want as the home directory.
As shown in Figure 14-12, be sure to change the directory listing style to UNIX. Most
users are accustomed to a UNIX look and feel from FTP.

FIGURE 14-11

Providing messages
for users of File
Transfer

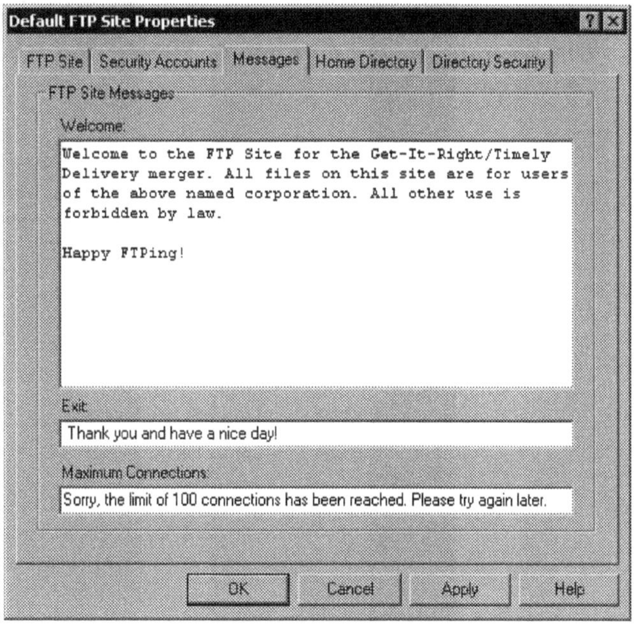

Changing
the Directory
Listing Style

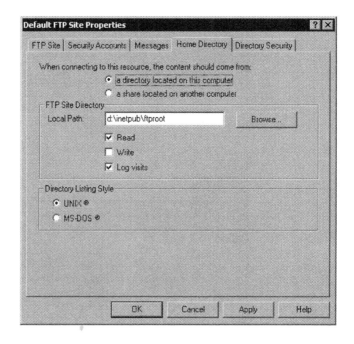

Click Apply, and then OK to return to IIS. Close IIS.

lab

Ⓗint

By setting the logon name to "timely," you retain anonymous logins and secure passwords. In addition, you limit site access to people who know or can guess the logon name. Using "timely" is a little more secure than using "anonymous."

ANSWERS TO LAB ANALYSIS TEST

1. Application server mode is appropriate in an organization that wants to deliver applications to the users' desktops. The mode has several advantages. One advantage is the need to install software only once. Given the length of time that software installation takes, the savings for the company can be significant. A second advantage is the guarantee that all computers will look and act the same. Nothing is more frustrating to a user or an administrator than a computer that acts differently from its neighbor. Finally, users can be provided with exactly the software that they need. Policies can be set that limit access to software based on number of licenses, individual user need, or geographic region.

2. IIS offers several technologies. One is the ability to host a web page. Another is the Active Server Page (ASP) technology. ASP allows an HTML developer to use Server-Side Includes (SSIs) that execute predefined scripts. The use of SSIs can greatly reduce development time for web applications. Finally, IIS allows an administrator to log activity on a web site. Good activity logs are crucial to understanding how visitors use a web site.

3. Remote control is a useful tool in any education or training environment. Administrators have the ability to watch how the user is performing a task. Such monitoring can help the instructor diagnose gaps in a student's knowledge. Additionally, the instructor can see what users might be doing wrong when they repeatedly fail at a task. Instructors can also demonstrate exact steps on the users' workstations. The student can watch while the instructor works, making the mouse and keyboard perform as they are supposed to.

4. A fat client is a typical computer. It has all the components that one would expect, including local long-term storage. The local long-term storage holds everything that makes the fat client work. A thin client, by contrast, has little or no local long-term storage. Instead, the thin client relies on a server to deliver all the software it needs to function. The thin client is very similar to a telnet session with a mainframe or UNIX account. The telnet software only sends commands and receives screen updates. The telnet program does nothing on its own. A thin client does nothing on its own; a fat client does nearly everything on its own.

5. The preferred method of downing a Terminal Services server is to use the command-line tool TSSHUTDN. TSSHUTDN notifies clients that the server is going down, and downs the server in 60 seconds.

cross
Reference   *See the "From The Classroom" subsection in Chapter 14 of the Study Guide.*

ANSWERS TO KEY TERM QUIZ

1. fat

2. RDP, TCP/IP

3. remote control

4. TS CAL

5. HTTP

INDEX

A

access
  remote, 278–279, 287–290
  to resources, 139–141, 147–149, 154–157, 163
access by policy, 262, 276
accounts
  user, 288–289
  See also user templates, creating
ACPI (Advanced Configuration and Power Interface), 68, 166–170
Active Directory, 48
Active Server Page (ASP), 341
adding
  counters, 336–337
  members to groups, 290
  Terminal Services, 333
addresses, 169, 179
  See also network services; TCP/IP
Advanced Configuration and Power Interface (ACPI), 68, 166–170
alerts
  problems with, 198, 212
  setting, 196–197, 210–211
Americans with Disabilities Act (ADA), 302
anonymous logins, FTP, 340
answer files, deployment (Windows 2000), 55–58, 69–73
application programs, removing, 206
application server mode, 331, 341
applications. *See* server applications
ASP (Active Server Page), 341
auditing, folders, 304–305, 312–316
authority, encryption, 285, 302

B

backup domain controller. *See* Windows 4.0 BDC
backups, server data, 214–215, 217–218, 222, 224–226, 229–231, 236
baselines
  creating, 188–189, 200–201
  See also alerts; counter logs; counters
boot disk, remote installation, 66
browser settings worksheet, 58

C

CAL (Client Access License), 27–28
certification, skill set evaluation, 2–4, 7, 9–10, 12
checklists
  networks, 108
  Windows NT 4.0 migration, 97
circular trace files, 198, 212
cleaning up, disks, 193–194, 204–206
Client Access License (CAL), 27–28
clients, fat versus thin, 331, 341
compatibility, hardware, 18–21, 33
compressing
  disks, 244, 254
  folders, 242–243, 250–253
configuring
  devices, 166–170, 179–182
  DHCP services, 106–110
  FTP sites, 329–330, 337–340
  remote connections, 255–276, 262, 266–269
connection sharing, Internet, 262, 276
control panel, disabling access, 282–283, 285, 298–299, 302

343

P

INTERNATIONAL CONTACT INFORMATION

AUSTRALIA
McGraw-Hill Book Company Australia Pty. Ltd.
TEL +61-2-9417-9899
FAX +61-2-9417-5687
http://www.mcgraw-hill.com.au
books-it_sydney@mcgraw-hill.com

CANADA
McGraw-Hill Ryerson Ltd.
TEL +905-430-5000
FAX +905-430-5020
http://www.mcgrawhill.ca

GREECE, MIDDLE EAST, NORTHERN AFRICA
McGraw-Hill Hellas
TEL +30-1-656-0990-3-4
FAX +30-1-654-5525

MEXICO (Also serving Latin America)
McGraw-Hill Interamericana Editores S.A. de C.V.
TEL +525-117-1583
FAX +525-117-1589
http://www.mcgraw-hill.com.mx
fernando_castellanos@mcgraw-hill.com

SINGAPORE (Serving Asia)
McGraw-Hill Book Company
TEL +65-863-1580
FAX +65-862-3354
http://www.mcgraw-hill.com.sg
mghasia@mcgraw-hill.com

SOUTH AFRICA
McGraw-Hill South Africa
TEL +27-11-622-7512
FAX +27-11-622-9045
robyn_swanepoel@mcgraw-hill.com

UNITED KINGDOM & EUROPE (Excluding Southern Europe)
McGraw-Hill Education Europe
TEL +44-1-628-502500
FAX +44-1-628-770224
http://www.mcgraw-hill.co.uk
computing_neurope@mcgraw-hill.com

ALL OTHER INQUIRIES Contact:
Osborne/McGraw-Hill
TEL +1-510-549-6600
FAX +1-510-883-7600
http://www.osborne.com
omg_international@mcgraw-hill.com

New Offerings from Osborne's
How to Do Everything Series

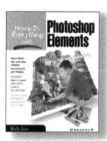